...941 in Rio de Janeiro ...phy before undertaking ... holds a literary doctor... and a PhD in sociology from the London School of Economics. His interest in the theory of culture matured at the Collège de France, where he attended Claude Lévi-Strauss's seminar for five years before turning to political sociology in England under the guidance of Ernest Gellner. A professor of political science at the University of Brasilia until 1982 and a former visiting professor at King's College, London, he is the author of several books, concentrating increasingly on the history of ideas. These include: *L'Esthétique de Lévi-Strauss* (1977), *The Veil and the Mask: essays on culture and ideology* (1979), *Rousseau and Weber: two studies in the theory of legitimacy* (1980), the Fontana Modern Masters Series *Foucault* (1985) and a forthcoming *From Prague to Paris: structuralist and poststructuralist itineraries*. A member of the Brazilian Academy and of the editorial board of *Government and Opposition*, he currently lives in London.

J. G. MERQUIOR

WESTERN MARXISM

SERIES EDITOR
JUSTIN WINTLE

PALADIN

Granada Publishing

Paladin Books
Granada Publishing Ltd
8 Grafton Street, London W1X 3LA

A Paladin Paperback Original 1986

ISBN 0-586-08454-1

Printed and bound in Great Britain by
Collins, Glasgow

Set in Baskerville

CONTENTS

For Leandro Konder,
who would only half agree

FOREWORD AND ACKNOWLEDGEMENTS

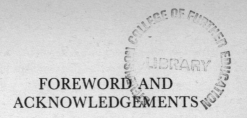

In his oft-quoted eleventh thesis on Feuerbach Marx enjoined philosophy to change the world instead of merely interpreting it. The trouble with post-Marxian Marxism is that historically it followed the advice to the letter: it certainly changed the face of the modern world, yet scarcely succeeded in interpreting it in an intellectually satisfactory way. When Western Marxism, born in the 1920s out of the spirit of revolution, gathered momentum in the three decades following World War II it voiced the dire need for rethinking both Marxist theory and its relationship with social praxis.

This short study is an attempt to assess critically the main results of such a theoretical endeavour. It reflects, I hope, many a pithy conversation on Marxism and its problems with a number of first-rate minds, none of which is the least responsible for the views presented here: the late Raymond Aron, Leszek Kolakowski, Ernest Gellner, Fernando Henrique Cardoso, Perry Anderson, Leandro Konder, Roberto Schwarz, Carlos Nelson Coutinho, John A. Hall, F. A. Santos. I am grateful to Helio Jaguaribe for the hospitality of his Instituto de Estudos Políticos e Sociais (Rio), where I briefly sketched most of the analysis of the Frankfurt School in 1984. Justin Wintle was a truly sympathetic editor, as always very keen on the biography of ideas, who actually much improved my text. Josette Priest took excellent care of the typescript. Ophelia Vesentini and J. M. Alkmin performed some detective-worthy jobs in pursuit of an often elusive bibliography. And I would like to thank the indexer, Rebecca Smith. In a sense,

Foreword and Acknowledgements

I have borne this book in my mind for many years – but I could scarcely have written it in just one Autumn without the help and encouragement of my friends and family.

JGM
London, June 1985

I

A CONCEPT AND ITS BACKGROUND

1. WHAT IS WESTERN MARXISM?

'Western Marxism' is generally taken to mean a body of thought, chiefly philosophical, encompassing the work of authors as different as Georg Lukács and Louis Althusser, Walter Benjamin and the later Jean-Paul Sartre. It also embraces theoretical interventions and historical analyses as distant in time, scope and spirit as those of Antonio Gramsci (d. 1937) and Jürgen Habermas, who began publishing only thirty years ago. It is at once a typical product of the creative inter-war culture and an ongoing theorizing, recognizable (if often deeply transformed) in the output of the second generation of the so-called Frankfurt school grouped around Habermas or, again, in what came to be known as French structuralist Marxism.

Such diversity makes critical interpretation difficult. But at least, roughly speaking, one knows *who* the western Marxists are: Lukács, Gramsci, the Frankfurtians, Sartre, Althusser, some 'new Left' theorists, and so on. It is much harder, however, to say *what* Western Marxism (WM) amounts to. When it comes to defining or even describing Western Marxism as a whole, as a common denominator among several trends in twentieth-century Marxism, the label itself quickly turns out to be a tricky one. For instance, it traditionally denotes non-Soviet, or non-Soviet-like, Marxist thought. Yet, if taken too literally, its geographical meaning becomes quite misleading. Several Marxist trends in the West, while very different from the Soviet canon, are

1

far from qualifying as 'Western Marxism' in the philosophical sense. Consider a few samples at random: a Trotskyist
like the influential Belgian economist Ernest Mandel; a
theorist of revolution like the early Régis Debray; or an
East German dissident such as Rudolf Bahro – arguably
the most important case of communist heresy to have
surfaced since Milovan Djilas's *The New Class* (1957). All
of these, in their most striking works (Debray's *Revolution in
the Revolution*, 1969, Mandel's *Late Capitalism*, 1972 and
Bahro's *The Alternative in Eastern Europe*, 1977), were at
loggerheads with the Soviet persuasion. Yet nobody has
ever tagged the badge 'Western Marxism' on to any of
them. Clearly, being a Marxist in the West does not alone
make one into a 'Western Marxist', any more than it
makes one automatically obedient to Soviet theory. To that
extent, the tag is just a misnomer.

However, as soon as we look at it from a *historical*
perspective, the label becomes much more meaningful. For
'Western Marxism' was born in the early 1920s as a
doctrinal challenge, coming from the West, to Soviet Marxism. The main founders of Western Marxism – Lukács and
Ernst Bloch, Karl Korsch and Gramsci – were in sharp
disagreement with the deterministic historical materialism
of Bolshevik philosophy defined by Lenin or Bukharin.
Both Lenin and Bukharin, as Engels and Plekhanov before
them, believed in objective economic laws as the driving
force of all human history; and they also held a view of
consciousness as being essentially a reflection of nature
and social reality. In the 1920s, these key theoretical
positions were shared, in the Leninist camp, in such widely
read Marxist treatises as Bukharin's *Historical Materialism*
(1921); and, on the anti-Bolshevik side, in Kautsky's *The
Materialist Historical Constitution of the State and the Development
of Mankind* (1927); but they were strongly opposed by
thinkers like Lukács and Gramsci, who took issue with the
overt naturalistic outlook of the more determinist brands of
Marxism.

Nevertheless, few things would be more erroneous than

2

to think of the original Western Marxists as anti-Leninists. Since World War II, the self-image of Western Marxism has tended to portray the movement as a liberal or libertarian kind of Marxism, infinitely closer to the humanist vision of the young Marx than to the grim political plight of 'real socialism' – i.e., of the communist regimes established under the banner of 'Marxism-Leninism'. Actually, the very phrase 'Western Marxism' seems to have been coined, by Maurice Merleau-Ponty, in an anti-Leninist spirit. By 1930, Korsch was already describing himself, Lukács and other opponents of the Comintern as 'western communists', and, even earlier, Comintern followers had branded Korsch and co. as 'West European' theorists. But it seems that the vogue for the phrase 'Western Marxism' did not pre-date the controversies within French Marxism in the mid-1950s. Yet the plain historical truth is that the great initiators of Western Marxist thought, Lukács and Gramsci above all, evinced a lifetime loyalty to the communist movement and – unlike German social democrats – were always proud of the Bolshevik triumph that came in the wake of the 1917 Revolution. For all their departures from Lenin's philosophy, both Lukács and Gramsci remained to the end impeccable Leninists as far as practical politics were concerned. And those founders like Bloch or Korsch who broke with Leninism had no decisive influence on the shaping of later Western Marxist theory. *WHY?*

Anyone who considers the credentials of Leninism to be less than impressive on libertarian grounds is bound to reach a similar conclusion about the mainsprings of Western Marxism. If anything, the first Western Marxists began as militants or sympathizers of various forms of Left communism (viz. Lukács's syndicalist inclinations, Gramsci's council communism period, etc.), then moved steadily to the orthodox pattern of vertical party rule. It was only later, with the emergence of the Frankfurt school, that Western Marxism ceased to be Leninist or even communist at all. And even so, at least one powerful group, the Althusserians, retained a clear desire to maintain strict allegiance to the Communist Party.

Political heresy, therefore, is far from providing an overall characterization of Western Marxism. In order to catch its peculiar flavour, we must turn to *theoretical* dissent. Here, the first thing to meet the eye is a consuming interest in culture. While the focus of classical Marxism was on economic history and the politics of class struggle, Western Marxism concerned itself primarily with culture and ideology. Instead of analysing processes of capital accumulation or the mechanics of crisis and the reproduction of social relations, most major Western Marxists have written extensively on the problems of alienation and reification within capitalist society. Of course, not everything under the gaze of WM was culture as opposed to politics and economics. Gramsci, for one, was adept at scrutinizing historical varieties of class struggle and class alliance; and the Althusserians thought hard on modes of production and social formations. But on the whole it is not inaccurate to describe WM as the Marxism of the superstructure, for even when its analyses are turned towards class domination it often tends to be conducted (as it is in Gramsci) largely regardless of any specified set of factors located in the techno-economic infrastructure, the world of what classical Marxism dubbed forces and (social) relations of production. As a rule, in its analytical performances, WM exhibits little sense of social constraints, particularly of an economic or socio-economic nature. Indeed, what sets WM apart, beyond a mere shift from economics into culture, is the combination of a cultural thematics and the near absence of infrastructural weight in the explanation of cultural and ideological phenomena.

Marx and Engels, Bernstein and Kautsky, Lenin and Bukharin – in other words, the two founders of Marxism, the leading revisionist, the high priest of orthodoxy at the time of the Second International, the leader of the first Marxist revolution and the best theorist of the Bolshevik regime – all upheld, within Marxism, the ideal of a master social science. Not so the Western Marxists. They preferred to regard Marxism not as a science but as a critique. To be sure, Marx himself, as Korsch was quick to stress, had titled or subtitled as such all his main works, from his youthful *Critique of Hegel's Philosophy of Right* (1843) to the *Contribution to the Critique of Political Economy* (1859), and last, but not least, *Capital* itself. Yet all that Marx meant was a 'sociologization' of the subject matter previously dealt with by less social-minded disciplines, for example idealist political philosophy or classical political economy. This Marxian sociologization was in turn an attempt to deepen that generalized historical approach which came to be a trademark of social science throughout the nineteenth century. Marx's critique of political economy endeavoured, therefore, to introduce social determinism into the explanation of economic processes and economic change. But with Marx, 'critique' was by no means intended as an alternative to 'science' – on the contrary, it was expected to clear the ground for a truly scientific historical account of social evolution and the fate of capitalism. In WM, by contrast, 'critique' is wielded as a philosophical weapon against any quest for social regularities endowed with causal power – precisely what Marx had been chasing in his mature work.

One can, indeed one should, distinguish the scientific outlook in Marx from the crude scientism of some of Engels's best-known formulae. Both Marx and Engels, however, did share a naturalistic conception of knowledge, and to that extent saw classical Marxism as a point of no return in the supersession of idealism – the philosophy, pre-eminently German by the early to mid-nineteenth century, that had insisted on the primacy of mind. Not content to stress the active role of consciousness in knowledge, the idealists had gone on to equate reality with mind, seeking to explain all phenomena in terms of the meaning-giving operations of human consciousness. In practice, therefore, idealism was the human viewpoint, and as such was scarcely compatible with the anti-anthropo-morphic detachment required by scientific thinking.

The hospitality shown by WM towards the classics of German idealism (above all, towards Hegel) is part and parcel of the stubborn rejection of the naturalist approach of Marx's Marxism. WM conspicuously opted for a human-ist epistemology: true knowledge, more than ever, came to be identified with the human viewpoint. Western Marxists were seldom after causes – but they were always after 'meaning', always in search of the 'human factor'. Hence their constant uneasiness about the materialist cast of mind of classical Marxism. Unwilling to disown materialism after the long discredit of idealist metaphysics, the Western Marxists were clearly embarrassed by its epistemological implications, which flew in the face of their humanist view of knowledge. On the other hand, as a speculative theory of being, the 'dialectical materialism' (diamat) of Engels and Plekhanov was no better than the metaphysics of mind in the idealist tradition. Matter or mind, no matter; mind or matter, never mind . . . the old conundrum catches the essential inanity of the worn-out dilemma. As a theory of knowledge, however, materialism had a lot to offer, for what it boiled down to was a naturalist strategy of explanatory analysis, frankly causal in direction and determinist in inclination. In analytical deed if not in philosophical rhet-oric, however, it was just not possible to square materialism with the humanist and anti-science bias of WM.

To a large extent, WM amounted to a restoration of the idealist element in Marxism, and I shall devote the next section to recalling the outlines of this idealist component by attempting to sort out the gist of the Hegel/Marx connection. The birthplace of WM was an essay (on class consciousness) in which the author, the young Lukács, aimed, in his own words, to achieve 'a Hegelianism more Hegelian than Hegel'.[1] Indeed, to some able commentators, notably Neil McInnes, the imprint of Hegel seems so visible in WM that the latter may be contrasted with previous versions of Marxist doctrine in that it evinces little taste for blending Marxism with other philosophical schools, except – precisely – its own Hegelian source. Thus while Kautsky was steeped in evolutionist thought, Plekhanov fell in love with monist ontologies epitomized by Spinoza, and the Austrian Marxists were very keen on Kant and Mach, WM stuck to the heritage. In many ways, WM was a Left Hegelianism redivivus, more faithful to the Master than the original Left Hegelians, not counting the greatest of them all – Marx himself.

Still, this marked fidelity to the Hegelian matrix did not prevent WM from borrowing important concepts from many different quarters of contemporary thought. If Croce's influence on Gramsci may be reckoned as one more case of Hegelianism (since Croce was arguably the foremost Hegelian of this century), much that was assimilated by WM came not only from 'maverick' philosophers such as Simmel or even Nietzsche, but also from the mainstream neo-idealist movement headed by Dilthey, who rebuilt the concept of historical knowledge in close kinship with a discipline fathered by romanticism: hermeneutics, the art of interpretation. Other strands incorporated into WM were originally foreign to academic philosophy: Weber's social theory; Freudian psycho-analysis; modernist aesthetics, to name but three. Thus, from the outset, WM eschewed that dogmatic, *a priori* avoidance of 'bourgeois' ideology so strictly observed by the diamat vulgate enshrined in Moscow.

The simplest description of WM seems bound therefore to underscore at least three characteristics: (a) its prominent cultural thematic; (b) its staunchly humanist view of knowledge; and (c) the broad eclecticism of its conceptual equipment. Obviously, then, WM is not just 'heresy' *vis-à-vis* Soviet Marxism: rather, it is a heresy with a special flavour. This becomes all the more conspicuous if one compares WM with previous collective departures from classical Marxism, or from that part of the Marxian legacy which was, in a rather sclerotic way, made into official wisdom by Soviet decree. For example, the so-called 'crisis of Marxism' moment (1897–9), dominated by the revisionist surge; or Austro-Marxism, born in the first decade of this century.

Each of the protagonists of the 'crisis of Marxism' debate – Antonio Labriola, the young Benedetto Croce, Eduard Bernstein, Georges Sorel and the Czech Thomas Masaryk, who invented the expression – was a fierce anti-determinist. As he thought Marx a blind believer in historical determinism, Masaryk (*The Philosophical and Sociological Foundations of Marxism*, 1898) was himself no Marxist. On the other hand Labriola (*Essays on the Materialist Conception of History*, 1896) took a non-determinist view of Marxism. Accordingly, he rejected Masaryk's notion of a theoretical crisis of Marxism altogether. In *Socialism and Philosophy* (1898) Labriola insisted that historical materialism was 'a philosophy of practice' opposed to both idealism (the thought-to-life instead of life-to-thought explanations) and 'naturalistic materialism'. His disciple Croce, who would give a radical twist to Labriolan anti-positivism by eventually developing an 'absolute historism', reduced the legitimacy of historical materialism to its being 'a simple canon of historical interpretation'. Much impressed by Croce's critique of historical determinism, Bernstein concentrated on refuting the Marxist prophecies of mass immiseration, class polarization and capitalist breakdown. Finally, Sorel inferred from the crisis of Marxism that Marxian historicism, as a theory of (economic) historical laws, was not a picture of reality but just a useful social myth – an active creed for the toiling masses, a rationale for revolution.

Now the striking differences between these thinkers (admittedly very dissimilar from each other) and most WM masters, from Lukács to Adorno and Sartre, is that none of them ever was or became a 'humanist' in the sense of rejecting the scientific ideal or denouncing scientific principles. Masaryk had a deeply religious mind which from the start ascribed the crisis of civilization to the decay of Christian faith. Nevertheless, he extolled science and went as far as contending, in the manner of Comte, that the task of philosophy was to build a new world-view grounded on scientific findings. Labriola, an ex-Hegelian, saw in Marx a healthy break with idealism; consequently, he had no quarrel with materialism *per se*, just with its mechanist variety. Engineer Sorel did not dismiss Marx's historical determinism because it was scientific, but because it was not scientific enough: it was unable to specify a convincing causal account of its assumptions and predictions. Croce's arguments against historical materialism *qua* historical determinism were similarly motivated. To Sorel, they seemed all the more cogent since they could be easily squared with Cournot's strictures against universal determinism, which were likewise of a perfectly logical and scientific character and greatly helped to shape Sorel's own epistemological ideas.

The second major heresy to be considered is that of Austro Marxism. During their first creative spell (1904–10), the Austrian Marxists did much to refine classical Marxism, or to bypass the coarse tenets of 'vulgar Marxism'. Thus, while Max Adler, resorting to Machian positivism, stressed that social causes normally operate through the mediation of consciousness, Karl Renner argued that bourgeois law was far from being a mere reflection of economic power. Later, between the two world wars, Austro-Marxism grew still bolder. Rudolf Hilferding expatiated on 'organized capitalism' as a new stage in socio-economic history; whereas Adler studied the metamorphosis of the working class, Renner identified new 'service' strata; and Otto Bauer did not baulk at pointing out the emergence, in Soviet socialism, of a new dominant class, the Bolshevik hierarchy. The upshot of such analysis was no less dissenting from Marxist-Leninist pieties than the drift of Western Marxist sociology. Yet the ideological framework of Austro-Marxism seems still further removed from the embattled humanism of WM than the *fin de siècle* crisis theorists. Adler tried to ground Marxist social science on Kantian epistemology, just as Bernstein had tried to base socialism on Kantian ethics. Moreover, like the Western Marxists

9

after them, they both saw their own politics as far more democratic than the reality of Bolshevik rule. But neither indulged in anything remotely like a full-blown repudiation of science, bourgeois culture and industrial society.

Let us call this missing element by its revealing German name: *Kulturkritik*. For WM is not just the Marxism of the superstructure: it was also, from the start, a theory of culture crisis, a passionate indictment of bourgeois civilization. That generous (and historically accurate) recognition of capitalist achievements which generated some of Marx and Engels' best pages since *The Communist Manifesto*, was nearly totally lost on WM philosophy. WM is a theoretical exercise whose cradle was the rekindled revolutionism that followed in the wake of October 1917, but whose habitat has mostly been, ever since those days, the humanist intelligentsia. WM grew out of, and continues to thrive on an obstinate rejection of the industrial ethos and, more generally, of the values of modern social culture, a rejection that, since the rise of the 'decadent' movement and the first intimations of modernist art a hundred years ago, has never subsided among humanist intellectuals in the West.

Western Marxist rhetoric did not condemn modernity as such, just capitalist modernity. But it is easy to show that a great deal of what went into its (often implicit) definition of capitalism belongs to the social condition of modern man in advanced industrialism. To that extent, WM launched an unexpected reprise from the Left of several leitmotifs in the conservative critique of industrial society. Recanting the philosophy of WM's oldest gospel – *History and Class Consciousness* (1923) – Lukács described it as 'romantic anti-capitalism'. What was romantic about it (and reminds one of the historical romantico-conservative rejection of early industrial capitalism) was that it conflated serious objections to bourgeois society with a rejection of industrial civilization based on modern technology and an ever more complex division of labour. And the point is, most of WM deserves the blame Lukács addressed to his own youthful outlook.

We shall see that this romantic stress on humanist pathos, besides doing less than justice to much of Gramsci's thought, also scarcely fits the work of Althusser; but we shall also see that Althusserianism is very much, in this respect, the exception that proves the rule.

For the time being, we must proceed from the broadest possible characterization of WM to recalling its main philosophical background: Hegel and Marx country. In so doing, I shall of course highlight what in Marx or Hegel most appealed to Western Marxists; but no attempt will be made to read either of them through the lenses of WM: for here the differences are at least as telling as the points of continuity.

2. THE HERITAGE: HEGEL

Of the Absolute, we ought to say that it is essentially an outcome.
Hegel

The poet Heinrich Heine once wrote that Kant was greater than Robespierre because while Robespierre had guillotined the king, Kant, by ruling out the speculative prowesses of metaphysics, had beheaded nobody less than God himself. However, added Heine, when Kant saw that his critical demolition of the concept of God's existence threw his loyal servant, Lampe, into frightful anguish, he took pity on him and restored the Creator (together with the immortality of the soul) as a 'postulate' of practical reason in his epoch-making *Critique of Practical Reason*.

Most of German philosophy immediately after Kant can be described as excellent news for good old Lampe: the majority of post-Kantians had no qualms about reasserting speculative metaphysics. Whereas Kant had severed absolutes from knowledge, Fichte (1762–1814), Schelling (1775–1854) and Georg Wilhelm Friedrich Hegel

(1770–1831) strove to make philosophy intimately acquainted with the absolute. Kant's epistemological scruples were simply brushed aside. To hold that no adequate grasp of ultimate beings (the famous 'thing-in-itself') can be rationally warranted came to be seen as an intellectual attitude lacking 'the courage of truth, the belief in the power of spirit'.

These words come from Hegel's inaugural lecture at the chair of the university of Berlin (1818). Hegel's impatience with Kant was a lifelong affair, showing that from the outset his own philosophy chose an entirely different path. Hegel's central thesis spelt a self-development of Thought where 'Thought' denotes the Absolute (hence the capital letter). It was a full-blown version of that equation of reality with mind which lies at the heart of idealism. While Kant had stressed the mind's active role in knowledge, the post-Kantian idealists went further than this: they saw the mind as the seat of reality, not just as a driving force in knowledge. German idealist thinkers differed from previous idealist thinkers (e.g., Berkeley) precisely because, instead of conceiving of mind as a prius offered at the beginning of knowing, they saw the primacy of mind as a programme unfolding in time (a 'process').

German idealism, then, was of a Faustian kind: it emphasized striving (*Streben*) and regarded Mind as the protagonist of a protracted drama – the agon of the spirit shaping the meaning of the world, or rather, the world itself. And here is another key aspect of post-Kantian metaphysics: the lofty accent on the spiritual. Not for nothing had its leaders Schelling and Hegel undertaken theological studies before coming to academic philosophy. If idealism in general amounts, as we noted, to the 'human viewpoint', German idealism served it with a religious vengeance. Metaphysical idealism deemed 'human experience' (as distinct from Revelation) the source where 'one can find the clue to an understanding of the ultimate nature of reality, and this clue was revealed through those traits which distinguish man as a spiritual being'.[2]

Hegel's specific contribution to this philosophy was that he greatly enhanced the idealist theme by presenting the self-development of Thought less as a reflection (the romantic and Fichtean work of the mind as 'experience') than as a 'positing', i.e., a process through which the subject of thought becomes its own object. We may call this positing (*Setzens*) the *thetic* element (from the Greek *thesein*, to put; cf. 'thesis', that which is put forward for discussion). It was the thetic element which earned Hegel's system the name of 'objective idealism', as against the emphatically subjective idealism of Fichte.

Yet in a sense the passage from subjective to objective idealism had already been started when Schelling, Hegel's former schoolmate at the theological seminary in Tübingen, projected mind on to nature as infinite self-activity – a move that so interested Hegel that he devoted his first published essay to explicating *The Difference between Fichte's and Schelling's Systems* (1801). What is specifically Hegelian is that the Absolute, in Hegel's mode of objective idealism, becomes intrinsically historical. To begin with, Hegel believed, as he said in the overture of his *Philosophy of Right* (1821), that all philosophy is 'its own time apprehended in thoughts'. Furthermore, faithful to the spiritual concerns of idealist metaphysics, he construed the self-development of Thought as a march of Spirit through – and within – history.

In Hegel's time, German culture was already disposed to a philosophy of history as an intellectual genre with more than a pinch of innovative religious inspiration. Take for instance G.E. Lessing, alongside Kant the greatest name in the *Aufklärung* (the German Enlightenment). His literary testament was a short philosophical tract called *The Education of the Human Race* (1780); in it, the orthodox Christian perspective of a history of salvation subtly gives way to a concept of salvation-through-history. This practically identified the divine with a set of stages in the ethical improvement of mankind.

But, as shown in another of Lessing's masterpieces, the

play *Nathan the Wise*, the historicization of religion, dictated as it was by an ethics of tolerance, focused as much on the width of historical experience as on its redemptive goal. By contrast, in Hegel's hands, the new, immanentist theory of religion as philosophy of history was to become a *historiosophy*, that is, a logic of history justified by a crowning stage which was also a state of social bliss. Hegelian history was strongly goal-orientated, a march of times heading for the present, each age a stepping-stone for the next. The word historiosophy itself was coined, in 1838, by a wildly messianic Hegelian, the Polish count August Cieszkowski. In the previous year, the notion, if not the term, had already provided the core of the highly eschatological thought of one of the main left Hegelians, Moses Hess (1812–75), author of a *Sacred History of Mankind* (1837).

Hegel's place in the gallery of western metaphysics is determined by his blending of ontology (the theory of being) with philosophy of history (the justification of the human adventure, a kind of secular theodicy). By defining the Absolute as an ultra-historical Spirit, Hegel historicized being. Henceforth, being could be thought of as pre-eminently a becoming. And later metaphysicians have seldom forgotten it. For example, it is hard to find so un-Hegelian an ontology as Heidegger's; and yet Heidegger always insisted on the historicity of his elusive Being.

Like the God of the old theology, Hegel's historical Spirit soars high above the limitations of finitude. In his view, the supreme task of reason (*Vernunft*) consisted in a takeover from faith, for reason's task was to promote the 'sublation' of the finite into the infinite of unfolding Spirit. Unlike reason thus defined, the understanding (*Verstand*), much praised by the *Aufklärung* – and roughly corresponding to analytical reason – seemed to him bound to the 'sadness of finitude' (*Trauer der Endlichkeit*), in the phrase of his *Logic*. The central problem of Hegel's philosophy was precisely the unity of finite and infinite. Hence the overwhelming importance, in his system, of mediation (*Vermittlung*), the crucial category he developed in his years at Jena

(1801–1807). Hegel was from the start enamoured of the absolute; he longed for a reconciliation (*Versohnung*), in this world, of finite and the divine infinite. But, being hostile to the romantic (and Schellingian) mystique of intuition, his way of superseding the wretched chasm between part and whole (since 'only the whole [*das Ganz*] is true') required the rational mediation of interlocking concepts instead of the leap into blind mystical faith or the raptures of poetical fantasy. Reconciliation by dint of an endless chain of mediations to be grasped by reason – *Versohnung* achieved by *Vermittlung* apprehended by *Vernunft*: such is the motto of Hegel's metaphysics. But more than that, his metaphysics are mildly salvationist as well, because mediation is an imitation of Christ: underneath mediation there lies the image of the greatest mediator, God turned man with his magnificent promise of Atonement[3].

The first commandment of idealist metaphysics was to posit as ultimate substance something partaking of the nature of the subject. As Hegel put it at the beginning of his *Phenomenology of Spirit* (1807): 'What matters is that truth be thought and expressed not only as a substance but also as a subject'. Such substance Hegel believed himself to have found in the Spirit which unfolds in human history. But this, of course, implied the idea of an Absolute which manifests itself by means of a non-absolute, finite reality. Now the concept of a positive, enriching self-alienation of the Absolute was a hoary notion of early medieval theology, and a tenet borrowed from the neo-platonic tradition by a contemporary of Charlemagne, John Scotus Eriugena. In so far as the necessary worldly incarnations of God, in this Christianized neo-platonic pattern, fall short of the infinite substantiality of the Absolute, God can be known only through what he is not: hence the concept of 'negative theology'. Like the idea of an enriching alienation, negative theology proved a decisive borrowing from neo-platonic doctrines into modern dialectics, the art of gaining insight from the grasp of contradictions. By stressing an *a contrario* way to reach the Absolute, the eternal Spirit returned to itself after a long pilgrimage in the realm of transient and contingent forms, negative theology provides dialectics with a model; and dialectics was the main method of Hegelian philosophy (besides being more than just a method).

Thanks to Leszek Kolakowski, we are now familiar with the shadow of negative theology in the metaphysical background of Hegelian dialectics, in Hegel as well as in Marx.[4] Others have chosen to stress, in the ancestry of dialectics, some gnostic motifs, especially the myth of a God of the Origins who, instead of manifesting himself in the world, exiles himself within his own inwardness, leaving to man the burden of restoring him to his pristine glory. This gnostic theme was endorsed, in Eriugena's time, by the Byzantine theology of St Cyril; next it penetrated the Jewish cabbala during the Renaissance, and then Christian mysticism, from Böhme in the early seventeenth century to pietism, the liveliest trend in German religiosity in the age of Enlightenment. The pietist theosophy of Friedrich Oetinger (1702–82), the 'Magus of the South', was a powerful influence among Hegel's masters at Tübingen.[5] And Hegel himself closed his *Phenomenology of Spirit* alluding to the 'lifeless loneliness' of God without man.

Both 'enriching self-alienation' and the gnostic rescue of the self-exiled deity share neo-platonic roots, even though, at first sight, these two mythical strands seem worlds apart. On the one hand, God is all a dynamics of exteriority; on the other, God flees the world. The God of negative theology is a super-extrovert; the God of the Gnosis, a morbid introvert. Yet the two do converge. In the myth of God's self-exile, the further he plunges inwards, the stronger becomes the world relinquished by him. In the event, therefore, we are left – just as in the myth of progressive alienation – with a situation dominated by the power of objectivity. Moreover, in both cases the strength of objective reality stems from the same source: it derives from a 'labour of negation' operating within an objectivity *subjectively grounded*, since it bears at each step the imprint of the Absolute-as-subject, acting as a historical process, or at the very least the mark of man's consciousness, striving to restore the divine amid the evil of the world.

For Hegel, the strategic role of externalization (*Entäusserung*) is tremendously important, since the higher a reality, the more it is actuality (*Wirklichkeit*). 'Genuine truth,' he wrote, 'is the prodigious transfer of the inner into the outer, the building of reason into the real world' (*Philosophy of Right*, para. 270). In the great *Logic* of 1812–16, which is in fact an ontology, the highest category, the Idea, is defined precisely by its need for actualization. Hegel's idea is not, as in Locke or Hume, a mere mental representation; rather, it is the concept in so far as the concept makes itself real.

One of Hegel's most famous, or infamous, declarations, coming right at the beginning of his *Philosophy of Right*, states that 'What is rational is actual and what is actual is rational'. Taken as an oracle of ingrained conservatism, as though it were the German pendant of Pope's celebrated phrase, 'Whatever is, is right', it stirred a flood of scornful comments; and Engels made things still worse by inverting the sequence of propositions, having Hegel say 'All that is actual is rational and all that is rational is actual'.[6] Yet to the first Hegelians, for example, Eduard Gans (1797–1839), Hegel's thesis, far from sacralizing the existing, simply meant that reason had power to realize itself.[7] Since his earliest theological writings, Hegel had made clear that philosophy had no truck with the crass legitimation of given realities. In the third edition of his *Encyclopedia of Philosophical Sciences* (1830) he stressed that actuality does by no means refer to sheer existence. Accordingly, the second half of the controversial dictum – 'what is actual is rational' – cannot mean that all existing ways of the world are rationally justified. Even so, Hegel was no latterday Plato. He did not think of the ideal as something out of reach, but as something, on the contrary, gradually embodied into the institutions of historical man.

Thus, without legitimizing all that exists in the present, Hegel wished to see his own times as the meaningful goal of the past. Hence the difference between him and the *Aufklärung* as concerns the concept of the present. For the Enlightenment, since progress means always a better state of affairs, the present can but free man from history. Hegel saw it another way. To him the present *fulfilled* the past because it realized (in both senses of the word) the essential content of history: the work of reason in the world. That is why he found fault with revolution and restoration alike. Both Revolution, by denying the past, and Restoration, by rejecting the present, seemed wrong in that both presupposed an unreal break between past and present, origin and future.[8] Like the Revolution, whose epochal significance he constantly underlined, Hegel sided with the present; but he extolled the present of the West for its deep historical meaning, not as a clean slate of history.

If we care to see this emphasis on historical actualization within the onto-theological framework briefly described earlier, we shall understand more fully why Hegel needed the dialectic method. The nodal point in this connection is the problem, already mentioned, of the ontological status of the finite. By stressing the need for Spirit to embody itself in historical forms, Hegel wanted to demonstrate that finite beings are not just a contingent reality but elements and stages in a plan endowed with necessity. The demonstration itself took two broad paths, well described by Charles Taylor as descending and ascending dialectic.[9] The task of ascending dialectic was to show that finite reality can be explained only by an increasingly wider network of relations, so that truth turns out to be a function of comprehensiveness. Yet growing interrelation is not enough, since by itself the dialectic ascending from the finite can never thoroughly overcome the original contingency of its starting point. At this juncture there comes, to the dialectician's rescue, a complementary descending dialectic, endeavouring to show that the apparently contingent finite actually *emanates* from a necessary development of the subject-substance, namely, Spirit.

Hegel's dynamic ontology gives us a two-way ladder:

while the Spirit comes down to the finite (or, better still, *as* finite), the finite climbs up the rungs of history, until it reaches the point where Spirit, without ceasing its constant externalization, attains the stage of its fullest self-knowledge – which is the time when the third great form of 'absolute spirit', philosophy, takes over from art and religion.

From what we have seen of Hegel's conception of the present, a rational fulfilment of the past, it is easy to infer that the dialectical progress does not simply suppress what is left behind. The German key term here, *Aufhebung*, means a 'lifting up' where surpassing is at one with preserving, *sublating* rather than suppressing. Such are the wonders wrought by the 'labour of the negative' when negation works under the spell of reconciliation. It follows that Hegelian dialectic is forever enamoured of *totality*.

In due course we shall see how crucial this holist view was to be for early WM, especially in Lukács, before becoming a true bone of contention for the Frankfurt school (particularly Adorno). But no discussion of Hegelian dialectics, however cursory, can avoid addressing itself to the notion of contradiction (*Widerspruch*), a veritable term of art in Hegel's philosophy, and one of his major legacies to Marxist language. Briefly, Hegel *did* indulge, a number of times, in a kind of dalliance with irrationalism, both by subscribing, as he did in Book II of the *Logic*, to the existence of contradictions *in re* (as opposed to logical contradictions) – a possibility explicitly and lucidly ruled out by Kant (*Critique of Pure Reason*, 1, 2, 1 appendix) – and by giving some bewildering examples of 'real' contradictions, as in his comments on physical movement (as he stated in the *Logic*, for something to move it must be both here and not here at the same time). Nothing is gained, however, by calling contradiction, with a hint of supralogical insight, what in fact boils down to mere oppositions, like the forces of attraction and repulsion in mechanics. Moreover, much of what Hegel deems contradictory is (as Croce perceived) nothing more than *distinct*. Engels brought dialectical thought into considerable disrepute by stating that resounding inanities such as 'the plant is the negation of the seed' were fine specimens of contradiction in nature.

But in Hegel's case there is a line of defence. Without denying the bogusness of the thesis of contradiction as the pith and marrow of reality, some commentators have drawn attention to the fact that Hegel did not usually assert that an object x always has at the same time a given quality and its contrary. Rather, he pointed to incompatibilities *over time*, like that obtaining, in a celebrated section of the *Phenomenology*, between the master who starts keeping his serf in bondage but ends up dependent upon his labour: master and slave are contraries, but as their relation progresses the initial sovereignty of the former turns out to be an acute form of dependency. In other words, as the logic of the situation unfolds, the master's position becomes 'contradictory'. More generally, Hegel tends to predicate such contradictions on stages between themselves, rather than within themselves. Following a suggestion by H.B. Acton,[10] it is tempting to say that contradiction may well have been Hegel's name (or misnomer) for the vital antagonism between competitive ideas and social forces – something that Hegel, as an attentive reader of political economy, deemed as positive in the history of civilization as in economic life. On the other hand, the work of mediation could hardly be accomplished if the 'labour of the negative' meant just a war of all things against all; and yet Hegel's system is, as much as the land of contradiction, a paradise for mediations.

One thing is sure: Hegelian contradiction, like Hegelian mediation, is a denizen of history. That is why, in the most spectacular and fascinating of his treatises, the *Phenomenology* – which he dubbed his 'voyage of discovery' – Spirit finds its being alternately through forms of consciousness (e.g. sense perception, self-consciousness), or philosophical stances and intellectual practices (stoicism, scepticism, scholarship) *and* through historical wholes (eg. ancient Greece, imperial Rome, early Christianity, the Protestant era, the French Revolution). In the eighth and final chapter, Hegel indicates that the task of philosophy in his day is no longer, as it was for Spinoza after Descartes, that of explaining the unity of thought and space; rather, it had become the task of explaining the unity of thought and historical time. What earlier 'was expressed as the unity of thought and space, should now be grasped as the unity of thought and time' – for the Spirit can reach perfect self-awareness only 'when it realizes itself as *Weltgeist*'.

Michael Rosen has drawn a skilful contrast between the assumptions of Hegel's 'voyage' in the great *Phenomenology* and Kant's idea of philosophical analysis.[11] According to Kant, experience – the stuff of analysis – is composed of two things: a content coming from outside, and a form imposed upon this by the mind's cognitive activities. Rosen stresses the psychological character of the philosophical enterprise thus conceived: philosophy, by inquiring into the mind's structures, gains insight into the structure of phenomena. By contrast, Hegel's concept of experience is historical, not psychological; and because of this, it does not allow for a Kantian separation between the form and content of experience.

Inasmuch as the *Phenomenology* discerns structures of consciousness underlying historical wholes – for instance, the 'unhappy consciousness' of early (Catholic) Christianity – Hegel's project in this 'Odyssey of the Spirit' (E. Bloch) may be said to resemble Kant's own. But the whole idea of a development of the mind in historical terms is anything but Kantian, as is the attempt to account for a spiritual structure of reality behind the world of phenomena.

The hero of the *Phenomenology* is the self-conscious Spirit, the 'universal individual' – 'an I which is a we, the we which is an I' – and its formulation sealed Hegel's final break with Schelling, whose brand of 'objective idealism', equated nature, not history, with mind. Later, Hegel, who did not share the almost unanimous contemporary preference, within his oeuvre, for the *Phenomenology*, described this dense welter of epistemology, anthropology, history and moral philosophy, as a propaedeutic to his full-grown system. Be that as it may, the doctrine of the Spirit, as put forward in the *Phenomonology*, historicized man in a sense deeply committed to the ruling principle of Hegel's mature social theory: the growth of freedom.

As with Rousseau, Hegel's social thought hinges upon freedom. The presupposition of freedom was to him the strength of individuality, and the attainment of individuality in turn was seen as no small achievement, something which could only have come very late in history. Among the more memorable passages of the *Phenomenology of Spirit* there is a picture of the ancient polis as a beautiful but undeveloped stage in history. Because in the polis there was still no real severance of the individual from the state, the Spirit reigned in youthful immediacy with itself. A morally *compact* community, the ancient city often witnessed the clash between different principles of legitimacy; yet it knew no inner drama, no individual 'schism in the soul'. Thus when Antigone challenged Creon, neither she nor he was in the grip of a conflict of values. She stood for divine injunction, he for human command – but neither struggled with two laws, nor endured a personal strife of duty and passion. This very absence of inner conflict, however, betrayed an underdevelopment of individuality.

On the other hand, in the 'soulless community' of the Roman empire, free individuals came to live between slavery and citizenry proper, for the state was thoroughly beyond their reach. Individuality was then compelled to take refuge in 'philosophical' inner liberty, or to dissolve into the 'unhappy consciousness' of the Christian beyond. Therefore, the citizen of the polis was free, but still undifferentiated from the state; the subject of the Empire dwelt in differentiation, but also in unfreedom. Only in the 'world of culture' of western Christendom before the French Revolution did there emerge a truly universal individualism. Just as he placed the Christian logos at the heart of his historicist metaphysics, Hegel made Christianity the cradle of the idea of liberty. 'The East knows', says his

Philosophy of History, 'that *one* single person (the despot) was alone free; Greece and Rome, that *some* were; the Germanic (Christian) world, that *all* are'.

This Christian principle of freedom did not materialize before Germanic feudalism. Until then, it remained co-cooned in religion, without any remarkable institutional expression. However, even among western peoples freedom did not reach a properly active stage until the Revolution and Napoleon. Only then did a 'civil society' composed of independent individuals receive its full juridical legitim-ation; only then did the idea of liberty – the freedom of spirit as universal will – find an appropriate form. And it is this kind of social order that, in its principle, Hegel extolled in the lapidary *Philosophy of Right* of 1821, his last complete utterance as a social theorist, and as such the object of critical reactions from Karl Marx and Lorenz von Stein.

Because of the *Philosophy of Right*, Hegel is often seen – and condemned – as an upholder of the state. And so he was; but it is of paramount importance to bear in mind that in his view the state, as 'the actuality of concrete freedom', ensures 'explicit recognition' of 'personal indi-viduality and its particular interests'; and that it is 'of their own accord' that, under the rule of the state, individual interests 'pass over into the interest of the universal' (*Philosophy of Right*, para. 260). The rational state consists in the 'unity' of objective freedom (the universal will) and 'subjective freedom', that is, freedom of everyone in their pursuit of chosen ends (para. 258, addition).

The main institutional prop envisaged by Hegel for building such uncanny unity of common good and particu-lar interest was a mechanism of representation of social classes. Thus for Hegel, unlike Marx, classes are not divisive but integrative social forces. This is why, in Hegel, there remain estates (*Stände*), i.e. legitimate clusters of status and/or crafts. Hegel's view of classes as pillars of the polity lend his political theory a strong corporatist flavour. In his Jena years Hegel distinguished three such estates: the peasantry; a mercantile class subdivided into craftsmen and businessmen; and the civil servants, a high minded, duty-bound 'public state' recruited and promoted on meritocratic grounds. Prior to the *Philosophy of Right*, Hegel's corporatism had little in common with the traditionalist ideal of a social pyramid topped by a hereditary landed aristocracy. In what is perhaps the best sociological reading of the *Philosophy of Right*, *Hegel's Theory of the Modern State* (1972) Shlomo Avineri claims that the introduction of an aristocracy as the upper part of the 'agricultural class' was a clear 'bow to Restoration ideology'. But the dutiful bureaucracy remained, in 1821, as 'universal' a class as before, an estate bent on knowledge and the common good, reflecting much of the public ethos of the German tradition of a learned civil service.

Later social theorists were less than convinced by this celebration of state officialdom. From Marx to Weber, German thought went a long way in de-idealizing bureaucracy. But in the case of the 'universal class', at least the notion of its enforcing the universality of 'objective freedom' seems clear enough: for, as a 'cognitive' estate, the state bureaucracy lives in the immediate neighbourhood of that universalist idea of freedom impersonated – precisely – by the state.

The whole picture becomes much dimmer, however, as one turns to that hopeful synthesis of universal will and particular individual interests adumbrated in the aforementioned paragraphs of the *Philosophy of Right*. Here the corporatist blueprint is to little avail, since, unlike the civil service, the other classes have no direct relation with the idea. How can we be sure, in Hegel's own terms, that individual freedom would not be threatened or destroyed in the process of such a synthesis – especially when we know that it is a synthesis *'von oben'*, that is, imposed from above?

For all the lack of specification, one thing is certain: Hegel did not countenance any reduction of that vigorous scope for individuality he was so keen on in the historical saga of the *Phenomenology*. Evidence for this is found in the passages of the *Philosophy of Right* (e.g., paras 185, 262, 299) where he goes out of his way to criticize Plato. In the *Republic*, he claims, the 'principle of self-subsistent particularity' was excluded from the state. Now Hegel pits the bourgeois stress on the free choice of occupation (the '*carrière ouverte aux talents*') against Plato's authoritarian ascriptive utopia, where people must work in the slots assigned them by their philosophical Guardians; and he does not baulk at comparing the *Republic*, in this regard, to oriental despotism – something as abhorrent to him as it had been to his beloved Montesquieu. Whatever the 'universal' bureaucratic estate might do, in Hegel it did not include anything like the absolute rule of despots, enlightened or otherwise.

Above all, Hegel's respect for individuality is warranted by his pathbreaking realization of the historical meaning of bourgeois society. The scholarly researches of Manfred Riedel have singled out the novelty of Hegel's ideas on two crucial points: the concepts of work and practice, and of civil society. Roughly speaking, Hegel put forward a new philosophical view of praxis. In classical thought *praxis* (the action of free men, which was an end in itself) is set high above *poiesis* (manual work, whose end lay beyond the activity, in useful products or works of art). Then Adam Smith turned it upside down: in *The Wealth of Nations* (1776), the praxis of politicians, jurists and soldiers is roundly demoted, whereas productive activity is exalted. In the early nineteenth century, this bourgeois–liberal dignification of work was to be wholeheartedly shared by the burgeoning socialism of Henri de Saint-Simon.

Hegel, from his Jena lectures of 1803/4 and 1805/6 onwards (the so-called *Realphilosophie*) gave work, beside speech and (communicative) action, a central role in the constitution of Spirit. To Riedel, this new poietics marks a felicitous fusion of political economy (with which, as we saw, Hegel was well acquainted) and transcendental idealism, with its accent on the productivity of the mind. In other words, Hegel endowed work with the lofty meaning

25

of a spiritual production. By the same token, he did not conceive of labour, as did Aristotle, in terms of its outcome but in terms of its origin: work arises from the 'negative' (i.e., creative) labour of the mind goaded by need and desire. In the dialectic of master and slave, the former embodies the classical contempt for production; but eventually it is the toiling consciousness of the shape-giving, object-producing slave which gets the upper hand. At the same time, Hegel does not limit his praise of the subjective meaning of productivity to the travail of conscience – rather, he projects it on to man's long struggle with nature.

Elsewhere, Hegel's dialogue with traditional practical philosophy was no less subversive. In particular, the *Philosophy of Right* sharply broke with classical views on family and civil society. Hegel sundered the concept of family from the last remnants of the '*oikos*' idea, the household as a system of economic subsistence and blood alliances; and he also boldly redefined 'civil society' as a vital, dynamic sphere of needs and interests distinct from the state. Until Hegel, '*societas civilis*' simply meant political association. As late as the mid-eighteenth century, in western political philosophy, state and society were welded, as witness the title of the seventh chapter of Locke's *Second Treatise of Government*: 'Of political or civil society' – a usage still running in Kant. To be sure, in the Scottish Enlightenment, Adam Ferguson, in his *History of Civil Society* (1767) – doubtless another main source of Hegel's social theory – presented a discussion of 'arts and sciences' under the label of 'civil society'; but Ferguson still identified the concept chiefly with the political order. 'Civil society' in the modern sense was a Hegelian invention dating from the Jena period and reaching a fully-fledged form in the third section of the *Philosophy of Right*.

Hence Hegel well understood the nature of modern society and the role of particular interests in its operation. Like his contemporary, the liberal Benjamin Constant, he realized the difference between ancient liberty, geared to political autonomy without much individuality, and manifold modern freedom which harnesses political liberty to protect the free enjoyment of civil liberties and, to that extent, is at root more social than political. However, this still does not resolve all our qualms about the fate of individual freedom under the Hegelian state. Significantly, Hegel did not go as far as Constant in his farewell to ancient models. As Judith Shklar has shown, his vision of Greece, in the context of the passionate Graecolatry of German humanism around 1800, sided with the 'political' not the 'aesthetic' classical ideal – though Hegel, characteristically, did not share the stern republicanism embraced by the 'Spartan' wing of political Graecophiles. Nor were all those who yearned for an aesthetic imitation of Greece always as politically conservative, as for example, Goethe; aesthetic Hellenism could lead straight to liberalism, as in Wilhelm von Humboldt's *Limits of State Action* (1792).

Unlike Humboldt, Hegel did not however entrust the state with a minimal and purely negative function (enforcing order, protecting rights) or even, like later, more social-minded liberals, with supplementary tasks (giving the economy a helping hand; broadening access to richer forms of freedom by equalizing opportunities). In his view, the state had a positive mission of the utmost significance: it was the bearer of human self-consciousness, the highest figure among the several incarnations of the 'objective spirit' – the objective spirit in turn being that substantial subject which, by actualizing its essential freedom, makes not just the law, but nature too, into posited objects (remember the 'thetic' element in idealism) filled with themselves; 'for freedom is being itself in another' (*Encyclopedia*, 3rd edition para. 24, add. 2).

The burden of this is that in Hegel's concept of the state freedom is equated with a power, not, as in liberal theory, with the absence of external constraints. True, Hegel angrily scolded those who, like the arch-reactionary Carl Ludwig von Haller, attempted to place an absolute state above law and modern constitutional thought; yet he, too, did not ground the legitimacy of the legal state primarily on citizenship, as did social contract theory from Hobbes to Rousseau. Instead of the legally capable citizen as an individual, now it was man *qua* man that, in the guise of a self-assertive Spirit, provided the foundation of modern politics.[12] Therefore freedom became for Hegel a Promethean force, irreducible to either self-rule (classical liberty) or absence of coercion in one's private affairs (modern civil liberty). Hegelian freedom was, like Fichte's, a power rather than either a franchise or a set of liberties.

The true ancient precedent for Hegelian freedom lies not in Greek political philosophy but in Aristotle's *Metaphysics* (982b), where the free man is said to be he who exists 'to himself and not for another'. Hegel takes over this concept in his own notion of the state as the supersubject of freedom, since he calls such a state (*Philosophy of Right*, para. 258) 'an end in itself' (*Selbstzweck*). But he adds to it, in typically idealist fashion, a reflective dimension: the autotelic state is the actuality of the moral idea 'clear to itself' in its capacity as a 'will thinking and knowing itself' (para. 257). Possibly, then, the only way out of the riddle posed by that uncanny 'unity' of general will and individual interests lies in the fact that ultimately Hegel's true subject of freedom, despite all his sincere acknowledgement of modern individualism, is man rather than the individual. At any rate, his central concept of universal history (*Weltgeschichte*) reinforces this impression: as Joachim Ritter has stressed, in Hegel history becomes universal in so far as its object is man in his essence.

Norberto Bobbio once drew an interesting contrast between Kant and Hegel as heirs to Rousseau's social contract, seen as a tool for establishing freedom as political autonomy. Kant, says Bobbio, accepted the Rousseaunian contract as a method but he preferred a state much closer to the liberal idea of a mere protector of civil liberties. Hegel, on the other hand, staunchly resisted the social contract as a political method, yet accepted the concept of autonomy as the main goal of the social order.[13]

However, the trouble is: *whose* autonomy? Hegel made a

point of dissociating his theory of the state as bearer of a universal will from Rousseau's, because in the latter the general will 'proceeds out of the individual will' as in a contract (*Philosophy of Right* para. 258, add.). A few lines earlier, he asserted somewhat ominously, that the state as a 'final end' (*Endzweck*) has 'supreme right against the individual'. Hegel's last political writing, a long critical commentary on the English Reform Bill (1831), opposed liberal demands for a broader franchise with two rather specious arguments: firstly, that universal suffrage led to political indifference, and second that in any case it gave the electorate no real power, since constituencies were not to control MPs' decisions. Some recent Hegel studies point out, apologetically, that this critique of the Reform Bill contained a lot of apt remarks on the class structure of early industrial England. Yet these valuable perceptions do not alter the fact that, from the viewpoint of democratic theory, neither his argument from apathy nor the argument from impotence seriously damages the legitimacy of the democratic principle. The truth is, whenever the concept of freedom (practical, not metaphysical: freedom as the opposite of coercion, not of determinism) ceases to be mainly social and political, and becomes 'anthropological' instead, stressing attributes of mankind rather than actions by concrete individuals, illiberal elements seem bound to arise; and something very much in this line was happening with the 'synthetic' level of liberty as defined in the *Philosophy of Right*. And the problem, as will be seen, did not exactly disappear in Hegel's successors on the left.

I shall now attempt the impossible and sketch an instant assessment of Hegel's contribution. We saw that, as a good post-Kantian, he wanted to make an honest woman of metaphysics. While Kant blamed the failure of metaphysics on metaphysics' own far-fetched aims, Hegel put the blame on the narrowness of the understanding, not on the search for absolutes *per se*. He played a leading rôle in the idealists' stubborn transgression of the criticist impeachment of sweeping metaphysical speculation. Like Fichte or Schelling, Hegel discarded the epistemological filter imposed by Kant on philosophical endeavours. Some make amends for Hegel by noting that his was a fundamentally different conception of knowledge – one that, detaching knowing from pure thought, integrated it within the general pattern of human action. But even if we grant this, we still have to ask: was this move justified? How much did we gain from such an 'anthropological' perspective on thought?

Whatever else it may have done, Hegel's approach to thought certainly helped to legitimize a historical view of man – something that, structuralist rhetoric apart, nobody seems willing to dispense with. There is no need to emphasize this point. But here Hegel had more than one important forerunner: Vico, Montesquieu, Herder all come to mind. Each was a great historicizer of culture and society. What none of them offered, however, was Hegel's 'reason in history' theme: his grand attempt to justify the present as a fulfilment of historical promise. So, the question again changes, to become: What can we save – if anything – from Hegel's historicism?

Hegel's Spirit was a worldly Providence. Its march did not evince any binding logical necessity, but displayed an overriding necessity for a purpose. An influential Hegel scholar early in our century, Theodor Haering, saw that whatever coherence there is between the figures of Spirit in the *Phenomenology* is of a purely historical, not logical character. Another great commentator, Nicolai Hartmann, set little store by Hegel's system-building, but valued highly the wealth of historical determinations of the objective spirit. Nowadays necessitarian theories of history, even in materialist versions, face widespread scepticism. Hegel's idealist brand of historical determinism fares still worse, although, in a sense, its very lack of causal claims (such as the base/superstructure one in Marx) renders it less plagued by epistemological objections than its materialist rivals. However, Hegel's theory of history can be seen from another angle, not as a demonstrative account of historical necessity, but as a persuasive invitation to legitimize one basic kind of society by means of historical comparisons.

'*Principium scientiae moralis est reverentia fato habenda*' (The principle of moral science must be a reverence towards fate). Hegel uttered this oracle in his inaugural lecture at Jena. He later repeated its core meaning in the famous dictum, '*Weltgeschichte ist Weltgericht*' (World history is the ultimate tribunal). But if this is so, how can we be sure that right is not just might? Hegel's philosophy of history and its progeny have often been invoked opportunistically, as though Hegel had not warned that in history's court of judgement 'world history is not the verdict of mere might' but of 'the necessary development of . . . the self-conscious-ness and freedom' of a rational mind whose progress he equated – in a clear bow to the Enlightenment – with the perfectibility of mankind (*Philosophy of Right*, paras 342–3). Yet in Hegel's own mind, as far as we can judge from his writings as a whole, reverence towards fate meant some-thing truly pioneering, coming so shortly after the big revolutionary upheavals and thoughtless restorations of the age. It meant a considered acceptance of the spirit of modern society, with its growing division of labour, its increase in individual freedom and its new sense of man's ability to shape history. Paradoxically, reverence for destiny inspired anything but social quietism – which may help to explain why Hegel never was a darling of conservative thinking. In his own time in Berlin he had to fight both wild reactionaries like Haller and sophisticated conserva-tives like Savigny, founder of the 'historical school' of legal philosophy.

It is precisely this element of trust in history which is missing in the Western Marxist Hegelians. Moreover, today, even sympathetic reappraisals of Hegel, most notably Charles Taylor's, tend to play down Hegel's pro-gressive acceptance of modern society. Professor Taylor's Hegel ends up by chiefly providing a yardstick by which to judge – unfavourably – our own liberal industrial world.

Claiming that Hegel wanted a reconciliation of utilitarianism with 'belonging', of bourgeois rationality with romantic 'expressivism', Taylor closes his remarkable study of him by concluding that contemporary western society has achieved nothing but a mockery of such ideals, since our social universe poorly combines a utilitarian public façade with a paltry romantic private life.[14]

This indictment has prompted a rejoinder by Ernest Gellner. There is nothing wrong, suggests Gellner, with having one's expression at home (paperbacks, hi-fi, etc.) and leaving the public sphere to soulless pragmatism. Especially if one cares to remember that the last bouts of social expressivism in the West were the Nürnberg rallies, and the Linksfaschismus fostered by the spirit of May 1968.[15] Yet Gellner concurs with Taylor in seeing Hegel chiefly as a response to, rather than a justification of, the emergence of modern society. Where he disagrees with Taylor is in his valuation: Taylor has a poor view of modernity, Gellner is basically sympathetic to it. Nevertheless, there are grounds to suspect that Hegel was far less close to the romantic uneasiness about modernity than either Taylor (approvingly) or Gellner (critically) seem to think.

In fairness to both Taylor and Gellner, it must be said that they are by no means alone in taking Hegel for a social theorist with strong romantic leanings. Perhaps the best-known modern attack on Hegel is Popper's denunciation (in Vol. II of *The Open Society and its Enemies*, 1945) not only of his historicism but of his *holism*, i.e., his alleged anti-individualist, and therefore illiberal, outlook. Popper's two arch-villains, treated by him as champions of holism, are Plato and Hegel, with Aristotle and Marx as minor, largely derivative culprits. This may sound rather ironical in view of what Hegel said of Plato's social utopia; but it still fuels a great deal of the present-day conventional wisdom about Hegel. Nevertheless, this view of things gets little support from modern Hegel scholarship. H.S. Harris, in the second volume of his minute perusal of *Hegel's*

Development, noting that after the 'philosophy of spirit' of 1805–6 Hegel approvingly recognized the 'protestant' character of the modern polity, based on the right to private judgement in the interpretation and assessment of law, stresses that such recognition marked a clear break with Hegel's own erstwhile holist ideals; from Jena onwards, says Harris, the 'Greek' model of a holist community became for Hegel 'subrational' because too impersonal. So much for viewing Hegel as a modern Plato.

One can, of course, keep the same basic interpretation and yet praise Hegel, instead of condemning him, for his holism. Thus Robert Nisbet, always keen on 'quests for community', greets Hegel as a main ancestor of a wisely holist 'sociological tradition'. The latest star in British neo-conservative political thought, Roger Scruton, has recently enlisted Hegel as a hero of conservatism – a healthy philosophical alternative to the empiricist, anti-philosophical line from Burke to Lord Hailsham and Sir Ian Gilmour. [16]

In its anti-individualist overtones, the community conservatism of Nisbet or Scruton strikes a note very different from the neo-liberal conservatism of Hayek – the high priest of the anti-holist party in contemporary social theory. But sometimes the Hegel-praising game puts community to less conservative uses. Taylor, for one, speaks of it as an invaluable framework for freedom – an expressivist, culture-bound kind of freedom, far superior to the abstract liberty of Marx and Sartre, precisely because it is rooted in community. Well before Taylor, in his *Hegel et l'État* (1950) – a little book which did much to destroy the reactionary image of Hegel – Eric Weil compared the Hegelian idea of freedom to Malinowski's encomium of the harmony of primitive society. Once again we find the holist reading of Hegel being used in a non-conservative direction: Weil's point was to *deny* that Hegel's statolatry meant to legitimize the status quo in Restoration Prussia. Yet what Weil implied by his analogy with Malinowskian societies – the 'tribal' nature of Hegel's social order – was just what led Popper to voice a strident revulsion against Hegel.

In any event, it is possible to be a 'philosophical' conservative and to like Hegel without indulging in community-hailing. Britain's leading academic conservative thinker, Michael Oakeshott, did just that. In *On Human Conduct* (1975) he speaks very affectionately of Hegel's concept of state. In his view, *der Staat*, in the *Philosophy of Right*, corresponds to a mode of association ruled by law (*das Recht*). Law, in turn, was to Hegel – claims Oakeshott – neither a simple command backed by force (as in classical legal positivism) nor a set of contrivances for satisfying wants; rather, it meant fundamentally a set of 'rules of recognition' to be observed by individuals in their actions prompted by a myriad of contingent wants. In this sense, Hegel's juridical state can be equated with Oakeshott's own concept of 'civil association', which, as Oakeshott himself always emphasized, is a notion harking back to the contractarian views of Hobbes – definitely *not* a holist thinker. Therefore a very positive conservative appraisal of Hegel can be kept, while moving far away from the holist mystique of community.

By late Victorian times, Hegel happened to be highly valued in the most unexpected of theoretical quarters – neo-classical economics. Marshall's *Principles of Economics*, the summa of neo-classical theory, are full of praise for him.[17] The praise, however, concentrated not on the apotheosis of the state but on the notion of continuous development as illustrated in Hegel's *Lectures on the Philosophy of History*. In other words, far from being thought a conservative, let alone a reactionary, Hegel was esteemed as a progressivist – exactly the characteristic which gets no prizes in contemporary Hegel-liking from Left or Right (i.e., not from Taylor or from Nisbet or Scruton).

I shall conclude my remarks on Hegel by suggesting why it could be worth returning to value this side of his thought. German philosophy from around 1700 devised two genres to cope with the sense of evil and tragedy in the world. The one was theodicy, the other philosophy of history. The master of theodicy was Leibniz; the virtuoso of philosophy of history was Hegel. The essence of his historiosophy was to incorporate historical tragedy into a deep awareness of the legitimacy of progress as embodied in youthful bourgeois society. Underpinning Hegel's system there is a will to salvation – but now 'salvation' came through historical self-knowledge. Hegel once went as far as stating that writing history without realizing the rationality of the process was just 'an idiotical divagation'. The saying may sound unfair to many forms of historical research, but it catches wonderfully the gist of his own philosophy.

Of all modern interpreters of Hegel, the one who most bluntly stressed this point was Alexandre Kojève (1902–68), a nephew of Kandinsky who emigrated to the West shortly after the Russian Revolution and, before becoming a French technocrat, ran a seminal course on the *Phenomenology of Spirit* at the Paris *École Pratique des Hautes Etudes* (1933–9) which was attended by Raymond Queneau, Eric Weil, Maurice Merleau-Ponty, Raymond Aron and Jacques Lacan. Taking Hegel's historicism quite seriously, Kojève thought that Hegelian truth is a child of the process, and as such 'is absolute only because it is the last one'.[18] Did not Hegel (in his lectures on the history of philosophy) say that the present was 'the highest thing'? Ten years after his death Hegel's disciples like Hess were already asking why on earth, since the Hegelian system had put even God and freedom within the grasp of reason, should the essence of the future be reckoned inscrutable. Such restless impatience with absolute knowledge as a recapitulation of the past and justification of the present was far from thriving only among Left Hegelians like Hess. For example, by 1843, Ludwig Michelet, every inch a moderate, a centre Hegelian, was writing thus: 'Philosophy is not just the owl of Minerva, which takes flight only at sunset; it is also the cock's crow, which announces the dawn of a new day.'

Kojève realized that on strictly Hegelian terms, this kind of question (intentionally addressed to the 'limitations' of the 'system') made little sense. Because in Hegel there are no criteria transcending history, only the historical process itself can answer queries about what comes next, or is better. Kojève gladly granted that this is blatant question-begging – in fact, a glaring vicious circle; but he saw no option to facing it. Either we have demonstrable extra-historical standards to gauge the worth of social reality at any given point in time, or we don't – in which case, all we can do is to follow Hegel and find solace in the retrospective wisdom of making sense of the past.

There was also another heady Hegelian theme which Kojève took very much in earnest: the idea of an 'end of history'. Here his sentence, just quoted, about the 'serial' nature of truth, with an absolute value set on the last episode in the historical series, says it all. He believed he was being thoroughly Hegelian in absolutizing the present. Accordingly, he tried to build on Hegel to sell the idea that our own age, having reached the peak where reason in history becomes self-conscious, witnesses a stabilization of historical movement. Events go on happening, of course; but history as a rational process has come to a halt. To Kojève, the wars and revolutions of the twentieth century, as well as the continuing rivalry between socio-economic systems, just certified Hegel's central insight on the unfolding of thought-history as a supreme stage of *Weltgeschichte*, that is to say, as the history of man *qua* man.

One may quibble a little here. Kojève could have put more weight on another of Hegel's themes: the 'cunning of reason', a shrewd philosophical ancestor of much that is most perceptive in sociology since Marx, Simmel or Weber, all of whom discussed at length great examples of the 'unintended consequences' of human action, collective as well as individual. After all, the achievement of thought-history belongs together with the 'owl of Minerva' leitmotif: salvation-through-knowledge comes only at the end of the journey. And the root meaning of the idea of a Spirit which as reason is lord of history is tied up with the uniqueness of humans as free beings. As the Kojevian, George Dennis O'Brien, says, because the 'story of history' (his description of Hegel's philosophical project) refers to free beings, 'it cannot be predicted ahead of time any more than one can predict new styles in art'.[19] Prediction is prohibited both by the philosophical thesis of the essential freedom of the I-we that is the Spirit, and by the sociological insight on the 'cunning of reason' (the paradox of unintended consequences of human action). Hess's naïve messianic claim that the future should be accounted for in Hegelian philosophical history is definitely out of step with Hegel's problematic. But so is, if less conspicuously, any interpretation leaning too much towards the idea of an end of history in a strong sense; for the temporal apotheosis of the present also involves a fair amount of 'prediction', discounting, once again, the intrinsic unpredictability of freedom inbuilt in the reason-in-history perspective.

To this extent, it might be wise to climb down from Kojève's historiosophic hubris and conclude, more modestly, with Karl Löwith, that the core of Hegel's philosophico-historical outlook was rather rooted in the 'bourgeois-Christian' culture of early nineteenth-century western society. When all is told, what Hegel did offer of more lasting value was: (a) a rational account of the direction, if not of the necessity, of historical movement (the 'story of history', that is, progress); and (b) a shrewd theory of bourgeois society. Hegel's blueprint of modern society even included, as Z.A. Pelczynski has suggested,[20] a dash of our contemporary 'social capitalisms', since it amply allowed for state regulation of the economy with a view to achieving social welfare. Again, by treating classes as estates, it harboured an intimation of our unions, which are 'estates of the realm' legitimized by state law. Thus Hegel's 'bourgeois-Christian' synthesis welded the acceptance of an advanced division of labour and serious provisos for community; it tried to keep rational drives and romantic impulses in balance, within a legal framework alive to the need for respecting the utilitarian growth of modern civil society.

The point, however, is: was this agenda for socio-political and cultural reconciliation, at bottom, felt by Hegel to breathe a replacement of or an improvement on the actual bourgeois society of the early nineteenth century, as a social formation born out of western history? Carl Schmitt once wrote that the day when, in January 1933, Hitler became chancellor of the German Reich marked the real death of Hegel. Schmitt was at the time closer to Hitler than to Hegel but his was indeed an apt saying. For the very first victims of the fascist furies were to be precisely the two components of Hegel's bourgeois-Christian weld: the Christian principle of individuality, nurtured throughout a long historical incubation in the West, and the bourgeois principle of an autonomous civil society, risen with the growth of modernity in culture and the economy.

Marx apart, the biggest influence on German thought since Hegel has been Nietzsche. Instead of justifying a cultural epoch, like Hegel's bourgeois-Christian society, Nietzsche launched a passionate indictment of modernity compounded by a devastating denunciation of Christianity; he mounted an all-embracing *Kulturkritik* for the sake of 'life' values. But the trouble is that this sweeping cultural critique lacks just what we find in Hegel: a proper theory of the institutional basis of modern society, and a reasonable account of historical movement, highlighting the birth of modernity. Like his rebel disciple Heidegger, who disowned the entire metaphysical tradition since Plato on the grounds that it concealed the true nature of Being, Nietzsche rejected whole eras yet had no theory of secular changes. By contrast, Hegel's insistence that the 'labour of the negative' always worked by means of *determinate* negations implied a deep attention to the historical concretum, to the rich internal differentiation of world history; and his pitting the power of the *concept* against romantic wholesale *intuitions* stemmed from his conviction that intuition grasped at best ahistorical identities instead of differentiated processes.

Hegel famously sneered at the triumph of intuition in Schelling's 'system of identity' because it dropped thought into 'the night of the Absolute, in which all cows are black'. Only the 'patience of the concept' could do justice to the complex inscapes and crooked paths of historical development.

In Nietzsche's brainchild, the *Kulturkritik*, all cows are rather blackish too, because, underpinning the *Kulturkritik*'s apocalyptic denunciations, there is no view of the process. Now, as we shall shortly see, mainstream Western Marxism – by which I mean its German-speaking branch, from Lukács to the Frankfurt school – espoused the *Kulturkritik* outlook. At the same time, most Western Marxists were proud of their allegiance to basic Hegelian categories such as mediation and negativity. Indeed, much of the thrust of WM could be described, as Georg Lichtheim realized, as a drift 'from Marx to Hegel'. Therefore, we shall have to address, as a central issue in our overview, the problem of ascertaining whether, by appropriating the *Kulturkritik*, the left neo-Hegelianism that most WM amounts to has not loosened too much that cogent grasp of historical wealth which encapsulates for us the enduring lesson of Hegel's thought. In particular, we shall have to provide an answer to the question: Has WM managed to combine its *Kulturkritik* with a new theory of the 'process'?

3. THE HERITAGE: MARX'S MARXISM

Marx was a creature of his time
       Yuri Andropov, 1983

A new theory of historical process was just what Hegel's main critical successor, Karl Marx (1818–83), gave to social theory after the decline of idealist metaphysics. Shortly after the death of Hegel, several of his former disciples showed an increasing dissatisfaction with what seemed to them a basic incoherence of the Hegelian system.

Taken together, their critical writings constitute what is known as the 'Hegelian Left' (1835–43). How come, they argued, that a philosophy lauding the 'labour of the negative' and presenting each historical stage as the seed of its own supersession, within the dialectic march of a self-realizing Spirit, teaches at the same time the acceptance of the social status quo, of the religious establishment and, last but not least, of the Hegelian system itself as a *nec plus ultra* of thought?

To Hegel, it will be remembered (see above page 17), what is rational is actual and what is actual is rational. Now the split among Hegelians in the mid-1930s was depicted by Michelet as a fundamental disagreement over this famous dictum. The Hegelian Right tended to think as though only the *already* actual, i.e. present reality, was rational – and therefore it sanctified the social order and the state of the 'system'. The Hegelian Left, by contrast, reckoned that only the rational still in an ideal state was truly actual. Consequently, to the Left Hegelians, the political and ideological status quo was but a vast mystification, which they set out to dismantle by means of several 'critiques'.

The opening salvo came from Ludwig Feuerbach (1804–72), author of *The Essence of Christianity* (1841). Feuerbach realized that Hegel's concept of religion was decidedly immanentist, for it identified God with a Spirit ultimately inseparable from the historical consciousness of mankind. He concluded that 'the secret of theology is anthropology': God's glorious attributes were just a mirror image of human needs and aspirations. But by this humanization of religion Feuerbach deeply altered one of Hegel's central categories, that of alienation or externalization. As already noted (pages 15–16), alienation, in Hegel, was something positive: indeed, the life of the Spirit was a ceaseless enriching self-alienation. Feuerbach put it the other way round: he saw alienation as a loss. God, as a product of man's self-alienation, signalled a deprivation of the human.

Feuerbach compounded his critique of alienation by a blunt materialist outlook. Breaking noisily with the spiritual world-view of German idealism, he poured out epigrams such as '*Mann ist was er isst*' (Man is what he eats). This meant a polemical return to certain trends of the French Enlightenment, clearly aimed against idealist philosophy. Prior to Feuerbach, another rebel Hegelian, Bruno Bauer (1809–82), had exposed religion as a fall of the mind – the mind's 'alienation' in the bad sense of the word. But Feuerbach materialist humanism gave it a more radical twist. Instead of opposing, like Bauer, philosophy (critical) and religion (alienated), he came to see philosophy as such, inasmuch as it meant theory divorced from the more concrete needs of man, as alienation. In this sense, materialist anthropology was intended as the undoing of philosophy.

The Essence of Christianity was not the only Left Hegelian bombshell to appear in print in 1841. There was also *The European Triarchy*, by the maverick messianic thinker Moses Hess, whom we have already seen chafing at the restraint shown by Hegel's philosophy of history as it came to theorizing about the future. Hess yearned to convert philosophy into revolutionary action – a proposition quite different from Feuerbach's. Feuerbachian materialism wanted to *abolish* philosophy; Hess's messianic historiosophy wanted to *fulfil* it in an impending revolution.

In addition, Hess made a decisive contribution to alienation theory. He discerned a third form of alienation, neither religious nor philosophical but economic. Following Proudhon, he contended that money could be as alienating as the belief in God – a point that Marx would use in his essay 'On the Jewish Question' (1843). Hess also went beyond Feuerbach in stating that, if the secret of theology is indeed anthropology, then it should be realized that the human nature underlying religious alienation is essentially *social*. Therefore, the critique of religion must be completed by a critique of socio-economic institutions: theology means anthropology, but anthropology, in turn, means socialism.

Hess was the man who converted Friedrich Engels (1820–95) to communism. But he conceived of communism – to Marx's fury – as 'the law of love', the final stage in the salvation saga of *The European Triarchy*; since 1837, Hess was reasoning in terms of a 'holy history of mankind' where revolution featured as an active Christian humanism, beyond all class interests. At the same time, Hess believed that the communist ideal varied according to national character. Thus, while French communism fed on the sense of justice and English communism on working-class interest, German communism expressed philosophical humanism. Paradoxically, Germany, by then a country politically and economically quite backward when compared to France and England, would have, in Hess's view, nothing less than the deepest revolution: the overthrow of class society for the sake of mankind as such.

This philosophical perspective on communism was not lost on Marx. In an 1844 introduction to his still unpublished *Critique of Hegel's Philosophy of Right* (1843) the young Marx described the German social revolution as the consummation of German philosophy. Seeing the proletariat as a class 'universal', a class 'that was not a class', because its sufferings made it just human, Marx stressed that while philosophy could not be achieved without transcending the proletariat (i.e. without abolishing class society), the proletariat could not transcend itself without achieving philosophy. 'Theory', wrote Marx, 'will become material force as soon as it seizes the masses.'

However, by 1844, Marx had also absorbed the materialist message of Feuerbach's humanism. One year earlier, his critique of Hegel's political philosophy had employed the typical Feuerbachian method of laying bare an 'ugly', material reality, made of passion and interest, behind a noble façade. Just as Feuerbach had shown human misery disguised under the celebration of God, Marx pointed to the war of all against all in civil society as the true reality underneath the harmonious semblance of the Hegelian state.

On the other hand, by the summer of 1844, when he drafted his *Economic and Philosophical Manuscripts* (the so-called Paris Manuscripts), Marx was also criticizing Feuerbach for his ahistorical stance. Materialism was not enough: it had to be combined with Hegel's precious insight on the active self-making of mankind throughout history, or, to say it in Marx's own words, on 'the self-creation of man as a process'. Not materialist anthropology, but a materialist history was needed, as the natural idiom of 'radical' thought; and radical was just what Marx wanted critical thinking to be.

Thus far we have four components of Marxian thought: (a) the critical thrust, which he shared with the other Left Hegelians; (b) the materialist drift of his critique, learned from Feuerbach; (c) the Hegelian stress (dropped by Feuerbach) on the Promethean power of negativity, that is to say, the dialectics of history as a process of human self-creation; and (d) the insistence, taken over from Hess (though this went unacknowledged) on a fulfilment of philosophy through social revolution and on the philosophical rôle meted out to the German proletariat.

Yet we began our discussion of Marx by saying that his great contribution *vis-à-vis* Hegel was a new view of historical process. But these four components alone do not amount to such an outcome. The missing link is the critique of political economy. It was Engels, in Paris, in September 1844, who drew Marx's attention to economics. Following in the steps of the greatest of bourgeois economists, David Ricardo (1772–1823), Engels made labour the source of economic value. He also claimed that under capitalism this truth undergoes an inversion, so that the value of labour, although it is the ultimate origin of prices, becomes itself dependent on prices. Later, Marx tried to work out a complex explanation of this inversion in his famous theory of the *surplus* value of labour, the linchpin of his original thinking on economics.

There is no need for us to go into even the outlines of Marx's economic analysis, since, besides being fairly well known, it has never been a central concern of Western Marxists. WM grew as a set of philosophical writings seldom engaging in sociological, let alone economic, issues. Of more moment to us is the fact that Marx's self-taught economics, after his academic legal and philosophical (Hegelian) studies in Berlin and Bonn, brought about a very significant change in the history of radical ideas. The change was in the relationship between communism and socialism.

Until Marx, communism was economically illiterate. It was an old ideal, harking back to some Fathers of the Church and a few Renaissance utopias (e.g. More's). Its principle of egalitarianism, social as well as economic, appealed to some figures of the French Enlightenment, like the abbé Mably. During the French Revolution Gracchus Babeuf (1760–97) strove to make the egalitarian utopia into the basis of an insurrectional politics. Henceforth the communist tradition became a radical revolutionism. Around 1840, its head was a notorious putschmonger, Blanqui (1805–81).

By contrast, socialism, a much later concept, was above all a reflection on industrialism – and as such a highly economic body of doctrine. Socialist thinkers such as the Englishman Owen, or the Left Saint-Simonians in France, worried about 'the anarchy of production' under capitalism. They proposed new forms of social and economic organization for the novel industrial world. Thus, while communisms were *political* movements, revolutionary and distributivist, socialisms were *economic* creeds, reformist and productivist. What *Marx did was both to economicize communism and politicize socialism*: he taught communism to speak the language of economics and injected the communist principle of revolutionary politics into the productivist tradition of socialism, dropping in the process the 'old socialist' custom of devising utopias, i.e. model societies.

According to the arguments used in the *Communist Manifesto* (1848), the main reason for Marx's choice of a communist rather than a socialist end-position was a fatal flaw in

what he and Engels called, at the close of the third
section of the *Manifesto*, the 'critical-utopian' school of prior
socialists (Saint-Simon, Fourier, Owen). The first adjective
was of course a commendation, denied, in particular, to
Proudhon, whom Marx had so severely criticized just a
few months earlier in *The Poverty of Philosophy* (1847),
the first printed statement of 'historical materialism' (the
previous one, *The German Ideology*, written in 1846 with
Engels, remained unpublished in Marx's lifetime). But the
second adjective – utopian – stressed that the erstwhile
socialists had recognized neither the need and inevitability
of social and political revolution nor the historical role of
the proletariat as its agent. Rather, writing at a time
when the working class was still underdeveloped, they
had naturally shunned mass politics and concentrated on
harmless small-scale experiments.

Did that mean that the *Communist Manifesto* itself was a
radical blockbuster? Far from it. In fact, in its *pars construens*
(the second section), the *Manifesto* was strikingly moderate,
largely demanding just what sounds to us very much part
and parcel of modern welfare states: income tax, state
schools, labour-protection laws . . . . Even the anti-capital-
ist measures proper – nationalization of industry, abolition
of inheritance – had long figured in old socialist gospels
(e.g. in Saint-Simonism) and were not seen as requiring an
earth-shaking revolution. Already, the rhetoric of revolution
was out of step with the political programme – a situation
which political Marxism would know quite often between
the aftermath of the 1848 upheavals and October 1917.

At any rate, the true singularity of Marx's thought was
not in its political programme; he actually ended up by
leaving no coherent blueprint for communist society. What
really singled Marx out was a particular way of looking at
revolution. But in order to understand this, one must bear
in mind what was specifically Marxian in the thematic of
the Left Hegelians. It will be remembered that the Left
Hegelian general theme was the concept of a bad alienation,
as opposed to Hegel's positive sense of alienation as a

45

healthy externalization. Here it is common knowledge that Marx's contribution was his theory of alienated labour. But of course Marx did not simply reassert the vapid generalities of Hess about proletarian destitution as the Passion of Mankind. Rather, he provided a *dynamic* view of economic alienation. The picture of alienated labour in the Paris Manuscripts became a scenario of exploitation of a 'reserve army' of workers since at least 'Wage Labour and Capital' (1849); later still, the notion of surplus value seemed to have enabled Marx to account for exploitation as a time-bomb as it were, an infernal mechanism leading capital to its own grave.

In the Paris Manuscripts, the motif of alienated labour is inserted into a Promethean vision, where industry is hailed as a great conquest of mankind, 'the open book of human faculties'. Marx and Engels always felt akin to the Promethean ethos of the liberal economists of the Manchester school. Saint-Simon's industrial prophetism was also dear to their hearts. The young Marx imbibed Saint-Simonian ideas – which were very much in the air in progressive circles – from his own father, his main Berlin teacher, centre Hegelian Eduard Gans, his father-in-law and Hess. Raymond Aron has said, aptly enough, that Marx wished for a synthesis of Saint-Simon and Rousseau, of industry with democracy – a self-rule of producers; but one might as well add that Marx also dreamt of another synthesis, that of Saint-Simon and Hegel: industrial growth as the medium of dialectical history, of history as a process propelled by contradiction to higher stages of social organization.

Hegel wrote in justification of modern society that it was, is the telos of history. Marx, too, saw communism – future modern society – as an apotheosis. He called it (in the Manuscripts) the 'solution to the riddle of history'. The abolition of private property 'and thus of human self-alienation' meant to him a 'real reappropriation of the human essence by and for man'. A social Eden would ensue, where freedom and equality would be twins. Yet historiosophies – logics of history culminating in social bliss – were rife among old socialists and young Hegelians like Hess. What made all the difference was the ability to grasp the eschaton as a fruit of the historical process itself, instead of merely pitting it, as an abstract ideal, against the social present. Hess, for instance, never properly deduced his 'communism of love' from the actual course of modern history. Marx, by contrast, seems to have understood very soon the need for an account of the process. He was only nineteen when he told his father, assessing his first year of studies in Berlin, that reading Hegel had taught him to go beyond the mere opposition between 'is' and 'ought'.

In Hegel's view, such an opposition – the Kantian divide between '*sein*' and '*sollen*' – only mirrored an impotence of Spirit (*die Ohnmacht des Geistes*). Therefore, as a firm believer in the power of Spirit, he spent all his life showing that the *sein/sollen* divide was overcome in history. Similarly, to Marx, the greatest error was to think of revolution as a duty or an ideal – it is a *tendency*, an inevitable historical force. In the words of *The German Ideology*: 'communism is . . . not an ideal to which reality will have to adjust. We call communism the real movement which abolishes the present state of affairs.' No wonder Marx matured by espousing economic determinism in such a natural way; the Hegelian mould of his thought made it perfectly easy. One is bound to agree with Iring Fetscher: 'in philosophical terms Marx has not deviated from Hegel but has simply given a practical, revolutionary turn to his thought.'[21] In Ferdinand Lassalle's shrewd remark, Marx was at once a socialist Ricardo and a Hegel turned economist (Lassalle to Marx, 12 May 1851).

As a Hegelian economist, Marx had a nice advantage and a serious disadvantage in relation to Hegel's own theory of the process. The advantage was of a cognitive character. Its name was historical materialism, whose best, classical formulation was given in the Preface to *A Contribution to the Critique of Political Economy* (1859): 'it is not the consciousness of men that determines their being, but, on the contrary, their social being that determines their consciousness.' It represented an advance in knowledge because, unlike Hegel's tale of the unfolding Spirit, it offered a causal hypothesis of – at the very least – genuine heuristic power. The 'economic structure of society' (the 'modes of production') as a 'real foundation' beneath a 'legal and political superstructure' with corresponding 'forces of social consciousness' – to continue quoting the Preface's famous terminology – provided the historian and the social scientist with a guiding thread for mapping out highly significant correlations disclosing a set of constraints bound to be involved in the necessary if not sufficient conditions for the working and change of societies. And it goes without saying that neither Marx nor Engels or Plekhanov ever thought of historical materialism in less than selective terms, that is, none of them ever dreamed of a ready-made key which would explain everything in history instead of accounting for just the big changes of macro-history. Even on a more modest scale, though, historical materialism, as a fruitful search for infrastructural relations, simply became standard procedure in sociological explanations at large.[22] By the same token, Marx must be reckoned one of the main founders of social science.

However, in Marx's hands, historical materialism was not just a general search for material constraints and economic conditions. It was presented by Marx and Engels as a causal theory in the strong sense, specifying a sequence of self-evolving modes of production: primitive communist, slave, Asiatic, feudal, capitalist. In other words, it was both a broad methodological prescription *and* a theory of social evolution. In this latter capacity, however, the Marxian theory was seriously vitiated. As even critical accounts most sympathetic to crediting changes in the productive system with a decisive power to shape macro-history openly admit, the very fact that Marx recognized that any given concrete social formation was only an imperfect embodiment of a mode of production (often mixing different ones), or that he never specified the timing of his main causal mechanism, namely, the necessary eventual adjustments of the (social) *relations* of production to changes in the (technical) *forces* of production, greatly reduced the testability of his explanatory account of history.[23]

Needless to say, economic determinism did not fare better when it featured as the prop of Marx's famous predictions about the evolution of industrial capitalism: immiseration of the working class, proletarization of society and the attendant intensification of class struggle, revolutionary break-outs in advanced countries, fall of the profit rate, collapse of the system entailed by the capitalists' self-inflicted crisis and by the widespread revolt of the exploited masses. Quite often, keeping their historicist faith forced the founders of Marxism to behave like stubborn prophets of doom. Thus, in the wake of the 1848 revolutions, at the dawn of the two golden decades of *laissez-faire* capitalism, the 1850s and '60s, Marx correctly surmised that the new wave of prosperity would weaken revolutionary drives. Nevertheless, as soon as the first crisis of conjuncture took place, he started predicting the arrival of the great red day over and over again. With great confidence, he anticipated an imminent widespread economic collapse in 1851, '52, '53 and '55. Engels spent the 1850s waiting for the outbreak of revolution – following or consummating the breakdown of capitalism – to relieve him of his job in his father's Manchester firm which enabled him to support the Marxes.[24] Yet the 'Great Depression' did not set in before 1873, and social agitation never recovered the level of the 'hungry forties'.

A still more ludicrous example of historicist hubris concerns the immiseration thesis. As Bertram Wolfe noticed, in the first edition of volume I of *Capital*, written in 1866–7, Marx displayed several British statistical data, from as recently as 1865 or '66 – but his data about wages stopped mysteriously in 1850. In the second edition he updated his statistics, except those about wages – which were, as before, readily available. That Marx was far from

49

being, as a rule, intellectually dishonest only makes it more telling. Little wonder he felt entitled to tell the First International, at the beginning of his inaugural address, that it was 'a great fact that the misery of the working masses has not diminished from 1848 to 1864'. Marx's determination to ignore wage statistics was all the more puzzling, since he used to stress that his surplus value theory of exploitation meant that wage labour remained 'a system of slavery irrespective of whether the worker is . . . better or worse paid.'[25] Be that as it may, Marxism had to wait until 1892, when Engels wrote a foreword to the second edition of his remarkable book, *The Condition of the Working Class in England* (1845), to hear the admission that, in almost half a century, there had been a substantial improvement in the material and moral state of British workers.

But here two things are worth remarking. First, none of Marx's prophecies, let alone his silly insistence on some of them, followed in any necessary sense from the general methodological principle enjoining the historical materialist approach. Second, besides being dictated by ideological bias, such forecasts were made possible, or indeed, encouraged, less by historicism in itself than by an immoderate application of the historicist cast of mind to the future – precisely the move avoided by Hegel (see pages above). In short: it was not because he had a theory of the process – the first grand one since Hegel's, and of far more cognitive interest than Comte's plausible but narrower 'law of the three (intellectual) stages' – that Marx sinned; rather, he erred because he stretched it too far.

What about the gist of Hegel's historicism – his acceptance of the spirit of modern society? We saw how wholehearted was Marx's approval of industrialism, how sincere his attachment to the democratic ideal. Does this mean that he too, like Hegel and unlike most romantics, sided with modernity? For a good answer, let us glance at his image of man.

Thomas Mann once said that socialism would be

redeemed when, so to speak, Marx had read Hölderlin.[26] A fine witticism; but, in a sense, slightly superfluous. For Marx, even without having read Hölderlin, held a definitely romantic and humanist view of man. From the outset, he adopted the humanist paradigm of the full, 'all-round' man, the manifold personality not enslaved by craft or profession, patterned after the Renaissance heroic model, akin to da Vinci's *uomo universale*. An often quoted passage of *The German Ideology* depicts communist society as the social arrangement that got rid of the division of labour and where nobody has an exclusive activity; such a society makes it possible for each one 'to do one thing today and another tomorrow, to hunt in the morning, fish in the afternoon, breed cattle in the evening, criticize after dinner, just as I like without ever becoming a hunter, a fisherman, a herdsman or a critic'. At the same time, 'society regulates the general production' – which comes as a relief after so much Bohemian fun, with almost no work in any conventional sense.

It seems that, for the young Marx, Proteus went hand in hand with Prometheus: communist man was to be a cheerful but highly productive jack-of-all-trades. This was obviously quite close to the romantic rejection of the work ethic and its ascetic emphasis on the narrow duties of each one's calling – a leitmotif in German moral thinking from Luther to Goethe's *Wilhelm Meisters Wanderjahre* (1821). But it meant no contempt for the *homo faber* as species being – hence our strange bedfellows, Proteus and Prometheus. Yet this blithe spirit did not outlive Marx's youth. In the *Grundrisse* (1858–9), his lengthy draft for so much of what eventually went into *Capital*, the 'universal individual' remains conspicuous. But now work is no longer a way of personal freedom. Significantly, Marx chided Fourier for holding too light a view of working, as an 'amusement'.[27] Work is essential to the self-creation of mankind but, for the individual, freedom begins with the 'economics of time' promised by the development of automation.

The *Grundrisse* are a turning point in Marxian thought. They brought the focus of Marx's critique of political economy to bear, for the first time, on production rather than on exchange; and they introduced the claim that what is exploited by capital is the worker's labour power, not just his labour. This cleared the ground for the theory of surplus value. But while it put the preparatory analysis for what eventually became *Capital* still more in keeping with Marx's old Prometheanism, with all its encomium of *homo faber*, in other respects his romantic streak continued unchecked: for example, his persistent dislike of money, merchandise and the division of labour.

Until the very end, Marx was hostile to the 'commodity form'. In *Capital* the 'fetishism of the commodity' section (vol.I, ch. 1,4) was to contain the masterpiece of Marx's critique of capitalism – and would become the Holy Writ of Western Marxism in its piety towards the founder. The *Critique of the Gotha Programme* (1875) stipulated in earnest the suppression of monetary currency, replaced by 'work certificates' enabling everyone to earn, for his own consumption, the equivalent to what he had contributed to social production. Finally, the *Grundrisse* show even a touch of nostalgia before the 'beauty and greatness' of the 'spontaneous interconnection' existing prior to the division of labour.[28]

Though the passage was deleted a year later in the *Critique of Political Economy*, presumably to avoid a passéiste impression,[29] the very fact that it was written at all betrays the extent of Marx's romantic unwillingness to accept the market economy as an institutional bedrock of the modern age. Joseph Schumpeter saw in him the last of the scholastics, ever obsessed by the idea of 'use value' and the chimera of a 'natural economy'. Thus the same thinker who extolled the benefits of industrialism and technological progress, upheld the capitalist bursting of the cake of custom and derided 'the idiocy of rural life', also nourished feelings of antipathy towards the nature of the modern economy as such – apart, that is, from any grievances concerning its capitalist social structure. As one of the best critics of Marxism put it: 'in Marx's view, the source of all evils of mankind lies in the commodity form more radically than in private property, which, it seems, is but the social condition for the existence of the commodity form ... Ultimately it is the very category of the economic that must be abolished.'[30]

For no other reason did Marx rebuke Proudhon, the anti-bourgeois who nevertheless wanted to preserve, in his anarchist utopia, all the concepts and institutions of the capitalist economy, from exchange and competition to credit, interests and taxes as well as wages, prices and profits. The Marxian critique of Proudhon shows that Aron was right: for Marx, the economy as such was evil. Time and time again, he showed an almost Carlylean revulsion against the cash nexus, as though a modern economy could possibly work without the agility procured by abstract systems of value.

On the economic side, then, there are grounds to say that Marx disliked part of the core of modern society. But what about his attitude towards modernity on the political side? Politically speaking, of course, what was 'modern', in Marx's day, was the rise of democracy, the spread of civil rights and the growth of nationalism. While Marx doubtless thought of himself as a democrat, when it came to human rights and free political institutions, his actual position was less than satisfactory. It is true that he used to criticize many a radical sect, from the Proudhonians and Hess's 'true communists' to the Lassalleans and Bakunin's anarchists, for their obdurate opposition to liberal movements. However, Marx's own stance was not in the least dictated by love for liberal principles but by his conviction, largely erroneous as it happens, that only political liberalism allowed capitalism a full expansion, just as only the completion of capitalist rule, making alienation thorough, would breed, as a necessary reaction, the revolutionary emancipation of the masses.

Very briefly, Marx's politics evinced at least three illiberal tendencies. First, as far as the economy is concerned, it incorporated much of the technocratic argument of Saint-Simon. Moreover, while in volume I of *Capital* he assumed that production and distribution in a post-capitalist society would be planned but spontaneously regulated by an association of free men, in volumes II and III he owned that the supervision of production through book-keeping would be 'even more necessary' than under capitalism.[31] Engels would strengthen this line of thought by stressing that efficient industry requires an almost military degree of control – a view not lost in the open admiration of Lenin or Trotsky for Taylorism.

Second, in the political field proper, Marx's ideas kept a number of disturbing authoritarian elements. To be sure, like Saint-Simon, he firmly believed that in a rational society there would be no need for *government* of people, just for an *administration* of things. As soon as 'organization' (a typical Saint-Simonian word) is introduced, says the Introduction to the *Critique of Hegel's Philosophy of Right*, 'socialism throws its political hull away'. The notion that under communism the state will perish still makes many people think of a basic kinship between Marxian Marxism and anarchism. Lenin wrote (in *State and Revolution*) that Marx's comments on the Paris Commune implied a view of the state that was ninety per cent anarchist.

In fact, Marx repelled anarchism in no ambiguous terms, as witnessed by his polemics with Stirner, Proudhon and Bakunin,[32] and he certainly did not concur with the anarchists in demanding an unqualified suppression of the state. As Avineri aptly observes, while for anarchism the abolition of the state was a forcible political act, for Marx the supersession of the state was the final outcome of a protracted process of social and economic transformations, 'introduced and sustained by political power'.[33] This temporal dimension is precisely what was underscored in the celebrated Marxian hope of a 'withering away of the state'. But the point is, state power would always be necessary for achieving universal ends – a conception of clear Hegelian origin, and completely out of tune with either the liberal or the anarchist views of his times. After all, it was Marx himself (in a letter to Weydemeyer of 1852) who included the concept of a dictatorship of the proletariat among his personal contributions to radical thought. Marx's proletarian dictatorship, it goes without saying, was intended to be just a temporary instrument; and Kautsky was perhaps right (against Lenin) in saying that its content was eminently social rather than political, i.e., power-wielding. A few Marxologists like Maximilien Rubel insist that while the idea of a statist Marx is but a Bakunist and Marxist-Leninist 'legend', the true Marx should be seen as a theorist of anarchism. Still, no anarchist has ever toyed with anything remotely similar to the dictatorship of the proletariat. To be sure, Bakunin, who accused Marx of proposing a repressive 'state communism', was silly enough to imagine a model society so drastically Spartan as to enable Marx to return the compliment (in his notes on Bakunin's *Statism and Anarchy*) by crediting the anarchist leader with devising a future, and ghastly, 'barracks communism'. However, if we grant that the form of revolution is itself the matrix of the post-capitalist polity, then Bakunin's charge was not groundless. For there is indeed a state-communist potential in the fateful idea of a 'proletarian' dictatorship.

Third, Marx defined communist liberty in such a way as to overlook, not to say despise, those civil rights and free institutions without which the modern world would not know any political freedom. Since his critique of Hegel's *Philosophy of Right* he rejected the principle of the separation of powers and the notion of individual rights. The latter he debunked in 'On the Jewish Question' as a mere ideological figleaf for bourgeois rule. Clearly, Marx was not above committing what Bobbio dubbed the 'genetic fallacy': for even if the rights of man and citizen were originally a bourgeois interest, it does not follow that they were to remain useful only to the bourgeoisie – as indeed the labour movement, already in Marx's lifetime, was to confirm, especially since the defence of workers' interests in Britain was given such a boost by the extension of suffrage in 1867.

Above all, Marx was not philosophically prepared to think of communism as a *moral* supersession of capitalism, as the 'social individualism' which Proudhon wanted, which would lose none of the liberal conquests. To begin with, his idea of freedom did not help him to see the point of individual rights: its accent fell on freedom conceived of as a power of self-realization, the self-actualization of human essence, not as a set of franchises or the pursuit of individual desires within a broad sphere of permissable behaviour.[34] Exactly the same problem cropped up in Hegel (see pages above 27–9) where we saw that the upshot of such a position was not beneficial to the true politics of liberty. But in Hegel, at least, the ambiguities of the freedom concept did not detract from a robust acknowledgement of the social worth of individuality. It would be difficult, though, to say something similar in the case of Marx. No more than Marx did Hegel share the Kantian respect for the person as an end in itself; but, as we saw, he fully realized that modern history meant an unprecedented – and welcome – growth of individuality. In Marx, this last element never enjoyed a comparable prominence. His free individual is more of a species-being than a singular personality. How could the spirit, if not always the letter, of his political views not reflect such a gap? It is difficult not to agree with Andrzej Walicki: to Marx, the ultimate legitimation of a social and political order came from the logic of history, not from the will of the people.[35] And unlike Hegel, his version of the logic of history did not particularly allow much room for individual assertion. All in all, it seems hard to avoid the conclusion that Marx's suggestions on rule, freedom and control under communism, though certainly not intended as a prop to tyranny, comprehended much that might be easily used by those who have built tyrannies in his name.

Classical Marxism – the most powerful attempt to date to combine a non-idealist theory of the historical process with wholesale social criticism – constitutes an impressive body of thought whose core is seriously amiss. As we have known ever since Eugen von Böhm-Bawerk's *Karl Marx and the Close of his System* (1896), the idea that capitalist profit rests on a surplus-value of labour has not been refuted – it *cannot* be refuted: the theory is untestable, it has no grip on empirical phenomena, any more than do Marx's inglorious endeavours to deduce the price structure from the level of surplus-value (the so-called 'transformation' problem in *Capital* Volume III). No wonder modern Marxists have been quite willing to ditch such a faulty construction. Piero Sraffa (1898–1983) told them to determine the rate of profit and the relative price of commodities by dint of hypotheses owing nothing to an exchange of commodities ruled by the amount of labour incorporated therein. Joan Robinson (1903–84) warned that the rate of exploitation depends more on the bargaining power of the workers than on the profit rate and the capital/labour relationship.[36] Georg Lichtheim, in his very perceptive *Marxism – an Historical and Critical Study* (1961), warned that there is no need for the surplus-value thesis to account for exploitation. The latter takes place whenever there is a monopolization of gains accruing to the employment of capital – whether this gain be attributed to labour or to all the factors of production; Marx admitted as much when he gave pride of place to ownership of means of production. This consideration has been pursued with full analytical rigour by John Roemer (*A General Theory of Exploitation and Class*, 1982), where he concludes that 'the labour theory of value is irrelevant as a theory of price, but it is also superseded in its role in the theory of exploitation.'[37]

Marx modelled his rising class, the proletariat, on the bourgeoisie. Just as the bourgeoisie had grown in the womb of feudal society, so the proletariat would grow out of capitalism. Each dying mode of production begat its successor as a child of its own contradictions. Yet in more

empirical historical terms the analogy hardly stands. The
rising bourgeoisie, besides being a new class, was an
economic élite, creating new forces and relations of production. The proletariat on the other hand was never
anything of the kind. Essential to industrialism as it has
been, it is not a technical or managerial élite devising a
new form of economic organization. (Technical élites in
modern production can and have considered themselves
exploited; but this is beside the point, since they obviously
do not correspond to the Marxian definition of a labour
force.) The late Raymond Aron thought that the historical
groundlessness of Marx's notion of the role of the proletariat
was the secret reason why Marxism was forced to conceive
of a revolutionary party as an unavowed ersatz of the
proletariat it was supposed merely to express and represent.

In the event, classical Marxism mistook its own historical
rôle. It saw itself as the product of a bourgeois and
proletarian revolutionary context – the industrializing West
of Victorian times. According to the historical record,
however, the decisive revolutionary class in the western
'age of revolution' (to borrow Eric Hobsbawm's title) were
not the urban workers, still very few in most of Europe,
but the peasantry, whose uprisings overthrew the Ancien
Régime society in the French Revolution and inflamed
Europe in the spring of 1848. To be sure, revolutions were
always started by urban strata – but they succeeded, or
simply went on, just where peasant participation followed
suit.[38] Summing it up: when Europe was indeed revolutionary, the proletariat counted for very little; and when the
proletariat became a weighty class, Europe ceased to
be revolutionary. Perhaps the social revolution that the
European Karl Marx placed in the near future belonged,
in historical reality, to the infancy of industrial capitalism.
The irony is that as soon as industrial capitalism came of
age, the working class won such victories as quickly to
surpass the dismal economic and cultural level of a
wretched proletariat – not least because it had been

equipped by Marxism with a cohesive and pugnacious ideology. *NO WAY*.

I referred to the European in Marx advisedly. In our own century the sociological truth of political Marxism gave the lie to the pieties of theoretical Marxism in a further sense. As Ernest Gellner shrewdly notes, far from being, as in its own belief, a solution to the evils of industrialism, communism ends up by providing a potent vehicle of forcible industrialization and primitive accumulation – the violent process so well described by Marx in chapters 26 to 28 of *Capital* Volume I. Marxism performs, under some nationalist regimes eager to build imitative industrializations, what in the past the Protestant ethic and its equivalents did for endogenous, spontaneous capitalism.

Yet, nowadays, Marxism is not just a creed time and again rekindled, in non-industrial countries, by the nationalist feelings of ex-colonial modernizing élites. It is also, within the advanced industrial world, the favourite ideological idiom of an intelligentsia deeply at odds with modern civilization. Western Marxism, in all its varieties, is the main form taken by this ideological language. We must now describe its birth in the wake of the Russian Revolution and its impact among western intellectuals.

II

THE FOUNDATIONS OF
WESTERN MARXISM

1. LUKÁCS AND 'CULTURE COMMUNISM'

Politics is merely the means, culture is the goal
Lukács, 1919

According to one of Karl Jaspers's reminiscences, in pre-war Heidelberg when people were asked, 'What's the name of the four evangelists?' the right reply was, 'Matthew, Mark, Lukács and Bloch'.[1] Young Lukács and young Bloch, founding fathers of Western Marxism, indeed ran a wildly messianic temperature in those days. Yet neither of them was – as yet – a Marxist. The story of their conversion tells much about the ultimate nature of WM.

Why begin with Lukács? Because, if the 'return to Hegel' and a highly 'cultural' subject matter were defining traits of WM in the original mould, then no one made more for its creation than the Hungarian György von Lukács (1885–1971), who having reportedly said that it was hardly possible to philosophize in his native language, wrote almost all his major books in German and came to be known as Georg Lukács.

Born in Budapest into the family of a Jewish banker ennobled by the Habsburgs, Lukács soon developed a cool relationship with his generous self-made father, and an icy relationship with his unloving mother. By the time he first went to Berlin (1906) in pursuit of philosophical studies, he had already little sympathy with official Hungarian culture. He was also deeply estranged from the secular and liberal cast of mind with which Magyarized Jews had played a big role in it, since the 1848 Revolution and the establishment of the Dual Monarchy in 1867.[2] In the years leading up to World War I the *pax liberalis* reached towards the middle of Franz Josef's long reign was increasingly challenged; and anti-Semitism became rampant throughout the empire. But the young Lukács was scarcely moved by the plight of bourgeois progressivism and its 'Philistine' culture – social democracy included.

Lukács's first book, a bulky *History of the Development of Modern Drama*,[3] theorized on the lonely characters of Hebbel and Ibsen by contrasting the atomist nature of bourgeois society with the organic social world of ancient Greece, the cradle of classical tragedy. Its two volumes contain pathbreaking insights. For example, Lukács skilfully relates the flourish of tragic drama to the feeling of historical decline on the part of social classes, without, nevertheless, reducing aesthetic quality to social basis. Accordingly, he attributes the lack of true tragedy in Goethe's and Schiller's otherwise very beautiful plays to the fact that they lived during the rise of the bourgeoisie.

As he made it clear in his pithy 'Notes toward the Theory of Literary History' (1910), Lukács wanted to follow the lead of Dilthey's *Experience and Poetry* (1905) by reading individual works against the backcloth of their *Zeitgeist*. But in so doing he sought to concentrate on form rather than on content. Being intrinsically historical, content was prone to be lost on readers belonging to different ages. Form, on the other hand, expressing general patterns of the human soul, enjoyed a timeless status. Euripides' tragedies, claimed Lukács, are less alive than *Oedipus Rex* or *Antigone* precisely because, in their own time, they were much more topical, much richer in content. Yet this does not mean that, as the object of literary history, form is not open to a historico-sociological interpretation. On the contrary: in so far as 'form is that which is truly social in literature', in human communication throughout the ages, aesthetic analysis is bound to be enriched by a sociological approach.

Lukács's own sociological approach owed much to the *Philosophy of Money* (1900) of Georg Simmel (1858–1918), especially its stress on the powerlessness of the individual within modern individualistic society.[4] In 1909–10, while attending lectures at Simmel's Berlin home (for Simmel, as a Jew, was denied a professorship), Lukács met Ernst Bloch. Ten years his senior, the wildly utopian-minded Bloch made him realize that 'it was still possible to philosophize in the manner of Aristotle or Hegel'. A year later we find Lukács, together with a modernist critic, Lajos Fülep, and with the financial help of his Philistine father, launching an unabashedly metaphysical journal, *A Szellem* (Spirit), devoted to questions touching 'the essence of culture'.[5] Such an essence he defined in an essay of 1910, 'Aesthetic Culture', as the 'meaning of life'. Indeed, Lukácsian culturology had from the start the most tense and intense existential overtones.

The essays he collected in *Soul and Form* (1910; German edition 1911) nearly all came, however, from a rather unphilosophical artistic magazine, *Nyugat* (West), to whose cosmopolitan tone *A Szellem* was meant to react. *Soul and Form* discusses a few large figures (Sterne, Novalis, Kierkegaard, Stefan George) along with some minor writers (Theodor Storm, Charles Louis Philippe, Rudolf Kassner, Paul Ernst). Throughout the book, however, there runs a stark antithesis between 'life' – equated with a thousand contingent relationships and marked by inauthenticity – and 'soul', a source of lofty existential choices trying hard to impose meaning on the facticity of sheer existence. 'Form' in turn meant the aesthetic imprint of such existential choice-meanings, so that literary works became symbols of moral gestures, as it were. Form gathers the bits of life into structures of moral meaning (*Sinngebilde*).

Lukács's view of art was therefore a far cry from naturalism (the mirroring of contingent facts), impressionism (the transcription of psychological surfaces or aimless inner quiverings) and symbolism (the main poetics of 'decadent' aestheticism). By the same token, the soul-and-form tandem was at loggerheads with vitalist thought (the *Lebensphilosophie* of Dilthey and Simmel) since 'soul', while being lived experience (*Erlebnis*), was by no means a surrender to the flow of (inner) life. In 'soul' the self evinces a moral fibre normally absent from the vitalists' master concept; absent, for instance, from that 'unlimited impressionability' which Simmel discerned in modern sensibility.

On other scores, by contrast, Lukács's essays did reflect some 'decadent' motifs, for example, in their fascination with death, so redolent of Viennese culture in the *belle époque*, from Mahler and Klimt to Schnitzler and Hofmannsthal (at any rate, Lukács's own milieu was already fairly thanatophilic, as witnessed by the *Death Aesthetics* (1907) of his old friend Bela Balázs, another guest at Simmel's seminar on the theory of culture). Significantly, Lukács thought highly of a hysteric decadent such as Otto Weininger (1880–1903), the misogynous rabid anti-semitic Jew who created a stir with the delirious pseudo-science of his *Sex and Character* (1903).

Lukács's Kierkegaardian ethicism articulated two conceptual axes. The first was the 'metaphysics of tragedy'. Tragic conflicts lay bare the soul's kernel. Lukács considered Novalis the greatest of the romantics because, besides expressing such a longing for community, Novalis's art fathomed the significance of death. The essay on Paul Ernst, a former socialist who came to embrace a tragic vision, encapsulates the outlook of *Soul and Form* as a whole – though, it has been argued, the essay on Theodor Storm considerably mitigates the rigidity of the tragical perspective and that on Sterne, a lively dialogue, deals an ironical blow to the latent puritanism of the soul-and-form mystique.

The second axis is the concept of 'the essay as form', proffered in the long letter to Leo Popper (Lukács's closest friend) which prefaces the book. True essayism faces ultimate existential issues while pretending only to tackle artworks, i.e., creatures of our imagination. In a culture without tragedies (here Lukács adumbrates George Steiner's theme in *The Death of Tragedy*, 1961), it behoves great essayists like Schopenhauer, Kierkegaard or Nietzsche to renew the tragic sense of life. But more generally the essay is the critic's weapon. Criticism guesses the 'fatal element', the soul-content of forms; in criticism, form becomes the voice with which burning existential questions are addressed, echoing the Pyrrhic victories of 'soul' over 'life'.

A few months after the publication of *Soul and Form*, Lukács's first love, the sensitive artist Irma Seidler, jumped to her death from a bridge on the Danube. Lukács had been introduced to Irma by Leo Popper at the Budapest salon of Mrs Polanyi (the mother of Karl and Michael) in 1907; but he chose to play Kierkegaard to his own Regine Olsen, avoiding marriage on the grounds that the task of 'understanding' was incompatible with a normal life. Irma's suicide was, in all probability, prompted by the ending of an affair with Bela Balázs; but our thinker, who had himself entertained suicidal ideas only a few months earlier, was deeply shaken; he dedicated the German edition of *Soul and Form* to her memory. Then, in a moving essay, 'On Poverty of Spirit' (1911), he placed the 'gift of goodness' he had found in Irma high above all ethics of duty. A grace beyond all forms, the 'poverty of spirit' is what shines in Myshkin or Alyosha Karamazov. Significantly enough, by this time Lukács was reading Martin Buber's mystical writings in praise of humility. Buber's Hasidic revival also showed that Jews were not – contrary to anti-Semitic clichés – the embodiment of modern rationalism, with its repulsive utilitarian ethos.

In 1912, Lukács went to Heidelberg to study under the neo-Kantian culturologist Heinrich Rickert. There he impressed the Max Weber household with his mystic temperament at odds with the *art pour l'art* cult of the 'Georgekreis', the sophisticated circle gathered round the charismatic symbolist poet, Stefan George. In Heidelberg too, between the years 1912 and 1914, he drafted his first aesthetics, posthumously printed as *Heidelberger Philosophie der Kunst*;[6] and he also enthralled himself to a neurotic Russian, the would-be painter Ljena Grabenko, whom he married shortly before the outbreak of the war. To Lukács, Ljena, a former member of the Terrorist Brigade of the Russian Socialist Revolutionary Party who had done a spell in the Tsar's gaols, embodied a fiercely messianic socialism based on personal sacrifice. However, by 1916, their marriage had become 'an unimaginable hell' as Balázs put it; for it so happened that Ljena chose to mount a *ménage à trois* with a disgruntled Viennese pianist whose lapses into physical violence eventually forced her to call – to no avail – a psychiatrist, a certain Karl Jaspers. Meanwhile, bearing it all with remarkable stoicism, Lukács was being urged by Max Weber to complete his systematic work on aesthetics in order that he could be habilitated as an academic philosopher under Rickert. So the thirty-one-year-old essayist returned to his desk and, amid all the din, imperturbably penned a new lengthy draft, the *Heidelberger Aesthetik*.

Heidelberg Aesthetics opens, in impeccable neo-Kantian fashion, by investigating problems of constitution: how are works of art possible? asks Lukács. The reply that Lukács gives is much influenced by the writings of a friend and tutor who was actually a rather rebellious neo-Kantian: Rickert's disciple Emil Lask (1875–1915). Lask insisted on a radical dualism between value and reality. Lukács posited art as an independent value-sphere (*Wertsphäre*) sharply 'bracketed off' (he borrowed Husserl's famous term) from the real world. The artwork was a 'self-contained, perfect and self-sufficient totality'. Consequently, art theory ought to be 'sphere-immanent', that is, 'oriented to the artwork'.

True to Leo Popper's pet idea, Lukács located the core of aesthetic meaning in the work itself, not in the artist's intentions. Yet Popper, a modernist who made a point of ranking Cézanne above Monet and Maillol above Rodin, had exalted 'form' in a formalist sense not far removed from the hymn to 'significant form' in Clive Bell's *Art* (1913) or the paean to 'structure' and formal 'purity' in

Roger Fry's *Vision and Design* (1920). Less steeped in the visual arts, Lukács stood closer to Lask's overriding concern with overcoming the Kantian separation between form and content and embraced Lask's attendant recognition of the fundamental irrationality of all contents. One might say that Lukács translated Popper's celebration of form into a Laskian form-content of a value-sphere, art, utterly divorced from worldly reality: a dualist metaphysics of neo-Kantian origins allows him to go on contrasting 'soul and form' with inauthentic 'life'. His *Heidelberg Aesthetics* carried on from the previous philosophy of art a conception of the artwork as a wholly utopian microcosm necessitated by the perennial human dissatisfaction with alienated existence. Thus, in his austere *Habilitationschrift* Lukács paid homage to his lost intellectual brothers: Popper, his Budapest alter ego, and Lask, his one Heidelberg intimate, killed in action in 1915.

In November 1917, exhausted by his life with Ljena, Lukács left Heidelberg for Budapest. But he did not intend his departure to be final, and placed a valise full of personal papers in the Deutsche Bank. The recovery of its contents, one year after his death, cast a new light on the genesis of Lukács's first masterpiece – the long essay entitled *The Theory of the Novel*, published in Hungarian in 1916 and in German in 1920.[7] Carefully reconstructed by two pupils of his old age, Ferenc Fehér and Agnes Heller, the notes in the Heidelberg valise leave no doubt that the slim 1916 volume was originally meant as the first chapter of a study on Dostoevsky.

Ljena's fellow-terrorists were not nihilists but Dostoevskyan militants. By killing one of the tsar's chief ministers, Plehve, and the Grand Duke Sergei (1904–1905), they had acted upon a conviction that for the sake of oppressed brothers, one should be prepared to sacrifice even one's own virtue. Far from thinking that the end justified the means, the Terrorist Brigade felt fully guilty for their acts; yet in their mystical ethic they saw themselves as a kind of moral kamikaze. Lukács was deeply impressed. As he told

Paul Ernst, he reckoned such attitudes as evidence of a 'second ethic', an imperative of the soul far superior to mere duties towards institutions. Had he not written on the glowing gift of goodness in the 'poverty of spirit'? Now the same basic abnegation turned social. To Lukács, it lent socialism a moral fervour sadly missing in the parliamentarian politics and evolutionary social theory of the Second International. For socialism to be truly redemptive, its anti-utilitarian, anti-individualist roots had to become a living, a daring creed.

What relationship did all this bear to Lukács theory of the novel? The immediate link was the theme of community. While *Soul and Form* enthused over the dream of a golden age in Novalis' lust for *Gemeinschaft*, *The Theory of the Novel* historicized it. With the help of Hegel's ideas on the contrast between ancient epos and modern fiction, it turned the story of western narrative into the tale of a Fall. In the pre-lapsarian state – the age of Homer – society was an organic totality and life, therefore, hospitable and meaningful: 'the world is vast and yet is like a home', writes Lukács. But soon after the soul, awake to its own essence, undergoes the experience of transcendence: with Plato, the Idea lives in exile from the actual social world. Modern history suffers it all with a vengeance; for modernity is the culture where 'the immanence of meaning in life has become a problem', the era of pervasive alienation. This age of 'transcendental homelessness' is the novel's habitat.

The second half of the book tells the story of the novel, a journey from 'world' to 'mind': from a former focus on outer events to a later obsession with consciousness. The novel's heroes display several general kinds of reaction to alienated reality. In 'abstract idealism' the self flees the world, as in the quixotic revolt depicted by Cervantes, or in Kleist's *Michael Kohlhaas*. In the 'romanticism of disillusionment' – a phrase Lukács first employed in a brilliant youthful essay on Ibsen – the self belittles the world and basks in its own self-absorption, as in the cynical narcissism of Frédéric Moreau in Flaubert's *Sentimental*

Education, or again in the passive resistance of Goncharov's *Oblomov*. Between these two extremes, the German *Bildungs-roman*, culminating in the second *Wilhelm Meister*, achieved a wise compromise between world and meaning. But Lukács's heart is with the great Russians. They alone managed to render a 'community of feeling' between 'simple human beings' (Tolstoy, the modern Homer); or, alternatively, to beckon us into new, mystical forms of brotherhood (Dostoevsky's Christian chiliasm). Although Dostoevsky gets no more thán the last paragraph of *The Theory of the Novel*, Lukács invites us to see him and Tolstoy as utopian narrators, masters of a 'projection beyond the social forms of life' (as he calls it in the title of his final chapter). Tolstoy looks for it in glimpses of a Rousseaunian reintegration within nature and its wise, soothing rhythms; Dostoevsky, in the social import of Christian love for the other.

While the tragic vision underlying *Soul and Form* stressed the 'high points' of existence, leading to failure, *The Theory of the Novel* prefers to pinpoint the hero's quest for value and meaning in an alienated universe – and here Lukács put a shrewd finger on a core structure of many modern fictions. Indeed, if the epic hero had an easy moral life, playing traditional rôles in his community, modern fiction swarms with solitary seekers often at war with their social environments. Lukács was also perceptive in his grasp of inner time as a structuring element in modern novels. His discussion of Flaubert's lyric sense of past and memory, like his brief comments on the often fragmentary aspect of fictional plots fraught with episodic events and unrelated characters loosely juxtaposed, proved truly seminal for later analyses of the genre. Again, he described well the ironical position of the omniscient author, detached from his heroes as much as from his own society. In their tacit search for human values, says Lukács, novelists are the 'negative mystics' of a godless age.

To a large extent, the tragic hue of *Soul and Form* gave way, in *The Theory of the Novel*, to a utopian glow; for, whereas, in the 1910 collection, 'soul' and 'form' properly coincided only in tragedy (whether in its dramatic form or otherwise) in the later book there are paths beyond the flights of idealism and the fate of embittered romanticism. A narrow, prosaic path leads into the German past: the *Bildungsroman*. Another one, however, points to the country where, in Lukács's view, the very fact that western progress had not yet destroyed for ever the roots of community held out a promise of human redemption. Such land was Russia, Ljena's – and Dostoevsky's – home.

Returning to Budapest, Lukács found himself established as a literary essayist: *The Theory of the Novel* had been quite a *succès d'estime* among German high-brow humanists. Out of the growing despair brought about by the endless slaughter of a monstrous, pointless European war, Lukács seemed to extract at once a proto-existentialist sense of the futility of life as 'normal business' and a passionate bid for its utter, utopian transformation. Broadly, the Hungarian intelligentsia had initially welcomed the war. To Hungary, the Triple Entente meant primarily imperial Russia – the country's barbarous oppressors of 1849. In 1914, Balázs, like Thomas Mann, saw the struggle as a clash between fine central European *Kultur* and an effete western civilization. As Lukács himself later recalled,[8] the intellectuals' mood, even when they were hostile to the war in principle, amounted to a soul-searching question: 'who was to save us' – in case, that is, of a victory of the West – 'from western civilization?' What a gloomy prospect indeed: 'Anglo-materialism' cum French decadence; Philistine industrialism and humbug human rights democracy ... Thus, though at a far remove from the traditionalism of conservative groups, the intellectuals displayed an ingrained revulsion against modernity in the sociological sense – the secular and utilitarian world of science, industry and democracy. In a word: they were much given to *Kulturkritik*. And in such a context, there was room enough for the ideological flavour of Lukács's anatomy of the novel – quite apart from its real analytical merits.

69

Certainly Hungary, between mid-war and the red inter-
lude of 1919 (the Bela Kun government), spawned many
contributions to the neo-idealist wave which swept European high culture in the last throes of the *belle époque*. In his
well-researched study, *The Young Lukács*, Lee Congdon has
aptly chronicled the social history of this 'revolutionary
culture' movement, which ended up with the conversion to
Marxism of some of its chief leaders. At the close of 1916, a
few months after a spell in postal censorship for the army,
Lukács and Balázs, also discharged, started to convene a
'Sunday Circle' at the playwright's flat in Buda. Regulars
of the circle included younger wits like Karl Mannheim,
later to be creator of the sociology of knowledge, and art
historians Frederic Antal, Arnold Hauser and Charles de
Tolnay, while the composers Zoltan Kodály and Bela
Bartók, the philosopher Michael Polanyi and the economist
Eugene Varga often sat in. By 1917, a 'Free School of
Humanistic Sciences' was formed, offering seminars and
lectures in keeping with a widespread ambition to surpass
positivism, naturalism and materialism in all shapes and
sizes.

All this culture-mongering remained by and large apolit-
ical. But early in 1918 meetings of the Sunday Circle and
the Sociological Society debated the kinship of 'progressive
idealism' and radical politics as stated by two philosophers,
Bela Fogarasi and Lukács. A prime concern of these radical
idealists was ethics. Borrowing from Kant's *Metaphysics of
Morals* to circumvent the stark ethical formalism of the
Critique of Practical Reason, Lukács stressed the Kantian
notion of virtue as an 'inner perfection'. He also seized on
Kant's distinction between 'external' legal duties of an
essentially instrumental nature and the 'internal' legislation
of self-enforced rules dictated by higher ends to build a case
for what Weber (in all likelihood impressed by Lukács's
example) would soon dub 'ethics of conviction' (*Gesinnungs-
ethik*).[9]

Among the sympathizers of the Free School was the
director of Budapest's Municipal Library, Ervin Szabó

(1877–1918). Deemed the father of Hungarian Marxism, but veering towards anarcho-syndicalism, Szabó led the anti-war wing of the intelligentsia. He also introduced Lukács to the work of Sorel. As a fervent believer in ethical socialism, full of contempt for the state and for political transactions, Sorel strongly appealed to Lukács's own leanings. And like many Sorelians, Lukács construed the ideas of the author of *Reflections on Violence* and *Illusions of Progress* in a distinctly irrationalist vein.[10] But for this very reason, Sorel's message, together with the *Kulturkritik* pathos and the overrating of 'conviction' ethics, gave Lukács a cast of mind anything but impervious to the spirit of millennial revolutionism. Add to this the intensity of his Dostoevskyan craving for brotherhood epiphanies in apocalyptic frameworks and it becomes easy to understand how alluring he could find the 'Light of October', that is, the immense moral hope spread by the Russian Revolution.

At first, however, Lukács had mixed feelings. When the radical journal *Free Thought* decided to address itself to the question of Bolshevism, just a couple of weeks after the formation of the Hungarian Communist Party (November 1918), Lukács contributed a piece entitled 'Bolshevism as a Moral Problem'. Bolshevism, he claimed, believed that proletarian power would put an end to all social forms of oppression; yet this was a pure act of faith, since nothing could ensure that good would come from evil, harmony from violence, the bliss of classless society from the barbarism of revolutionary terror. Therefore, as a moral problem, a Bolshevik regime posed an 'irresolvable dilemma'. Nevertheless, a few weeks after the printing of his article, Lukács, in the company of Ljena, Balázs and Fogarasi, joined the CP. Many of the other members of the Sunday Circle were simply flabbergasted on hearing the news.

On closer inspection, however, Lukács's decision was not such a volte-face. After all, having never been a liberal or a social democrat reformist, he shared much of the communist outlook. His only objection to Bolshevism concerned its violent methods, his Sorelian misgivings about the party-state (Sorel himself, mistaking Leninism for the realm of soviets, gave his full blessing to the Russian Revolution). But in the autumn of 1918 Lukács read Lenin's tactical masterpiece of anarchist rhetoric, *State and Revolution*, and this may have assuaged his qualms about the Bolsheviks' attitude towards state power. Also, he was introduced to the CP's leader, Bela Kun, by Irma Seidler's brother – so the Beatrice of his first youth, the very muse of the 'poverty of spirit' mystique, seemed to be gently pushing him towards the communist cause.

While in Heidelberg, Lukács's respect for Kierkegaard had deepened. Now he found himself facing one of those agonizing dilemmas for which the Dane so recommended dramatic, clear-cut choices, engaging all of one's existence. Nor was the historical moment propitious for compromises. With Leninism fighting for its life and the new-born Weimar Republic resorting to bloodshed to nip socialist revolution in the bud (viz. the murders of Karl Liebknecht, Rosa Luxemburg and Kurt Eisner) there seemed to be little point in shunning violence: neither side had clean hands. In his first convert's essay, 'Tactics and Ethics', Lukács just turned the argument of 'Bolshevism as a Moral Problem' upside down: if there was no way to preserve virtue, if avoiding support for communist force meant conniving at bourgeois repression, then the right thing to do was to sin on the side of hope – the prospect of a regenerated mankind in the promise of the October Revolution.

Thus Lukács committed his half-tragic, half-utopian *Kulturkritik*, his mystical need for ethical absolutes, to communism. Had he not stated, in his book on modern drama, that by its own religious, messianic nature, Marxism was quite distinct from other, more naturalist brands of socialism? Moreover, even his strictly *moral* evaluation of communism had been for some time less negative than the 'Free Thought' article might suggest. True, as late as 1917 he still found the proletarian ideology too abstract to provide as comprehensive a morality as the Christian ethos rekindled by Dostoevsky[11]; yet such an opinion did not prevent him from envisaging the Russian Revolution as – in Ernst Bloch's words – a 'fulfilment of destiny'.[12]

'Tactics and Ethics' also gave Lukács's newly acquired Marxism a Hegelian framework. This made him see revolutionary goals not as a distant normative ideal but as part of the historical process itself. Unlike his former moral utopias, revolution was less a dream than an actual tendency. The Hegelianism of such a view needs no stressing. Bloch used to boast that in their Heidelberg years he had coaxed Lukács into improving his knowledge of Hegel. Now at last the result was visible. But thinking of revolution in Hegelian terms meant a dialectical revaluation of the present – an outcome hardly akin to the wild futurism of Bloch's super-utopian perspective (Bloch's *Geist der Utopie* was issued in 1918). For a long time, Lukács had thought of the present as 'the age of absolute sinfulness' – a Fichtean phrase much to his liking, as indeed was the missionary pathos in Fichte. Hereafter he would try to make his peace with the present – not, of course, as a status quo, but as an actuality pregnant with drastic social change.

The work which captured the new orientation of his thought, and which launched Western Marxism, was *History and Class Consciousness* (1923). Reckoned by many the most important Marxist book of our century, it comprises eight essays written (in a rather awkward German) between March 1919 and December 1922. As Michael Löwy has shown, several of the essays were extensively rewritten – and the rewriting always embodied a departure from Lukács's erstwhile ethicism, his abstract, 'Fichtean' moralism.[13] But Lukács's new revolutionary realism was combined with an exceedingly heretical posture *vis-à-vis* Marxism as codified by Engels and Lenin.

To begin with, Lukács ruthlessly ruled out Engels's notion of a dialectic of nature – this, in a book subtitled 'Studies in Marxist Dialectics'! Again, he tacitly disavowed Lenin's 'reflection' theory of knowledge. Furthermore, he bluntly suggested that economic determinism held true only for capitalist society, not for history as a whole. Deterministically interpreted, he claimed, historical materialism simply ceased to be truly historical. It followed that no two ages could bear the same pattern of socio-historical explanation. Now Marx and Engels had granted that in primitive, classless societies kinship can be as determining as any economic factor. But Lukács was implying that even class societies could do without the causal primacy of the economy – provided they were pre-capitalist. On top of which, he had the gall to challenge nothing less than the principle of materialism itself. He even went as far as quoting his Heidelberg master, Rickert, to the effect that materialism was but 'inverted Platonism'.

Genuine Marxism, wrote Lukács, does not consist in any specific tenets but in a method: the dialectic. Marxism, in other words, was to be read against its Hegelian roots; and quite naturally the revival of the idealist tradition meant a new understanding of the role of consciousness. The philosophical Philistines who were Marx's successors had 'turned historical development into a wholly automatic process, not only independent but even qualitatively different from consciousness'. Yet Marx himself, in his first thesis on Feuerbach, had warned against leaving 'the active side' to be 'developed abstractly by idealism'. What was wrong with Feuerbachian materialism was precisely its conception of reality in terms foreign to activity. Lukács believed that the same old mistake had been repeated, this time within Marxism, in the positivist, mechanist and determinist views of Engels and Kautsky – the evangelists of the Second International. Their kind of thinking paid lip-service to the dialectic, yet was at bottom a-dialectical.

In Lukács's view, dialectic as method instead of dogma was much more than just a set of rules. Rather, it meant a way of thinking based on the realization that true thought both grasps the world and changes it. Hegel showed that knowledge is deeply involved in reality as a process; thought is at once the self-awareness of the world and the world's ultimate nature. It follows that thought very much takes part in the making of the actual process. Therefore, the cognitive and the normative can hardly be severed from each other: they are the two faces, so to speak, of the dialectical coin. Thought is ontologically, and not only epistemologically, productive. Ergo, *theory is not just knowledge – it is praxis*. But conversely, praxis is consciousness.

Now the question was: consciousness (mainly) of what? Lukács's reply was straightforward: of alienation. More than forty years after the publication of *History and Class Consciousness*, he proudly said that in it, 'for the first time since Marx', alienation was 'treated as the central question of the revolutionary critique of capitalism'.[14] Alienation was the subject of the longest essay in the whole collection, 'Reification and the Consciousness of the Proletariat', written especially for the book. Its opening section describes alienation as tantamount to *reification* (*Verdinglichung*), a concept from Simmel linked by Lukács with Marx's analysis of 'commodity fetishism'. Reification makes human relations into thing-like phenomena. The rule of the commodity 'objectifies' men, disguising history as nature. The human universe becomes impersonal; man stops recognizing himself in his own works and becomes estranged from his fellows.

The second part of the Reification essay purports to show alienation as ideology. To Lukács, ideology is less a bias dictated by class interest than a structural limitation of the mind imposed by class position. Thus, bourgeois thought cannot help being reifying. It is bound to fall prey to unbridgeable 'antinomies', like Kant's celebrated distinction between the phenomena and the inscrutable thing-in-itself, or again, Kant's abstract, formal ethics, which Lukács saw as leaving the actual world unchanged, unyielding to human initiative. Even when a bourgeois thinker is able to overcome these antinomies, as Hegel did, there remain other ideological barriers. Thus, Hegel brought history into the theory of being and knowledge, but mystified the real subject of history by talking of Spirit instead of flesh-and-blood men.

All this only proved that the bourgeoisie was doomed. The new, higher form of historical consciousness, which bourgeois thought repeatedly failed to achieve, was 'the point of view of totality'. In Lukács' own words:

It is not the predominance of economic themes in the explanation of history that decisively marks off Marxism from bourgeois science. It is the point of view of totality. The category of totality, the universal and determining domination of the whole over the parts, constitutes the essence of the method Marx borrowed from Hegel ... For Marxism there is not, in the last analysis any autonomous science of law, of political economy, of history, etc.; there is only one science, historical and dialectical, unique and unitary, of the development of society as a whole.

Concrete totality as conscious praxis is for Lukács the fundamental category of reality; and totality as praxis is self-activated: it is a *subject*. If the function of the point of view of totality is to provide a global meaning to history and life, totality-praxis cannot possibly be atheoretical; it must be a living knowledge, an understanding as well as a course of events. On the other hand, such a cognition cannot have an individual for a subject. Since knowledge of totality is historical praxis, and it is classes rather than individuals which bear the burden of shaping history, the true subject of totality must be a class. The viewpoint of totality as subject belongs to class consciousness.

But why is it a privilege of the proletariat? Here Lukács resumes the old Marxian argument about 'the class that is not a class' (see above page 42), able to speak for the whole of mankind. Only workers, realizing that their labour is simultaneously a commodity and their own life, can experience objective reality as something derived from a debased, alienating human activity. The proletariat is the only class that, while being a subject as is every class, is able to know itself as an object: for in its deprivation it directly perceives the essence of the dehumanizing, reifying process which is modern society at work; its self-knowledge as alienated labour points to the very source – however unwilling – of universal reification under the sway of commodity. Hence the Passion of the Proletariat redeems, cognitively as well as actively, all mankind; out of its wretchedness the proletariat becomes the only class to grasp the real, global nature of the process – the meaning of totality. And as totality is both a subject and a dynamic directional whole, the self-knowledge of the proletariat means at once a true picture of the world and the praxis whereby it will be transformed.

All this heady subject/object dialectic grafted on to class struggle was presented by assertion rather than by any demonstrative logic. A vast number of begged questions are buried beneath the march of peremptory sentences. Take, for example, the beginning of the first section of the first essay:

> Only when a historical situation has arisen in which a class must understand society if it is to assert itself; only when the fact that a class understands itself means that it understands society as a whole and when, in consequence, the class becomes both the subject and the object of knowledge; in short, only when these conditions are all satisfied will the unity of theory and practice, the precondition of the revolutionary function of the theory, become possible. Such a situation has in fact arisen with the entry of the proletariat into history.[15]

Lukács freely admitted that the *actual* consciousness of the proletariat might well be very far from the revolutionary wisdom of the subject-totality. But he tried to bypass the problem. Max Weber had suggested that the concept of 'objective possibility' was a useful, indeed necessary, tool in the methodology of social science, as a set of thought-experiments leading to a grasp of relevant causal connections and enabling the adjustment of ideal-typical constructs to empirical data.[16] Boldly borrowing from this idea, Lukács postulated an 'imputed' class consciousness for the proletariat. If the working class proved revolutionary so much the better. If not, there was always a historical meaning of its situation – a meaning that, as a function of

77

totality, could only be revolutionary; and such meaning, as a consciousness ascribed to, rather than experienced by, the proletariat will be sensed by an insurrectional élite – the revolutionary Marxist vanguard, a natural interpreter of the true proletarian mind.

The Lukácsian equation of subject with class placed heavy demands on individual conscience. Lukács made no bones about it: his subject-totality as revolutionary praxis required a 'conscious subordination of the self to that collective will that is destined to bring real freedom into being ... This conscious collective will is the Communist Party.'[17] Indeed, in *History and Class Consciousness*, the apotheosis of totality turns out to be a blatant hypostasis of the Leninist party. However, Lukács's politics, in 1922, when he was living in exile in Vienna after the fall of the Bela Kun government in August 1919, was slightly more complex than the Bolshevik party-worship foisted on western communists by Moscow. On the one hand, his position implied rather a substitutionism with a vengeance: not only did he replace class by party (as the source of revolutionary power) but he also replaced the party by its vanguard. On the other hand, Lukács also seemed eager to combine this ultra-élitism for the sake of revolution with a Luxemburgian preference for 'spontaneity' over 'organization'.

Since the dawn of the century, the socialist movement in central Europe had been politically divided into three currents. Some, like Rosa Luxemburg (1871–1919), believed in spontaneous revolutionary action coming from the toiling masses. Others had no such faith. Either they concluded, with Bernstein, that mass revolution, having become unlikely, was also unnecessary and therefore socialism should openly evolve into social reformism by established political means; or, like Lenin, they stuck to the idea of a necessary revolution which, given the masses' inertia, had to be aroused in them and conducted by an insurrectional avant-garde – the Communist Party. The appeal of Luxemburg's view lay in its attempt to avoid both the surrender of class war entailed by reformism and the perils of authoritarianism inherent in the vanguard theory – a theory coupled, since Lenin's *What is to be Done?* (1902) with a strong centralist power structure within the revolutionary party. Luxemburg was adamant that red parties were supposed to accelerate but not initiate revolutions. The latter was an inalienable right of the masses – a belief, let us note in passing, perfectly in line with classical Marxism.

In the period 1919–22 Lukács began, politically speaking, as a Luxemburgian. As such (and, of course, as a Sorelian) he was very fond of workers' councils, but not of 'strong' parties. Then, after the failure of the so-called March Action which tried to repeat in 1921 in Germany the Spartakist uprising led by Luxemburg and Liebknecht two years before, he moved away from orthodox spontaneism. The last of the essays in *History and Class Consciousness* defended the role of the Leninist party. But the point is, was the defence tempered? Some think that even then Lukács was reaching out for a compromise between the Kautsky-Lenin view of 'organization' as a prius to revolutionary struggle and Luxemburg's idea of it as a mere product of such a struggle. Other political essays by Lukács, contemporary with those in the book, from 'Party and Class' (1919) to 'Organization and Revolutionary Initiative' (1921) berated party organizations as hostages to capitalist society (in so far as they were bound to become reifying institutions). Lenin himself singled out one of these essays, 'The Question of Parliamentarianism' (1920), as a sample of 'Leftism' – the very 'infantile disorder' of communism he roundly condemned in his famous pamphlet of April 1920. Significantly, in the organization essay, Lukács, while accepting organization, stresses that it is by no means a technical issue related to bureaucratic means, but 'the supreme spiritual question of revolution'.

When all is told, however, one gets the impression that Lukács's end position was as 'vanguardist' as Lenin's. He places such a weight on the gnostic vanguard as the true history-maker (in the name, of course, of the proletariat

79

whose 'imputed consciousness' it represents) that class ends up by providing little more than an inert precondition of vanguard action.[18] What marks off Lukács from Lenin is his accent on ideology instead of organization, on the degree of belief rather than on the realities of *rapports de force*. Suffice it to say that, in Lukács's view, revolution was prevented by ideological confusion rather than bourgeois strength. Typically, he refused to acknowledge that the March Action had come to grief because it was isolated from the masses. Mass ripeness was nonsense: all that counted was the determination of the vanguard. Of objective conditions, to which Lenin paid such shrewd attention, Lukács had nothing of consequence to say.

There is something profoundly stubborn about *History and Class Consciousness*. Its conspicuous purpose was to provide a philosophical legitimation of the Bolshevik revolution. Lukács drew on Hegel in order to justify Lenin in the teeth of social democratic scruples. Yet it was all done out of an obsessive ethical and 'cultural' motivation. Lukács's full embracing of Marxism was preceded by an ardent mood of 'revolutionary culturalism', in David Kettler's phrase.[19] Culturalism, with all its idealist implications, was in fact a driving force of Lukácsian thought. Consider, for example, his important essay of June 1919, 'The Old and the New Culture'.[20] It contends that the proletariat's task is the re-creation of community. But 'community', in turn, was seen as primarily a cultural rather than a social phenomenon: a matter of spiritual meaning instead of a given pattern of social relations. This was quite distinct from, though not unrelated to, Toennies's seminal concept of *Gemeinschaft*, as opposed to the cool, atomistic encounters which are the rule under *Gesellschaft* or 'society'. At bottom, revolutionary politics was to Lukács little more than a means for the renewal of a long lost cultural harmony.

Besides, the cultural amounted to the spiritual; culture as high culture was a lay surrogate of spirituality. Lukács explicitly avoided the materialism of the anthropological culture concept and instead subscribed to Alfred Weber's influential antithesis between (spiritual) 'culture' and (technical) 'civilization'. To Lukács, culture was 'the ensemble of valuable products and abilities dispensable in relation to the immediate maintenance of life'. While the liberating proletarian praxis is pre-eminently a high-cultural consciousness, the humble, daily materiality of needs in the pragmatic prose of life is just an obstacle and a nuisance, since 'immediate evils and miseries block the ultimate questions from consciousness'. 'Ultimate questions' feed culture just as the *imago dei* and the problems of salvation and theodicy used to feed spirituality in olden times. What is more, Lukács made a point of placing the cultural goal of the proletariat as far as possible from the economic: 'liberation from capitalism means liberation from the rule of the economy.' And culture so conceived is anything but a superstructure. During capitalism, no doubt, ideologies were just the superstructure of the historical process leading to the collapse of capital. In the proletarian dictatorship, however, 'this relationship is reversed', says Lukács: thought, the culture-bearer, takes command. What Lukács offered as a philosophy of Bolshevik revolution deserves indeed to be called *culture communism*.

What kind of reception did *History and Class Consciousness* get? From his Viennese exile Lukács could notice the impact of his message among the Left radicals. His old Berlin and Heidelberg friend, Ernst Bloch (1875–1977), wrote a long, appreciative review of the book, hailing Lukács's revaluation of 'the philosophical heritage' of Marxism. Leninism was doing philosophy as Monsieur Jourdain spoke prose: the Russians, said Bloch, were 'acting philosophically' but thought 'as uncultured dogs'. He also praised the theory of reification and the stress on totality, 'the metaphysical total theme of history'.[21]

In the spring of 1922, in Thuringia, and in the summer of 1923, in the Black Forest, Lukács met among other founders of the Frankfurt school (see below, Chapter 3), Karl Korsch (1886–1961). Korsch's *Marxism and Philosophy*

(1923) was greeted by many as a companion volume to Lukács's much lengthier work. Did he not insist that Marxism was the achievement, instead of the negation, of Hegelian thought? Did he not exude the same enthusiasm about the 'light of October', emphasizing that Marxism was above all a theory of social revolution? What could be more in keeping with Lukács than an enthusiasm for idealist philosophy and an impatience with the economic determinism of Second International Marxism?

It has become almost commonplace to view Lukács, Korsch and Bloch as the three magi of Western Marxism, the three wise men who broke with the unphilosophical quietism of the Second International and restored Marxism to the humanist wealth of its idealist origins. Certainly all three shared, in the 1920s, a messianic mood and a Hegelian mind. The former is conspicuous enough, but the Hegelian element needs to be drawn out. In 'Tactics and Ethics' and most emphatically in *History and Class Consciousness*, Lukács was driving home the point that consciousness is not just any knowledge, but a type of knowledge in which the mere fact of knowing 'produces an essential modification in the object known'.[22] In other words, consciousness-knowledge is world-shaping – a central Hegelian position. Korsch too took pains to stress, especially against the Austro-Marxists, that dialectics forbade conceiving of theory as something extraneous to social reality: true theory is social reality in the making. And Bloch's ontology of utopia followed the same direction: it posited knowledge as an active, world-shaping hope which is at once a cognitive power and a cosmic – let alone social – force. Science, of course, and historical materialism *qua* scientific intention, are scarcely cast in such a mould – but Bloch did not care. Historical materialism was just part and parcel of the 'cold stream' of Marxism; the 'warm stream', which he tried to rekindle, was humanist, utopian and unabashedly religious. In addition, like Lukács, only more so, Bloch's primary concern was with culture, and he had no time whatsoever for the materialities of economy and society.

Nevertheless, the truth is that differences among the true *philosophical* founders of WM (Gramsci, the fourth founder, was essentially something else) are as important as those wide areas of agreement. Bloch, to begin with, was always less of a Marxist, western or otherwise. In *Spirit of Utopia* he actually chided Marx for reducing history to its socio-economic dimension. This was different from Lukács's or Korsch's polemics with Marxist economic determinism: while they appealed to Marx (rightly or wrongly) in order to combat the Marxism of Engels, Plekhanov, Kautsky or the Austrians, Bloch was questioning the Master himself. In the 1920s, Lukács and Korsch, who joined the CP, saw themselves as fundamentalists; Bloch did not – indeed, he hardly could. Moreover, although he lived ninety-odd years, he never became a registered communist. It is true that up to his defection to the West in 1961 he unflinchingly defended the Bolshevik regime, even during Stalin's terror, whereas Korsch broke with it in the 1920s; but his was a strange case of political sympathy without philosophical commitment. Bloch's background as well as his major influence bears witness to this heretical position: for he started in the ranks of the Expressionist movement (and all his life defended – against Lukács – avant-garde art) only to become one of the godfathers of Liberation Theology – in both cases, far from the Marxist canon.

Thanks to a recent and very competent study, by Wayne Hudson, of Bloch's formation and work, we can see how steeped he was in the neo-romantic ideology of the *Belle Époque*. Bloch's ambition was eventually to build a Marxist metaphysics; but in fact, as Hudson notes, most of his basic ideas were formulated before the end of the Great War, before he became a Marxist. Never a friend of sustained argument, Bloch filled many books with highly allusive and metaphorical notions: the best way to consider his prose without exasperation is to regard it as a musical composition, a pot-pourri of motifs dazzlingly gleaned from several sources in the wealth of the idealist tradition.

Bloch shared with Nietzsche the conviction that the 'death of God' required a positive, daring and heroic attitude towards life and value-building. But he also embraced another influential stream of reaction against the alleged decadence of the bourgeois West: the Dostoevskian, Messianic cult of the mystical East. And, equally important, he was convinced that there was a need for the reconstruction of metaphysics if cultural renewal was to take place. Thus motivated, Bloch combined many a borrowing from early modern mystical theology, romantic and expressionist literature, nineteenth-century philosophy and modern speculations on the occult to concoct a heady brand of utopian Marxism.

From German mystics and German romantics he learned to stress the utopian subject, the 'soul', which he calls (in *Spirit of Utopia*) 'the moral mystical Paracletic I'. The soul's natural enemy is the 'occlusion of the subject' imposed by capitalism. But at the same time Bloch wanted to go beyond subjectivism. From Eduard von Hartmann (1842–1906), the link between Schopenhauer and Freud, he borrowed the idea of an unconscious apprehension of the external world. Then he took pains to describe the objective pole in starkly antipositivistic terms. He fully shared the Heidelberg neo-Kantians' concern with 'values' well above facts, their enthronement of a 'creative' practical reason; and from another neo-Kantian, Hans Vaihinger, author of the striking *Philosophy of As-If* (1911), he adopted the idea of a need for fact-transcending postulates. Bloch's central concept – the 'not-yet' (*noch-nicht*) – can be reckoned a robust ontological version of Vaihinger's as-if.

Finally, Bloch wrote in constant dialogue with a whole tradition of 'process philosophies', i.e. 'dynamic' ontologies. From his beloved Schelling, whose pages on the pregnancy of the dark recesses of inwardness meant so much to his own subject theory, he took the crucial theme of the force and wisdom of a self-evolving Nature; from Schopenhauer he took the theme of the cosmic will; from Bergson, the motif of emergent reality in close association with inner, 'felt' time. But Schopenhauer's will seemed to him too blind, and Bergson's time too directionless. Therefore Bloch turned to the finality of Schelling's nature and Hegel's history. He found Hegel's conception of reality as a permanent interaction of subject and object utterly strategic for the new metaphysics – Hegel was the *echt* process thinker. However, Hegel had overlooked the not-yet. Bloch charged him with 'anamnesis', a Platonic term he redefined to mean knowledge restricted to what has already become. True Marxism was, in Bloch's view, a futuristic rephrasing of the Hegelian play of subject and object. As for the 'scientific' Marxism of the II International, it was just a relapse in anamnesis.

All of this converged into an ecstatic exaltation of man. Bloch concerned himself with the 'anthroposophy' of Rudolf Steiner (1861–1925), then a charismatic doctrine of the occult which claimed to be a non-confessional theory of the divine, a theosophy without a god. Bloch's syncretist system proposed utopia as a blend of cosmogenesis cum social eschaton within an apocalyptic anthropolatry. His opus magnum *Principle of Hope* (*Das Prinzip Hoffnung*, 1949) often reminds one of the visionary work of the Jesuit palaeontologist, Teilhard de Chardin (1881–1955) – especially in view of the fact that Teilhard's 'cosmogenesis', unlike Bergson's *élan vital*, is, as Bloch's hope-as-being, a convergent, not a divergent, evolutionary force – converging, that is, in man's triumph over imperfection. Understandably, Bloch tried to restructure rather than to reject the Marxist dialectic of nature – a spurious tenet in the eyes of all Western Marxists, from Lukács to Sartre. As a 'Marxist Schelling' (Habermas),[23] Bloch held a highly romantic view of nature and a deeply disparaging view of technology. But the former is irrelevant to, and the latter incompatible with, classical Marxism.

In the young Korsch, by contrast, there was no sign of the romantic *Kulturkritik*. *Marxism and Philosophy* was every bit as messianic as *Spirit of Utopia* or *History and Class Consciousness*; and Kautsky, in a review, blamed Korsch for neglecting the fact that revolutions depend upon a set of specific conditions, instead of being always possible everywhere.[24] Yet unlike Lukács or Bloch, Korsch was not keen to harness the philosophical pedigree of Marxism to the neo-romantic revolt against modern civilization. Further, for all his Hegel-worship, he did not build anything remotely similar to the Lukácsian totality as a master subject of history, majestically hovering over the petty facts of empirical class consciousness. On the contrary: as a former Fabian sympathizer, Korsch retained a no-nonsense approach to the social question and construed the unity of theory and practice, reasserted by WM, as the primacy of proletarian *practice* over abstract historicism. This alone points to a conspicuous gap between his kind of return to philosophy and the Lukácsian way of doing it. No wonder Korsch, in the late 1930s (*Karl Marx*, 1938), came to value Marxism as an empirical-minded social science shorn of all speculative gnosis, in particular Hegelianism. In short: while the lay theologian, Bloch, was no true founder of WM because he was never more than half a Marxist in the first place, the revolutionary Fabian, Korsch, was not one either, because he soon ceased to be a philosophical Marxist and in any case was never a full *Western* Marxist, i.e., a standard-bearer of philosophy as humanist *Kulturkritik*. As a result, instead of three magi we are left with just one: Georg Lukács.

Scolded by Lenin, Lukács (together with Korsch) was roundly excommunicated, ideologically speaking, by Gregory Zinoviev, Guardian of the Faith after Lenin's death, during the fifth congress of the Comintern (1924). But while Lukács repented and eventually in 1933 repudiated *History and Class Consciousness*, Korsch refused to do any such thing and was expelled from the Communist Party soon after. In the early 1960s, however, Lukács's troublesome book started a second public life. Along with Sartre's *Critique of Dialectical Reason* (1960), it fuelled the renaissance of Marxist philosophy. Even before this, as already mentioned, it had provided the main theoretical grounding of the Frankfurt school. Therefore no other work stands so much at the centre of WM in each one of its three generations: that of Lukács himself, that of Adorno and Sartre, and that of Habermas nowadays. Nor should we think just of the major figures: for it was also *History and Class Consciousness*, more than any other work by Lukács, which inspired several Lukácsian schools, from Budapest (the Agnes Heller group), Italy (e.g. Cesare Cases) and Latin America (L. Konder, C.N. Coutinho) in the 1960s to California in the 1970s (the Telos group led by Paul Piccone).

It is worth noting that Merleau-Ponty, Western Marxism's greatest renegade in its second generation, shared the general regard for *History and Class Consciousness* as a *fons et origo*. To Merleau-Ponty, the book's invaluable significance lay in its bold break with Marxism-Leninism; but what he stressed was chiefly its epistemology and dialectics. He saw in the Marxism of the young Lukács a healthy dismissal of Lenin's crude reflection theory of knowledge and Engels's coarse dialectic of nature. However, in regard to politics Lukács appears under a less heretical light, so that it is still hard to disagree with those who find the underlying meaning of *History and Class Consciousness* distinctly Leninist.[25] If the theory of vanguard power in the name of proletarian revolution is Leninism, then the young Lukács is Leninist indeed.

His actual rôle was to conceptualize Leninism distilled by 'culture communism' – to concoct a version of Leninism highly palatable to the humanist mind.

As often remarked, Lukács's cultural Leninism has an unmistakable pathos about it: the same extremist drive runs from the tragic vision of *Soul and Form* to the blind party allegiance enjoined by *History and Class Consciousness*. Prior to his conversion, Lukács's ingrained ethicism had made him protest against the moral amorphousness of life. By addressing ultimate questions adumbrated in literature, critical essayism strove to avoid the 'psychological nihilism' of our knowledge of people, which muddles through myriad relationships without ever grasping real meaningfulness.[26] Once turned Marxist, Lukács went on evincing that 'neo-classical passion for (moral) order' which Bloch saw smouldering in his Heidelberg friend.[27] His old anti-individualism lent itself to a sectarian dismissal of dissent. Thus the Kronstadt insurgents, those inaugural victims of Leninist dictatorship, were referred to in *History and Class Consciousness* as 'a corrosive tendency in the service of the bourgeoisie'.[28]

Whoever is impressed by the broad-mindedness of Lukács's reply to the question 'What is orthodox Marxism?' (the opening essay of the book) – namely, that true orthodoxy lies in method (see above page 74) – would do well to remember its context. In fact, Lukács was combating the sensible Austro-Marxian injunction to distinguish within Marxism between social science and socialist ethics; and he asserted the orthodoxy of method as a strategy of immunization against 'eclectic' refutations of Marx's prophecies about the future of capitalism. Even if each of the conclusions arrived at through the dialectic method were proven false, he said, the method would still be valid. By stating that orthodoxy 'does not imply the uncritical acceptance' of Marxist theses, he only seemed to exhibit intellectual liberalism, for in fact he goes on immediately to assert 'the scientific conviction' that dialectics was 'the road to truth', its methods being allowed to develop and deepen only 'along the lines laid down by its founders'.[29] Besides, he makes a point of discrediting 'all attempts to surpass or improve' such a method. One is left wondering what can possibly be called 'scientific' about a method which is declared unalterable and mysteriously survives every single refutation of its past as well as future applications.

So much for broad-mindedness. The irony of it is that such a bunch of heresies *vis-à-vis* the diamat of established Marxism should voice so loud a concern for orthodoxy.

But fuelling the dogmatism was an extremist craving for absolute moral certainties allowing little room for cognitive detachment.

As it turned out, the extremist pathos seems to have generated a pent-up imperativeness scarcely compatible with the new Hegelian realism flaunted by Lukács from 1919. A long lineage of interpreters, from Joszef Revai's memorable review in 1924 to Michael Löwy and Lee Congdon in our own time, have stressed that *History and Class Consciousness* marked a resolute shift from utopia to dialectics. Certainly the letter of the book supports such a reading. But its whole spirit tells a very different tale. If dialectic realism meant Hegelianism, then it is instructive that, for all his praise for Hegel, Lukács actually departed from him on crucial accounts. There are two vital issues at least where *History and Class Consciousness* ends up by being ultimately un-Hegelian.

First, *subject theory*. Already in *The Theory of the Novel* Lukács's Hegelian bent was much qualified in this respect. While the strongly historicized notion of the novel was doubtless rooted in Hegel's *Aesthetics*, the novel's content as 'transcendent homelessness' in a 'godless age' sprung rather from the Schillerian and romantic obsession with 'sentimental' art, i.e., artforms deeply at odds with their own surrounding social culture. In like manner, much of the core of *History and Class Consciousness* tells of an embattled subject much closer to Fichte's ego with all its moralist activism than to the objectifications of Hegel's more realistic reason.

In his *Negative Dialectics* Adorno criticized Lukács for assuming that reification springs from the acts of a unified social subject, so that a change in social consciousness would be sufficient to transform the world.[30] Again, in their recent study of Lukács, Andrew Arato and Paul Breines found that his discovery of dialectics did not abrogate the Fichtean characteristics of his concept of subject.[31] Moreover, *Soul and Form* had embraced a perspective akin to Simmel's 'tragedy of culture', stressing the unbridgeable gap between the subject's intentions and the fate of his works. Yet in 1923 Lukács, having acquired a taste for Fichte in Heidelberg, replaced such a perspective by the arch-idealist notion that objectifications faithfully mirror the subject's acts. Thus bad objectification (reification) mirrors the bad (capitalist) subject; good objectification, by contrast, will reflect the good subject once the revolutionary consciousness of the proletariat comes of age. In both cases, the social subject's act and product have become transparently loyal to the subject's own intentions – which is plainly Fichte rather than Hegel.

A second, equally revealing, area of evidence that shows Lukács a non-Hegelian *malgré lui* is his *process theory*. Reification was told as the story of a Fall rather than a progressive though contradiction-ridden movement, as in Hegel or Marx. So the present age – capitalism – remained after all indicted, Fichtewise, as an epoch of absolute sinfulness (see above page 73). Understandably, the Marxism of the young Lukács held considerable appeal for the uncompromising *Kulturkritik* of the Frankfurt school[32] Now in so far as the *kulturkritische* outlook is, as I intimated (see above pages 38–9), deeply antithetical to a proper theory of process, the young Lukács may be said to lack a reasonable account of the historical process – by which I mean a theory of *differentiated* historical evolution. This contention stands or falls largely regardless of the content, positive or negative, of such a process. In any case, few things could be more un-Hegelian than to be found wanting in this connection.

Bloch's injection of *Kulturkritik* into Marxist historiosophy was too idiosyncratically religious to succeed; not surprisingly, in the long run it attracted more theologians than Marxists. Lukács's case was far subtler. In *History and Class Consciousness*, he managed to put a Hegelian framework, built on consciousness, dialectic and totality, at the service of what was essentially a Fichtean position, and as such it was alien to the best virtues of Hegel's objective idealism, particularly as regards depth of historical discernment. If

Bloch went too far in his religionization of Marxism, Lukács put forward a forceful but highly arbitrary romanticization. He granted as much when, in his own final assessment of his Marxist youth, he identified his main sin as 'romantic anti-capitalism'.

As noticed by one of his first critics, Siegfried Marck, Lukács's blend of Marxism and romantic cultural critique worked to the detriment of Marxism as a sociological heuristics. In exchange, Marxism was transmuted into a 'world-view' fraught with dogmatism, revolving around a mythology of class consciousness.[33] Modern critics have not ignored the exacerbated romanticism underpinning this 'world-view Marxism'. To Lucio Colletti (*Marxism and Hegel*, 1969), the central theme of *History and Class Consciousness* is the equation of capitalist reification with science and industry in themselves; Lukács, in his judgement, was a Luddite of the mind. But while Colletti, at the time, was still keen to stress the gulf between this neo-romantic *Kulturkritik* and Marxism, to Leszek Kolakowski these same elements gave the work of the young Lukács the power to contain an unwitting 'exposition of Marxist mythology'. Lukács's Hegelian standpoint on the unity of thought and praxis decisively unearthed the deeply prophetic and utopian nature of Marxism, minimized by the scientific leanings of the Second International.[34]

To put it bluntly: Colletti thought that Lukács smuggled romanticism into Marxism; Kolakowski, that by so doing Lukács disclosed the hidden romanticism of Marxism itself. But of course what Colletti calls 'romantic' is the anti-industrial, anti-modern ethos, whereas what Kolakowski dubs 'mythical' is the gnostic root of the Marxist utopia – the myth of alienation as Fall and of revolution as Redemption. Perhaps there is a potential link between their views in Raymond Aron's realization (see above page 53) that Marx's ultimate aim required the abolition, and not just the transformation, of the economy. For if the goal of redemptive revolution turns out to be a suppression of the economy, then the essence of Marxism would strike at the institutional heart of modernity, thereby integrating Lukács's *Kulturkritik* into the inner truth of Marxism – classical as well as Western.

Reduced to their bare bones, the two main intellectual interpretations of Marxism in force thirty years ago, that is to say, just before the revival of *History and Class Consciousness*, ran as follows. One, held by Joseph Schumpeter, viewed Marxism as a lop-sided Ricardian economics. The other, fostered by Karl Löwith, viewed it as a *Heilgeschichte*, a history of salvation in economic language.[35] Since the revival of Lukács's early work, however, it is no longer possible to overlook the philosophical, as opposed to the economic, nature of Marxism. On the other hand, in acknowledging the prophetic, utopian cast of mind of Marxism, it is no longer usual to stress its economic language. The lesson is clear: the upshot of Lukács's philosophical recasting of Marxism has been the establishment of Marxism as a humanist lore; and for no other reason was 'culture communism' so partial to the *Kulturkritik* mentality.

If Lukács is rightly adjudged the chief founding father of Western Marxism, it needs to be emphasized that Lukács himself played little or no further part in what he had inspired. After *History and Class Consciousness* he largely ceased to be a Western Marxist. Of course, he kept many idealist traits: an enduring fondness for totality, and a dualist epistemology: his erstwhile contempt for science and analytic reason led a kind of softened after-life. But overall he dropped the stark *Kulturkritik* stance – so much so, that he discovered several virtues in capitalism's past, distinguishing between good and bad, progressive and reactionary bourgeois traditions in art and culture. While it would be grossly unfair to his work between 1923 and, say, 1963 (the year of publication of his outstanding *Aesthetics*) to suggest that he complied unswervingly with the dogmas of Marxist-Leninism, he did move steadily closer to whatever the latter kept of classical Marxism. Then it was that he finally exchanged his early utopian messianism for a dialectic vision of history – the vision, for instance, that informs such a masterpiece of literary criticism as *The Historical Novel* (1938, published 1955). But as a whole his fierce struggle against irrationalist trends, coupled with his stern rejection of avant-garde art, set him worlds apart from the second and third generations of WM.

It has been *de rigueur* to dismiss the high polemic of Lukács's *The Destruction of Reason* (1954) as a piece of Stalinist sectarianism, the more so after Adorno suggested that, by equating irrationalism with decadence, Lukács had simply joined hands with fascist ideologues. Yet this dismissal was perhaps too hasty. Guilt-by-association is hardly a good criterion for discarding theories of whatever kind. The fascists were also and notoriously enamoured of Nietzsche: ought we to throw him overboard too purely on this account? Still more important, there is a problem of irrationalism, in and out of 'bourgeois' thought. And Western Marxism's reluctance to face it, beyond the admittedly faulty diagnostics of the post-WM Lukács, says a great deal about WM itself.

2. GRAMSCI AND MARXIST HISTORISM

> . . . The ashes of Gramsci . . . Between hope
> and my old distrust, I approach you,
> chancing upon this thinned-out greenhouse, before
>
> your tomb, before your spirit, still alive
> down here among the free

Pasolini's *Ashes of Gramsci* was published in book form in 1957, exactly twenty years after Antonio Gramsci, following a decade of imprisonment, had died. But the bulk of his *Prison Notebooks* – his remarkable and decisive, if fragmentary, contribution to Marxist thought – was only printed between 1948 and 1951, when Pasolini was still in his formative years. Both as a writer and a film-maker, Pasolini (1922–75), with his pagan primitivism and his 'savage' leftism, embodied the spirit of the counter-culture at its wildest. The poet's homage reflects the unique status of Gramsci's image within the world of the Left. Whereas the best-known portrait of Lukács, the other main initiator of WM, is a fascinating but unlovable character in Thomas Mann's *Magic Mountain* (1924) – Naphta, the red Jesuit, a sharp intellect craving authority – Gramsci, by contrast, became the saint of Western Marxism: a warm, humane figure hallowed by martyrdom – like Rosa Luxemburg – at the hands of Reaction.

Born into the lower strata of the Sardinian petty-bourgeoisie in 1891, Gramsci studied philology in Turin on a scholarship. With one-third of its population composed of industrial workers by the end of the war, Turin was the heartland of socialism in Italy. The young Gramsci joined the Party and, with Palmiro Togliatti, an old friend from Sardinia, launched a radical weekly, *Ordine Nuovo*, much ' read during the widespread strikes of the '*biennio rosso*' of 1919–20. The following year, outraged by the socialists' coyness before the strike movement, he helped create the PCI (Partito Comunista Italiano). He was in Moscow, at the service of the Comintern, when the fascists seized power (1922). Two years later he was appointed leader of the PCI, and in 1926 he was sentenced by Mussolini's regime to twenty years in gaol, on avowedly political charges. Always a sick man, he spent a large part of the sentence in hospital.

Gramsci's major theoretical contribution is to be found in his *Prison Notebooks* – the famous *Quaderni del Carcere*. There are thirty-three of them, stretching to well over 2,000 pages. Gramsci's sister-in-law managed to smuggle them out of the clinic where he died and send them to Moscow. The notebooks were begun in 1929; in 1935, illness forced Gramsci to give up writing. The earliest notes are primarily a response to victorious fascism. In the early 1930s they become more theoretical, less immediately political. Finally, in the last two years or so, the focus falls on Italian culture and linguistic issues. The very nature of the notebooks, not to speak of the circumstances under which they were written, makes them sometimes scrappy and repetitive. Yet how much more rewarding their reading is, as compared with many a treatise, leisurely composed, of academic WM!

Initially Gramsci shared the messianic impatience of the other early Western Marxists. In the best-known of his articles, 'Revolution against Capital' (1917) he hailed Lenin's conquest of power as the revenge of revolutionary will against the economic-determinist creed of the Second International. But he also consistently discredited the historicist statements associated with classical Marxism: 'One knows what has been and what is, not what will be', as he bluntly put it; and devoted many paragraphs in his notebooks to combating the 'superstition' of 'historical economism',[36] the particularly crude version of Marxist historicism popularized by Achille Loria (1857–1943). Gramsci never tired of thundering against 'the iron conviction that there exist objective laws of historical development similar in kind to natural laws, together with a belief in a predetermined teleology like that of religion' – an illusion which, in his judgement, always led to fatalist inaction on the part of revolutionary forces.

As much as Lukács or Bloch, he cut a highly sophisticated figure, a friend of revolution who was no foe to highbrow culture and modernist trends in art or literature. His lifelong concern with political education was also, as it had been for the patron saint of Italian progressivism, Giuseppe Mazzini (1805–72), a matter of lifting politics to an elevated cultural level, an enlightened, universalist humanism.

What Gramsci, both to avoid the censor's suspicion and to honour a tradition in Italian Marxism established by Labriola (see above page 8), called a 'philosophy of praxis' was conceived – just like Lukács's totalist class consciousness – as a comprehensive world-view. 'The philosophy of praxis', he wrote 'contains in itself all the fundamental elements needed to construct a total and integral conception of the world, a total philosophy and theory of natural science, and . . . everything that is needed to give life to an integral practical organization of society, that is, to become a total integral civilization.'[37] He also shared with central European WM an animus against materialism. In the phrase 'historical materialism' it was the first term that should be stressed, not the second, which, in Gramsci's view, smacked of 'metaphysics'. The philosophy of praxis, he insisted, was 'an absolute humanism of history'.[38] No less than Lukács and Korsch, he strongly opposed Bukharin's techno-economic determinism, discussed at length in the *Prison Notebooks*, and gladly quoted from Croce's critique of the Russian theorist. This uncompromising humanism was reflected in his strange way of upholding the dialectic of nature: for Gramsci argued that since the meaning of nature and its history was altogether, in virtue of the truth of absolute historism, a function of *human* history, there was no reason – *pace* Lukács – why the dialectic should not also apply to nature.[39]

Yet within this *generic* idealist outlook Gramsci showed little inclination to prefer, as the young Lukács so often had, idealist to materialist explanations in social theory proper. A good instance of this arose out of the controversy between Trotsky and Masaryk *à propos* the un-European course of Russian social evolution. When, in *Russland und Europa* (1913) the Czech Masaryk traced the brittleness of Russian civil society to the absence of a religious Reformation, Trotsky retorted that this in turn was due to the non-existence of a sizeable, vigorous urban economy in the early modern period. Significantly, Gramsci agreed with Trotsky's rejoinder, which he even translated (1918). In addition, ideology could be useful without in the least being true. Thus, Gramsci pointed out the parallel between the belief in God's providence and more especially in predestination in early modern times, and the fatalistic brand of socialism up to a certain stage in the history of industrialism as witnessing a necessary form of rationalizing the meaning of life (*Prison Notebooks*, pages 337–43).

While refusing to see ideology as merely a reflection of

an economic position or the weapon of a class's false consciousness, Gramsci (unlike Lukács) was far from accounting for the autonomous rôle of ideas by means of a metaphysics of history. Instead of the grand opera of the subject-totality of *History and Class Consciousness*, his prison fragments outlined analyses of concrete political and ideological development. Intellectual historians such as James Joll have rightly contrasted the wealth of historical study inbuilt in the *Prison Notebooks* with the abstract epistemological exercises of later WM (e.g. the Frankfurt school). The point is that Gramsci, albeit often an original and shrewd thinker, was no professional philosopher. His intellectual equipment was of a more empirical variety: historical and philological. Not for nothing had his chief linguistic mentor, Matteo Bartoli, taught him, in the face of 'neo-grammarian' orthodoxy, to stress the *social* context of language.[40]

However, Gramsci did have a towering philosophical influence behind him – that of Benedetto Croce (1866–1952). A great deal of the *Prison Notebooks* is a sustained debate with Croce's own view of dialectics and historism. Croce's idealism appealed to Gramsci on three counts: its secular cast of mind, its anti-positivism, and its strong historical perspective. Moreover, Croce was at heart a *historist* rather than a *historicist*: he emphasized historical contexts and historical developments, but avoided seeing history as a Long March towards a supreme goal. Even so, Croce's interpretation of modern western history seemed to Gramsci too idealistic. Gramsci chided the Naples philosopher for commencing his *History of Europe in the Nineteenth Century* (1932) at the Bourbon Restoration, overlooking the background represented by the economic and military upheavals of the French Revolution and the Napoleonic wars, and his *History of Italy* in 1871, without discussing the struggles of the Risorgimento.[41] Both criticisms were basically sound. Croce's historical works coincided with his espousal of liberalism in fascist Italy. Yet as Croce turned liberal, in the mid-1920s, he replaced his erstwhile 'philosophy of practice' by a far less earthly focus on 'the ethico-political' – the historical manifestations of freedom. Therefore, in a sense, the later Croce was indeed more 'metaphysical' than the early one.

Gramsci's own analyses in the *Prison Notebooks* can be deemed a valiant attempt to marxify the ethico-political by correlating it to class-ridden socio-economic infrastructures. These in turn were undertaken with so keen a sense of national context that Gramsci's historico-political theory seemed to stem as much from an Italian problematic as from classical problems of proletarian revolution. For instance, a major concern of Gramsci's was the need for a Jacobin-like revolution in Italy. He longed for a movement capable of using the state to carry out the national transformation which the Italian bourgeoisie had failed to lead. And because of his Italian problematic, Gramsci's attention was drawn to two issues in particular: the role of élites and the function of class alliances.

Gramsci believed that ruling classes can be either leading or simply dominant. In the Risorgimento, the new ruling class from Piedmont, almost by legerdemain, took control of a unified Italy without seeking a proper national consent. Subsequently, the kingdom's political élite, still dominant rather than leading, absorbed the Mazzinian and Garibaldian wings by dint of 'transformism', a politics of compromise chiefly destined to deprive extremist parties of their leadership by luring the latter into the 'system'. Transformism was in turn but a form of a complex socio-political process, 'passive revolution', which Gramsci identified in at least two guises. *Either* it meant just revolution without mass participation, as in the Risorgimento, *or* it corresponded, in addition, to a covert progress of social classes prevented from advancing overtly, like the bourgeoisie in Restoration France (hence Gramsci's alternative label, 'revolution-restoration'). His conviction that fascism was a transitional form of bourgeois rule, a sort of Italian Second Empire, led him tentatively to apply the concept to Mussolini's regime; yet here, as he was the first to admit, there were more questions than answers. Gramsci discerned a

'Piedmont-type function' in passive revolutions, by which he meant political and social change conducted by the state in the absence of classes able to mobilize popular support. In such cases, one had rule, even strong rule – but no leadership.[42]

All this theorizing went well beyond even the famous, anomalous and half-hearted attempts of classical Marxism (in its theory of Bonapartism) to cope with the phenomenon of autonomous state power, i.e., the state as something more than the executive committee of the bourgeoisie. To a large extent, Gramsci's insights may be considered a Marxist challenge to the central theme in Italian political thought as it has been developed by Mosca and Pareto, the fathers of élite theory. While they stuck to the ruler/ruled axis, Gramsci strove to combine this angle with a flexible political sociology of class. On the other hand, as Walter Adamson has suggested,[43] the different perspectives – Marx's normal derivative view of the state, and Gramsci's often 'politist' view of class – can be seen as complementary rather than mutually exclusive. For Marx, dealing (as in *Capital*) with *ongoing* societies, politics would ordinarily count as the manipulation of class interests at the surface of a social structure. For Gramsci, on the other hand, whose subject was more often than not socio-political *change*, the play of the superstructure naturally carried a much bigger weight. It goes without saying that whenever Marx did tackle major political changes, as he did in *The Eighteenth Brumaire of Louis Bonaparte*, his view of politics became clearly less epiphenomenalist. Be that as it may, one thing is certain: to Gramsci, politics was ultimately neither an epiphenomenon nor an omnipotent prime mover.[44]

Class alliances, which Gramsci dubbed 'historical blocs', entered the picture because leading ruling classes are supposed to enlist the support of 'subaltern classes'. Thus, while the urban Jacobins won over the French peasantry to their cause, in the Risorgimento the Mazzinians failed to arouse the peasantry, thereby hamstringing the bourgeois-democratic revolution in Italy. Modernizing blocs were, at any rate, a staple theme in Italian progressive political thought, from the advanced wing of the Risorgimento (Pisacane) to reforming liberals who wanted to foster northern industrialism with the help of the southern peasantry (Gobetti). But in Gramsci, popular support is a two-way street. Occasionally, in open revolutionary processes, it refers to the mobilization of mass consent. Usually, however, it builds a whole set of values around a broad consensus, customs and practices engineered by the hegemony of a ruling class.

The concept of hegemony had wide currency in Russian Marxism, denoting the political primacy of the proletariat within the lower classes. While 'proletarian dictatorship' was supposed to be aimed against the bourgeoisie, proletarian 'hegemony' was meant to be wielded over the peasantry. Gramsci's usage introduced three changes into the meaning of hegemony: (a) the term came to designate an *inter*class relationship rather than, as in Russian Marxism, an *intra*block one – for Gramsci freely refers to *bourgeois* hegemony over the masses; (b) it was emphatically extended into the cultural sphere; and (c) it was generally placed within the orbit of civil society, in contradistinction to the state.[45] Moreover, though he warned that hegemony needed a root in economic activity, as a rule Gramsci hinted that its essence is of an 'ethico-political' character. Hegemony is to the ethico-political what force is in the arena of economic interests.

Gramsci's *Prison Notebooks* also indicate a further correlation: hegemony, it was claimed, is the mainstay of rule in the West, where a robust civil society is not dwarfed by state power. He attaches more than one meaning to 'civil society'; but his dominant sense plainly connected it to private institutions such as the church, schools and trade unions, whereas the state consists of public institutions like government, the courts, the army and the police. Now in the West, wrote Gramsci, the state was just an 'outer ditch' in a formidable network of fortresses – the social, economic and cultural world of a sturdy civil society. In imperial Russia, by contrast, the state was all-powerful and civil society merely 'gelatinous'. Therefore, in the West, the revolutionary struggle could not follow the same strategy. While Lenin had succeeded in a frontal attack, a brisk 'war of movement' on Russian society, revolutionary socialism in the West has to wield a complex and subtle 'war of position'. The working class and its allies must first conquer hegemony; social predominance must precede political domination. Seizure of power can then ensue as the culmination of a protracted revolutionary process. Aware of the draconian repression which followed the revolutionary adventurism of the German March Action – an ill-starred attempt at a 'war of movement' (see above page 79) – Gramsci also wanted to make amends for his own recent past: between 1921 and 1924 he had actually resisted the over-cautious united front line of Lenin's Comintern – only to see the triumph of fascism. Now he came firmly to oppose those who, like his rival within the PCI, former party leader Amadeo Bordiga, stubbornly clung to the divisionist tactics of 'Left communism' berated by Lenin.

Gramsci's concept of hegemony, as primarily a phenomenon of civil society, has been criticized by Perry Anderson. Anderson interprets the thrust of Gramsci's argument as stating that 'since hegemony pertains to civil society and [Western] civil society prevails over the state, it is the cultural ascendancy of the ruling class that essentially ensures the stability of the capitalist order.'[46] Anderson also claims that while Gramsci was perfectly right in stressing the role of consent in the survival of capitalism he was wrong in locating it within the sphere of civil society. Justifying his critique, he points out that there are two components of popular assent in bourgeois society: a *material* one, fuelled by the rise in standards of living and the so-called welfare state; and a *juridico-political* component, equated with the 'democratic code', i.e. the idea that the liberal state represents the totality of the population, regardless of class divisions. But material assent, he tells us, is far less stable and decisive than political assent. Belief in the classlessness of the state is the hub of ideological power in capitalist orders, and the influence of the media and other cultural agencies just clinches this ideological effect.

In Anderson's view, to infer from the efficacy of this ideological view of the state that the latter is not, in bourgeois democracies, a repressive machine whose main function is to ensure the reproduction of class exploitation, is a social-democratic illusion that Gramsci, in so far as he tended to place bourgeois hegemony within civil society, came close to sharing. As Anderson recalls, Kautsky, in his 1910 polemic with Rosa Luxemburg, employed concepts (borrowed from strategic theory) strikingly similar to Gramsci's: he spoke of a 'strategy of attrition' (cf. 'war of position') befitting revolution in the West and of 'strategy of overthrow' (cf. 'war of movement') as proper to the Russian situation. Yet, unlike Gramsci, Kautsky thought that the Russian state was weaker than its western counterpart; he stressed that, if anything, the German army and bureaucracy were stronger than the tsar's weaponry.[47]

One does not need to endorse the Marxist premise that the state is fundamentally a repressive instrument of class rule to acknowledge Anderson's point: the state, as much as civil society, is the pivot of consent and consensus in liberal capitalism. But it can be said that Gramsci's analysis was truly ground-breaking in as far as it uncovered the wealth of determinations belonging to civil society in the bourgeois West, and here the Weberian concept of the patrimonial state, as opposed to the state born of bourgeois revolutions, suggested itself as encapsulating a convergent problematic. Moreover, Gramsci did allow for an interesting degree of variation in his western model, for he saw Italian civil society, too, as largely 'gelatinous', though obviously not to the same extent as Russia's. In his eyes the Italian syndrome betrayed a conjunction of a weak civil society and a weak state,[48] because no previous Jacobin leadership had occurred, attaching the country to a leading central power. Quoting Weber's *Parliament and Government* (1920), Gramsci set great store by the weight of socially representative parties as transmission belts between state and society. And so, his diagnostic of the Italian case proves that hegemony involves the state as well as civil society.

There is an intriguing page in the *Prison Notebooks* where Gramsci, explicitly comparing inter-war Europe with the post-Napoleonic Restoration, asks: 'does there exist an absolute identity between war of position and passive revolution?'[49] Here Gramsci is apparently hinting, if not at reformism, then at least at an institutional growth of a working-class-led bloc that could eventually dispense with forcible revolution altogether. Cultural and juridical gradual takeovers were indeed countenanced by Marxist heretics like Sorel; and it is worth noting that Gramsci in fact described Sorel as being to the passive revolution after the Commune what Sorel's master Proudhon had been to the former post-revolutionary age in the first half of the nineteenth century.[50] Sorel, however, was prepared to forego revolution (while sticking to its rhetoric as a functional myth of social rejuvenation) because, as a good Proudhonian, he despised politics and loathed Jacobin parties. Not so Gramsci. He shared the Sorelian concern for ethical socialism, but was also very keen on parties and on Jacobin politics. This only makes his cryptic remarks on 'war of position' and 'passive revolution' all the more tantalizing.

Gramsci construed Lenin's critique of trade-union 'economism' as an almost Sorelian invitation to build socialism as a new morality fed on a new world-view. But this could be done only through 'an apparatus of hegemony'[51] where the role played by intellectuals was to be of prime importance. Gramsci thought that there is no such thing as an independent social category made up of intellectuals. Rather, intellectuals are always class-bound, but class-bound in two distinct ways: either they are 'organic', i.e.

103

'organic', i.e. an active organizing force in a given class; or 'traditional', professionals of the mind enjoying the appearance of being above classes but in a position actually derived from the past of the social structure; for once upon a time these intellectuals, too, acted as mouth-pieces and ideology-caterers for the then rising bourgeoisie. Thus, 'organic' intellectuals are above all organizers of hegemony in the making.

Gramsci's position lies mid-way between Kautsky's idea of intellectuals as indispensable bearers of revolutionary ideology on behalf of a class to which they do not necessarily belong, but which does not reach revolutionary consciousness by itself, and the leftist anti-intellectualism of Sorel which, incidentally, was shared by Bordiga. Much has been made of the originality of his views on this point. [52] To some, Gramsci's theory of intellectuals constitutes his 'greatest achievement' as a Marxist thinker.[53] To me, it seems a relatively uninteresting area of his thought. For unlike his theory of state and society, here Gramsci's focus is often less critical and sociological than normative – a wishful thinking geared to building proletarian hegemony. One would like to read more about the intrinsic possibility that 'organic intellectuals' as ideologists and apparatchki can behave as an interest group and eventually as a power-élite – like the 'service intelligentsias' described by G. Konrad and I. Szelenyi in *The Intellectuals on the Road to Class Power* (1974, translated 1979). Naturally, Gramsci did not have this kind of animal in mind. But then, neither did other radicals at the time (for example, the Polish anarchist Wactaw Machajski) who were less lyrical about the power of 'organizers'.

Croce once called Marx the Machiavelli of the proletariat. A substantial portion of the *Prison Notebooks* bears the title 'Notes on Machiavelli'; and we know that Gramsci planned to write a 'Modern Prince'. To him, the modern prince, the 'Prince-myth', had to be collective. In fact, it would be the Communist Party as an organ of class will. Gramsci saw Machiavelli's political thought as a creative response to the failure of the Renaissance (as against the Reformation) to reach the masses in order to build modern nations. Machiavelli's myth of the Prince aimed at providing an Italian 'pendant' of what modern monarchies were making in western Europe: a momentous alliance between crown and the third estate. Once again, we have the motifs of leadership and historical blocs intertwined. Finally, the great Florentine also provided Gramsci with the centaur image: like Machiavelli's centaur, the Party as modern prince would combine force with cunning, stick and carrot. Critical of both the liberal emphasis on consent in Croce and the fascist fetishism of force in Gentile, Gramsci was perhaps mindful of his feuds within the PCI, where the leftist Bordiga embodied violence and the rightist Angelo Tasca stood for persuasion and transaction.

With his meditations on Machiavelli, Gramsci reached the classical source of an abiding Italian concern with state-building and leadership. Four stages have been discerned in the evolution of his theory of leadership and élites:[54] (a) an early standard élite theory, shared with Mussolini (still a socialist at the time) in his youth; (b) a period with workers' councils featuring as élites, from 1916 to the '*biennio rosso*'; (c) a turn, in 1921, towards the Leninist concept of a revolutionary vanguard; and (d) a stress on the educational function of the party as élite, not very different from Lenin's famous last misgivings about the bureaucratic dangers threatening his 'democratic central-ism' model.

It is fair to say that Gramsci significantly surpassed Lenin in this anxiety. In his strictures against bureaucracies he went so far as to reject the *substitution* of party for class inherent in Leninism and uncritically accepted by Lukács. One might say that the drift of Gramsci's analyses went clearly towards restructuring the concept of revolutionary party in a from-sect-to-church direction: in his view, the party was to be an élite but had at the same time to be deeply permeated by society at large. Like the church, the Gramscian party has a catholic embrace about it. In

Kolakowski's phrase, Gramsci was a 'communist revision-ist' who shunned the idea – shared by Lenin, Kautsky and Lukács – of 'scientific socialism' as the grounds for a manipulative role of the Marxist party.[55]

Neo-Gramscians think that Gramsci's refusal to merge party and state under socialist rule, as well as his insistence on the need to strengthen civil society after the conquest of power, put him 'beyond Lenin'.[56] Some even depict Gramsci, in strong de-Leninized terms, as a proponent of a constitutional path to socialism, a 'western way' where hegemony means a peaceful, gradual acquisition of power.[57] Others are more sceptical. Joseph Femia, in an excellent recent study, suggests that a distinction should be made between Gramsci the intellectual, a broad-minded inquisi-tive spirit, and Gramsci the politician, still tied to a faithful and dogmatic revolutionism: thus he remained committed to the anti-parliamentarian and insurrectional approach later abandoned (often in his name) by the 'Eurocommun-ism' of the PCI; and he never dissented from Marxist expectations about the growing size and increasing homo-geneity of the working class which, of course, did not come true.

Sober sympathetic assessments nowadays tend to acknowledge that Gramsci's modification of Leninism was 'expansive but certainly not pluralistic'[58] – a point that most neo-Gramscians should grant, since everybody seems to agree that Gramsci did not formulate an explicitly pluralist conception of socialist power. Certainly he seemed unprepared to envisage sharing power with other parties. Lucio Colletti put it in a nutshell: if for Gramsci there should be no dictatorship of the proletariat without hegemony, neither should there be any communist hegemony without dictatorship of the proletariat.[59] When all is told, there is indeed much that places Gramsci well 'beyond Lenin' – but also well to the right of Rosa Luxemburg. BY WHO'S DEFINITION.

All the same, Gramsci's concern for enlarging the com-munist constituency has endeared him to the leaders of communist liberalization throughout the world. Both the now declining Eurocommunist wave and the ideas on 'mass democracy' defended, on the Left of the PCI, by Pietro Ingrao, are rooted in his thought. And so is, in contemporary Latin America, the search for 'national-popular' blocs, which has replaced the idea of development led by national bourgeoisies in league with 'Bismarckian' modernizing states. With the discrediting of the authoritarian bureaucratic regimes, many eyes have turned to the concept of 'civil society'. Gramscian analyses, coupled with 'dependency theory', hog the intellectual stage. Nothing even remotely similar was ever enjoyed, in terms of political prestige, by any other Western Marxist master.

But then, Gramsci was the odd Western Marxist. His thought distinctly lacks a major ingredient of WM: the *Kulturkritik* element. His fondness for futurism and Americanism betrayed a productivist and technological vision akin to Sorel's, yet deeply alien to the neo-romantic phobias of Lukács and Bloch or, later on, of the Frankfurt school. Typical of him is his emphatic realization that in America there is no sizeable unproductive pre-capitalist stratum, no large body of 'pensioners of history'. In an important section of the *Prison Notebooks* entitled 'Americanism and Fordism' he considers the ideas of Frederick Taylor on 'scientific management' which so interested Lenin and Trotsky. Mechanization of labour, said Gramsci, enables the worker to attain 'a state of complete freedom' – for the very routine of his chores gives him greater opportunities for thinking, and his realization that the capitalists would like him to behave just like a robot makes him at best an unwilling conformist.[60] Could anything sound less like Herbert Marcuse?   *Good Point*

Equally, one looks in vain in all the notebooks for that denigration of science that from Bloch and Lukács to Adorno and Marcuse is as tiresome as it is frequent. Gramsci believed formal logic to be wrongly despised by idealist philosophers, since it was, like grammar, 'a necessary condition for the development of science'. Such contentions are simply unimaginable in the pages of any other classic of WM with Hegelian roots. Above all, one senses crucially that in Gramsci (again as in Sorel) there is no theory of alienation – the very philosophical linchpin of the *Kulturkritik* stance.

However ambiguous or even erroneous his positive political views, there is little doubt that within the Marxist tradition Gramsci has had a profoundly liberating effect. He brought the class struggle theme to bear in analyses devoid of all the shortcomings imposed by the dogmas of historical materialism. Better still, as Chantal Mouffe says, Gramsci tolled the knell of class reductionism: with him, class becomes a powerful heuristic perspective and *magna pars* in suggestive attempts at explanation; but it doesn't get into the way of the 'thick description' of historical contexts. True, his tribute to historism may have cost him – paradoxically – a firmer grasp of some historical trends: as Femia observes, the absence in Gramsci of any developed economic analysis blinded him to the adaptive potential of capitalism; and he mistook the *laissez-faire* economy for capitalism itself. No more than other true believers Gramsci had no intimation about its impending Keynesian metamorphosis.[61] Still, no Marxist thinker of comparable stature had such an 'empirical cast of mind'.[62]

Italian Marxism after Gramsci, by breaking with his historism, cut itself off from his historical political sociology in the process. This was something of a pity, for in the main post-Gramscian development – the anti-idealist school of Galvano della Volpe (1895–1968), where Lucio Colletti (b. 1924) was brought up[63] – epistemological concerns (admittedly often fruitful) were not substantiated by historical inquiry. Colletti himself specialized in the demystification of Marxist historiosophy, and ended up by altogether rejecting the idea that Marxism should be nothing less than a world-view.[64] But Colletti is by now an ex-Marxist, or at the very least a thinker placed, somewhat uneasily, '*tra Marxismo e no*' (between Marxism and non-Marxism), to quote the title of one of his most recent books. In spite of the rich diversity of Marxist culture in

Italy, it seems too early to tell whether or not it will beget a thinker able to jettison Gramsci's idealism while at the same time matching his achievement as a historical analyst.

III

THE POST-WAR SCENE

Let us summarize the story so far. Its conceptual hero has been Hegel's brainchild, the *theory of process*. By saying that Hegel had, whereas other thinkers, notably Nietzsche, had not, a theory of process we mean basically two things: (a) that in Hegel philosophy aimed at making sense of history as a whole and (b) that in so doing it strove to present a rational vindication of modern society, not as a crass defence of the social status quo but as a justification of an overall trend towards an enlarged individual freedom.

We saw further that Marx, as distinct from other Left Hegelians, tried to stick to social theory as primarily an account of historical process; but his attempt was marred by some unwarranted causal claims as well as by a half-hearted acceptance of the dynamic principle of modernity (thus he had no quarrel with industrialism, *per se*, only with its economic institutions as such). As for Western Marxism, it was born, especially in central Europe, out of an unmistakable abandonment of the dual thrust of Hegelian thought: for the young Lukács had no real theory of process, and certainly never dreamt of writing in justification of modern society, not even in the limited yet important sense in which Marx did. Therefore WM, while rekindling the revolutionary spirit of Marxian thought, did away with Marx's own link-up of revolution and historical process. Gramsci alone among the founders of WM was truly bent on historical sociology – but the very nature of his analyses put him closer to the *historist* tradition of Weber or Croce than to the *historicist* concerns of Hegel and Marx: accordingly, he was much keener on specific historical configurations than on the logic of history as a whole.

In the next stage of WM the drift away from a theory of process continued still further. It dates from the 1930s and is generally known as the 'critical theory' of the Frankfurt school – the main idiom of WM since World War II.

1. THE CLASSICAL FRANKFURT SCHOOL

Philosophy is the attempt to consider everything from the viewpoint of redemption.

Adorno, *Minima Moralia*

Herr Professor Doktor Theodor Wiesengrund Adorno was a chubby, bald little man. Former pupils of his tell that, during his Frankfurt lectures, whenever he felt he had reached a crucial stage in the argument, he stood on tiptoe and entreated the general attention by saying in a raised voice: '*Meine Damen und Herren: das ist sehr dialektisch!*' Dialectics was indeed the core of the Frankfurtians' philosophical idiom, so much so that it is sometimes referred to as 'the neo-Hegelian school of Frankfurt'. As for the viewpoint of redemption stated above, it dictated the outlook of all Frankfurt's greatest dialecticians – Horkheimer, Adorno, Marcuse – to the very last. Thought, with them, was 'critical' because, although they had no positive image of a redeemed society to offer, they did stick to the idea that the world as it is remains in dire need of redemption.

The cradle of 'critical theory' was the Institut für Sozialforschung (Institute for Social Research) officially opened in Frankfurt, thanks to the largesse of Felix Weil's wealthy father, in June 1924. Its initiators were Marxisant intellectuals like Weil and the economists, Friedrich Pollock and Karl August Wittfogel. Its first director, Carl Grünberg, 'the father of Austro-Marxism', had been for many years the only Marxist professor in Europe besides Labriola, and as such had taught Karl Renner, Rudolf Hilferding and Max Adler.[1]

During 1930s, however, under the directorship of Max Horkheimer (1895–1973), the main regulars of the Institute and chief contributors to its periodical, the *Zeitschrift für Sozialforschung*, held a theoretical profile that was very different from Austro-Marxism and which came rather from the humanities. These knights of critical theory were sociologists of literature, like Leo Lowenthal and Hans Mayer; trained philosophers, like the musicologist Theodor W. Adorno and the Left Heideggerian Herbert Marcuse; and even psychoanalysts, like Erich Fromm. Little wonder they shifted the focus of the Institute's studies from its original intention of conducting research on the German labour movement to 'cultural criticism' at large. By the same token, political scientists with a legal background such as Franz Neumann or Otto Kirschheimer eventually found themselves out of step with mainstream Frankfurt theory. Their institutional focus jarred with the sweeping psychological assumptions with which the critical theorists built their grim vision of mass culture as a medium for repression and domination.

The knights of critical theory were in thrall to the Left humanism of *History and Class Consciousness*, and particularly mesmerized by the concept of reification (see above page 75). Later, Adorno would define dialectics as the 'intransigence towards all reification'.[2] But, as Franz Borkenau, once a maverick collaborator of the Institute, was to realize, Lukács's 'pure theory of communism' was starkly élitist in two respects. First, it inferred from Lenin's doctrine of the vanguard the logical conclusion that, as the proletariat lacked a proper class consciousness, it had to get it from theory-mongers, i.e., from intellectuals who by totality-gazing would teach the workers what 'their' class consciousness ought to be like. Second, Lukács had produced a theory which, unlike the vulgate of the Moscow dispensation, was a kind of 'code Marxism', hardly intelligible outside the small circle of those philosophically educated at, say, Heidelberg.[3] Like Lukács and Korsch, and unlike Bloch or Gramsci, most of these Frankfurtian radicals were born and brought up in the (Jewish) upper middle-class – and much of their output and outlook reflected a highbrow attitude full of ill-disguised contempt for popular culture of all kinds. WHY NOT?

For the messianic Lukács there was no contradiction between his ultra-Leninist vanguardism and the belief that any transformation could come about only as the product of the free action of the proletariat. The Frankfurtians were far less sanguine in their expectations. Eventually they spoke of 'the historical obsolescence of the theory of the proletariat's revolutionary potential'.[4] But already by 1930, seeing no social upheavals in the offing despite the world crash, they had shed any real faith in the proletariat as a revolutionary force. They might – as did Horkheimer and Marcuse in their reviews of Mannheim's *Ideology and Utopia* (1929) – criticize bourgeois thought for severing class consciousness from a totalist *revolutionary* perspective; but theirs was at most a lip-service allegiance to the class struggle theme. Given the 'impotence of the workers', admonished Horkheimer, 'truth sought refuge among small groups of admirable men'[5] – admirable and, no doubt, mutually admiring; but strictly within the narrow limits of a coterie utterly devoid of links, social, political or cultural, with the toiling masses. Had these sophisticated academics been able to read what Gramsci was jotting down in prison they would have realized that they stood no chance whatsoever of turning into 'organic intellectuals' of the quiescent working class at the close of the Weimar regime.

Horkheimer's programme for the Institute, laid down in 1931, was 'social philosophy'. Social philosophy, unlike philosophy *tout court*, saw itself as an empirical undertaking; but it also took pride in its commitment to 'grasping the whole' – a clear imprint of the Lukácsian totality cult. Vowing himself to be as materialist as he was Hegelian, Horkheimer dispensed with the demiurgic subject, the grand unfolding of the Idea, for the sake of concrete human interaction in history. Soon, however, the real thrust of social philosophy as 'critical theory' found its true target: it was aimed at destroying the concept of progress. 'Dialectic', wrote Horkheimer, 'is not identical with development . . . the end of exploitation . . . is not a further acceleration of progress, but a qualitative leap out of the dimension of progress.'[6] By 1940, with the unleashing of Hitler's war, most Frankfurtians agreed with Pollock that the historical mechanism leading to the breakdown of capitalism was no longer working. Instead, a 'state capitalism' had emerged, which seemed capable of preventing social and techno-economic contradiction from exploding the system. In vain did Neumann, in his painstaking anatomy of Nazism, *Behemoth* (1942), protest that the notion of a state capitalism was self-contradictory, and that the empirical reality of German economy, where cartelization rather than national-ization remained the rule, gave the lie to the statist interpretation put forward by Pollock in an extrapolation from his previous analyses of the Stalinist way to industrial-ism.[7] Most Frankfurtians sided with the state capitalism thesis not because it was more accurate but because it carried a profoundly pessimistic inference about the course of history, and so best suited their own musings about the universality of authoritarian power. This in turn they saw as being rooted in 'technological domination' feeding on widespread psychological repression (as in the sado-maso-chist character of the Nazi mind, according to Fromm).

Within such an outlook, there was of course no room for the idea of social progress predicated on the inevitable supersession of the property economy. Technical and econ-omic progress was no longer a vehicle of liberation – quite the opposite.

Such debunking of progress was a major instance of that encroachment by *Kulturkritik* upon the analysis of the histori-cal process which typifies so much of WM. The state capital-ism thesis adopted by the Frankfurt school stood almost as a pretext for a posture of *Kulturpessimismus* so emphatically asserted that it made previous prophets of cultural doom, like Burckhardt or Spengler, seem, by contrast, positively cheery. Further props to this gloomy vision were the Weberian theme of increasing rationalization, i.e. the growth of instrumental rationality, which the Frankfurtians construed as a factor of domination of man over man and not just of alienation in the 'iron cage' of rampant bureaucracies, and Husserl's picture (in his *Crisis of European Sciences*, 1936) of western reason having lost its way in many inadequate and on the whole insufficient cognitive disciplines. In Frankfurt, the *loss* of the unity of reason became its *perversion*. The school's classic *Dialectic of Enlightenment* (1947), jointly written by Horkheimer and Adorno during the war years, equated reason – the very principle of the Enlightenment – with repression. Husserl had hoped that a new philosophical method, phenomenology, would bring about the latent rationality of the western logos, thereby putting an end to the disorientation of the present. But for the Frankfurtians, rationality had come true – only, its real meaning was a long tradition of betrayal. In their view, rationality had presided over the growth of the division of labour, yet all the attendant material progress was vitiated by the coercion of instinct and nature; for the Frankfurtians, despite their staunch anti-naturalistic stance *vis-à-vis* knowledge, were resolute naturists in morals – and they saw technology as an irrevocable denial of nature.

With progress favouring repression and a non-revolutionary proletariat, the historical totality could but spell disaster, and the unsociological generality of their holistic ideas about technological domination enabled the Frankfurtians to stick to their futile exorcism of alleged vicious totalities well after the defeat of Nazi barbarism or the end of Stalinist terror. Their demonization of reason and technology as well as their disparagement of all mass culture (including jazz and Chaplin's films) licensed them to include the societies of advanced liberalism in the same league as the fascist tyrannies of 1922–45. No wonder they felt compelled to ditch Marx's famous eleventh thesis on Feuerbach (philosophy should change the world, not interpret it). Instead they reverted to a strictly contemplative view of theory as critique. The goddess Praxis, in the sense of liberating social action, had, in their eyes, become terribly lazy.

But this was a gradual realization. As late as 1935, truth was still to Horkheimer 'a moment of correct praxis'.[8] In his most important essay from the 1930s, 'Traditional and Critical Theory' (1937), he stressed that while the former, from Descartes to Husserl, aimed always at a description of reality, and envisaged activity, as in Bacon, as at most technological control, the latter, critical theory, shunned every attempt to place knowledge above action. Yet ten years later, in *Eclipse of Reason*, he would have none of this: the book is a stern warning against conflating critical thought with social activism – especially if political. Quite logically, Horkheimer devoted a great deal of his later reflections to extolling the conservative withdrawal of Schopenhauer over the revolutionary engagement of Marx.

If Horkheimer's evolution displays the characteristic mood of the classical Frankfurt school – *Kulturkritik* in a gloomy vein – its method and flavour were best exemplified in the writings of Theodor Adorno (1903–69), the virtuoso of abstruse dialectics as a language of thwarted redemption. Although he only joined the institute in 1938, on the eve of its exile, his influence weighed decisively in shifting its labours to a culturalist perspective overwhelmingly dictated by a high culture problematic akin to avant-garde art yet conspicuously alien to Marxism, both as political theory and social science. When Adorno came to Marxism, in the late 1920s, he avoided the base/superstructure approach as much as Lukács had in *History and Class Consciousness*. Unlike Lukács, however, he was far less given to comprehensive vistas of cultural wholes. Rather, through his mentor Siegfried Kracauer (later, author of *From Caligari to Hitler*) he learned to dissect minor, even minute cultural phenomena with the microscopic precision pioneered by Simmel in his impressionistic sociology.

It was Kraucauer, too, who introduced Adorno to the

living master of critical cultural microscopies: Walter Benjamin. As has been shown,[9] Adorno's inaugural lecture at the University of Frankfurt, 'The Actuality of Philosophy' (1931), was in the main a Marxisant translation of the epistemology sketched by Benjamin in the first chapter of his near-arcane book on German baroque drama, his so-called *Trauerspielbuch* of 1928. In *Negative Dialectics* (1966), his chief philosophical labour, Adorno defined dialectics as 'the sense of non-identity'. Now what Benjamin had hinted at in the first paragraphs of the *Trauerspielbuch* was the primacy of 'philosophical experience' (*Erfahrung*) over the 'possessiveness' of knowledge (*Erkenntnis*) as the conceptual subsumption of particulars. By committing most of Frankfurt Marxism to a hyper-culturalism whose paradigm was the modernist utopia of avant-garde art, Adorno devised a philosophical organon basically derived from Benjamin. If only for this reason, we must pause to consider the work of Benjamin himself, an interwar *oeuvre* whose wide impact came much later.

The Lonely Work of Walter Benjamin

The construction of life is at present in the power of facts far more than of convictions, and of such facts as have scarcely ever become the basis of convictions.

One-Way Street

Walter Benjamin (1892–1940) is the most romantic of all Western Marxists. His impoverishment, his exile and eventually his suicide in order to escape the Gestapo on the Spanish border of a fallen France make him as much a martyr of radical culture in the age of modern tyranny as the imprisoned Gramsci. Moreover, he was all his life a loner, a misfit among academics and a rebel among radicals – a sort of *poète maudit* of thought, whose lucid, engrossing prose shines like a melancholy jewel in the literary litter of WM screeds.

Probably one of the very greatest critics, certainly the

best German essayist of this century, Benjamin was a Jewish Berliner born in a well-to-do Philistine home who became involved in the counter-culture of his day – the wild student movement of the Wilhelmine Reich. At twenty-five, he wrote an essay as a birthday gift to Gershom Scholem (1897–1982), destined to become a lifelong friend and an outstanding historian of the Cabbala, and who tried hard but in vain to make Benjamin embrace Zionism. The essay, 'On the Programme of the Philosophy to Come', committed philosophy to the foundation of 'a higher concept of experience' – 'higher' in the sense of more comprehensive than the Kantian one, which was perception-bound. 'Kantian' knowledge, though decisively revolving round experience rather than naïvely geared to an impossible grasp of the nature of reality, seemed to Benjamin limited by logic as much as by perception. In the already mentioned 'epistemo-critical prologue' to *The Origin of German Tragic Drama* he also opposed the cognitive value of essayistic 'mosaics', composed by 'immersion' in 'minute details of subject matter', to the 'shallow universalism' of scientific philosophy; he called for an 'art of interruption in contrast to the chain of deduction'.[10] Philosophers had long been too close to scientists; the present task of thought, claimed Benjamin, was to show their affinities with artists, those great dealers in particulars.

The *Trauerspielbuch* redefined 'idea' in a way oddly at variance with philosophical jargon. To Benjamin, idea is neither a pure form, as in Plato, nor a mental shadow of perception, as in Locke, nor is it a regulative principle, as in Kant. In Benjamin's simile, 'ideas are to realities what constellations are to stars': they are uncanny monads, representations of particulars which, since they are no moments in a becoming, are not even concrete universals à la Hegel.

This elusive association of truth-content with hidden details became the linchpin of Benjamin's criticism. Such an aesthetic model of epistemology provided the subject of his 1919 dissertation, *The Concept of Art Criticism in German*

Romanticism. Discussing the theoretical fragments of Friedrich Schlegel and Novalis, he stressed that for the romantics criticism was less the evaluation, by external standards, of an artwork, 'than the method of its completion': true criticism was 'immanent' interpretation, uncovering the 'secret dispositions' of the work. Critical reflection fulfilled literary meaning.

The romantics, as good idealists, combined this immanent perspective with the theme of the subject, the sovereignty of the creative and ironical consciousness. Art was for them both a higher organon of knowledge and the seat of triumphant subjectivity. Here, however, Benjamin departed from romantic theory. Following in the footsteps of Ludwig Klages (1872–1956), a member of the Georgekreis (see above page 64), he instead gave pride of place to the spontaneity of the object – a symbolist doctrine in sharp contrast with the Kantian and post-Kantian stress on the subject's activity.

Klages was a 'telluric' thinker, risen against the Platonic tradition of looking for truth beyond matter. He lectured on arcane subjects like graphology before the youth movement in Berlin, and advocated direct insight into the materiality of the object, without conceptual mediation. Privileged 'moments', epiphanies of 'primal pictures' reflected a 'nimbus' – the radiance of the active object, shining conceptless in all its dense significance.[11]

The same symbolist, Orphic note inspired Benjamin's mystical theory of language, formulated from 1916 onwards. It saw the essence of the word as a pristine mimesis of meaning, over and above mere communication. To him, meaning was imparted 'in language, not just through it'. But in Benjamin such Mallarméan views on Orphic verbal mimesis were clothed in Jewish myth, especially in his ideas on translation. Each genuine translation meant the rekindling of a primeval code, echoing the names Adam gave to a virgin world.

In the Georgekreis circle these symbolist beliefs added up to a kind of cosmic aestheticism. Benjamin, by contrast, put them into a firm ethical framework. His affair with Jula Cohn, a friend of Georg Gundolf, brought him close to the Georgekreis, where Gundolf reigned as critic. Yet his first major venture in critical essayism (1925), a lengthy comment on Goethe's novel *Elective Affinities*, read primarily as a polemic against their naturist aestheticism. Benjamin was not deaf to Kierkegaard's accent on the ethical. Above all though, as Julian Roberts has pointed out,[12] he was deeply impressed by the highly moral philosophy of religion of the Marburg neo-Kantian, Hermann Cohen (1842–1918).

Cohen stood for an enlightened Judaism tantamount to the universalist commandments of Kantian ethics. He wanted full emancipation for Jews, but saw no great difference between Judaism as a 'religion of reason' (to quote the title of a book of his) and an ethical Protestantism based on a strictly individual, eminently responsible spiritual access to God, with no room for ritual and church hierarchy. These latter bore for Cohen the mark of 'cultic' crypto-polytheism, the smack of Catholic idolatry. Like Adolf von Harnack, the great Lutheran historian and theologian, Cohen tended to see Catholicism as 'heathen', and therefore supported Bismarck in the *Kulturkampf*. Faith meant to him a belief in utter transcendence, nourished by fervent hope – the prophetic confidence in mankind's power to free itself through God. Going beyond Kant, Cohen conceived of freedom as something more than a hypothesis for ethics; he wanted it to be world-producing, 'a real force for living men'.[13]

As Benjamin's *Trauerspielbuch* moves from Greek tragedy to the German Protestant 'mourning-play' (*Trauerspiel*) the dawn of morality in myth gives way to the full ethics of the Christian conscience, which opposes the pure transcendence of an empty heaven to the welter of worldly sin. Thus Cohen's ethical Judaism lent a new light to that 'redemptive criticism'[14] Benjamin learned from the romantics. It also merged with a central element in Klages: the glorification of epiphanies at the expense of linear time.

Messianic pathos in Benjamin always points to glowing instants, never to the unfolding of a cumulative temporality. When it looks to the past, it refuses to see the origin as a genesis; as it contemplates the future, it denies all evolution. As such, this anti-historicist cast of mind is akin to the revulsion against Hegel-like historiosophies voiced by Franz Rosenzweig (1886–1929) in *The Star of Redemption* (1921), an outstanding work of Jewish philosophy which left an imprint on Benjamin's writings of the 1920s. To Rosenzweig, the grim truth of Hegel's historicism was a race full of violence, the march of the nation-state towards the Great War. Whereas Christianity expected salvation through history, Jewish piety lived redemption as a messianic vigil that would have nothing to do with progress and its pageant of victims.

Benjamin was the Rosenzweig of culture. He used redemptive criticism as a strategy for the retrieval of humanity. Meaning had to be salvaged, for human longing, especially as a quest for freedom and happiness, lies buried under many layers of repression. Was not the work of civilization, as Freud so well perceived, a colossal repressive effort? If so, truth can only be, as the *Trauerspielbuch* prologue puts it, 'the death of intention'. In the same book he coined his key aesthetic concept, allegory, as the cipher of the dim truth of the repressed. 'Allegories are amidst ideas what ruins are amidst things.' Unlike the symbol, which unites subject and object in blissful harmony, both in creation and contemplation, allegories thrive on the dark distance between form and sense, meaning and intention. In the allegorical, time is felt as a Passion; oblivion wreaks havoc on expression. 'The purity and beauty of a failure' – this phrase of Benjamin, written a propos Kafka, could well be generalized as the gist of his allegorical poetics.

Benjamin wove a unique mix of social critique and historical nostalgia into his essays. As he put it in his *Theses on the Philosophy of History*, written in 1939–40: 'the past carries with it a temporal index by which it is referred to redemption. There is a secret agreement between past generations and the present one. Our coming was expected on earth.'[15] This sounds like a messianic Edmund Burke: a social contract has been made with the dead, but this time in the name of redemption, for the past has been victimized and betrayed. Critical history, says Benjamin, ought to know how to rekindle 'the sparks of hope in the past'.[16] The closing aphorisms of *One-Way Street* (1928), a collection of fragments written almost immediately after his *Trauerspielbuch*, identified the main culprits of historical betrayal: 'This immense wooing of the cosmos was enacted for the first time on a planetary scale, that is, in the spirit of technology. But because the lust for profit of the ruling class sought satisfaction through it, technology betrayed man and turned the bridal bed into a bloodbath.'[17] Here is the Frankfurt school's way of serving an old dish, romantic anti-capitalism from the Left: as in the young Lukács, class rule is indicted. But at the same time the protest against technology *qua* mastery of nature is enhanced: for, unlike Lukács, the Frankfurtians display still another romantic streak – a veritable mystique of mother nature. Reification, in Lukács, is bad just because it is inhuman; technological domination, in Benjamin, Adorno or Marcuse, is hideous because it works 'against nature'.

Cultural nostalgia does colour some of Benjamin's most cogent essays. In 'The Storyteller' (1936), for instance, oral narrative is described as a highly personal form of verbal entertainment in which the narrator leaves the imprint of his experience on the tale just as the craftsman leaves his mark on his pottery. Printing and the dispersal of feeling in modern urban society – what Benjamin described as a growing inability to exchange experiences – killed such forms of verbal art, which were both exemplary and authentic, personal and authoritative. As countless commentators have stressed, the moral impoverishment implied by Benjamin's idea of a loss of 'the epic side of truth' presents striking similarities with the contrast between the 'integrated civilization' of yore and the 'transcendental homelessness' of the modern world, depicted by Lukács'

Theory of the Novel (see above page 67) – a work actually quoted by Benjamin. Even the modern novel is construed against this nostalgia-ridden background. In 'The Storyteller', the real focus of analysis is not its declared subject, the minor Russian writer Nikolai Leskov, but Proust; and Proust (whom Benjamin translated) was seen as at once the terminal point in the dissolution of objective plots and as a passionate attempt to restore, through memory, the authority of that 'narrator's face' ever present in traditional storytelling.

As we have seen, *allegory* was the centrepiece of Benjamin's aesthetics. With the help of these *Kulturkritik* bearings, we can see now that Benjamin discerned two historical types of allegory: while the Christian one, exemplified in baroque drama, basically referred to the creature's sense of finitude, of the meaninglessness of the world, the essential message conveyed by modern allegory since Baudelaire was *alienation*. Modern allegories bask in the enigmatic because their true meaning partakes of the nature of repressed impulses; they are dim epiphanies, half-choked cries of revolt and despair. In a sense, they replace another pattern of aesthetic experience: the *aura*.

The term 'aura' was borrowed from Klages, for whom it denoted a given kind of nimbus (cf. page 119, above). Benjamin defined the aura as 'the unique phenomenon of a distance, however close it may be'.[18] For a long time our experience of art mirrored the practice of religious worship, not the least because, more often than not, the main artworks were religious images. Now this *cultic* function, Benjamin explains, lent contemplation a ritual status, surrounding the hallowed work with an aura of special authority by virtue of the uniqueness of its location and the actual experience of it – exactly the kind of attribute lost when techniques of reproduction brought images ever closer to desecrating visual manipulations.

Given the romantic remembrance of tradition and oral culture in 'The Storyteller', one would expect that Benjamin would expatiate ruefully on the 'decline of the aura'.

In fact, however, he did nothing of the sort. The aura concept was launched in an essay written shortly before his mini-theory of the novel: 'The Work of Art in the Age of Mechanical Reproduction' (1935), first published (in French, for propaganda reasons) in the then Paris-based *Zeitschrift für Sozialforschung*. The ideological stakes were clear: cultic, auratic art had been extolled by the rites of *l'art pour l'art*, a trend seeking to restore the aura by dint of an *à outrance* aestheticism. Fascism, on the other hand, aimed at making politics into an 'artistic' spectacle. By greeting rather than lamenting the demise of the aura, Benjamin wished to reply to the fascist aestheticization of politics with a full-blooded politicization of art. The shock aesthetics of the film, breaking with the slow tempo of contemplation or reading, as well as with the privacy of the traditional experience of secular art, opened up a new, revolutionary path in aesthetic communication. The film made it possible to extend Brecht's 'alienation effects' to a whole perceptual structure. Mechanical art could thus become a weapon of social liberation.

Benjamin's main work throughout the 1930s, the so-called *Passagenwerk*, is permeated by his views on aura and allegory. The title refers to the arcades of Paris as the 'capital of the nineteenth century', seat of the primal history (*Urgeschichte*) of our own modernity. The unfinished *Passagenwerk*[19] amounts to over a thousand pages of largely disconnected fragments on urban architecture, fashion and prostitution, bohemian life, human types like the dandy and the *flâneur* or writers such as Fourier, Hugo and, above all, Baudelaire. Its method, so dear to Benjamin, was literary montage: nothing is said, everything is 'shown' by means of quotations (Benjamin was, beside Karl Kraus, whom he criticized sympathetically, a master of the unexpected quote). The general purpose was to dissect the phantasmagoria of Victorian 'lived' ideology, the social-grounded self-delusions of the bourgeois mind under the rule of commodity fetishism, with the 'arcades' harbouring many masks of such fetishism.

By pointing out the possibility of transparent revolutionary art, the 'Work of Art' essay set off a utopian reversal of those allegories of bourgeois alienation. But allegory itself could be used in a liberating perspective. Thus Benjamin hailed the 'profane illuminations' of surrealism for their alleged power to rescue objects from the state of commodity by decontextualizing them. In his crucial essay on surrealism (1929), Breton's movement is praised for its 'revolutionary nihilism'. Perhaps Benjamin sensed that revolution itself was about to be appropriated by the nihilism of cynical barbarians – a prognosis already supplied by Hermann Rauschning's portrait of the Nazi regime in *The Revolution of Nihilism* (1938); revolutionizing the nihilist temper of the allegorical avant-garde seemed to Benjamin a way of pre-empting the moral annihilation of political revolutionism.

However, the dominant position in Benjamin's later aesthetics was 'Brechtian', for all that to Brecht himself the 'Work of Art' essay was 'all mysticism, out of an attack against mysticism'. In the mid-1920s, Benjamin, who since his youth movement days had kept away from political socialism, moved towards the Marxism of *History and Class Consciousness*. Then, in 1928, he met Brecht, introduced by the playwright's Latvian assistant, Benjamin's mistress Asja Lacis. While beforehand he had sometimes written as a Sorelian (witness his essay, 'Critique of Violence') but was no communist, by the end of the decade, after a trip to Moscow, he had become a commited 'red' intellectual. And his communism expressed itself chiefly in a creative theoretical development of Brecht's utopian *engagé* aesthetics. Instead of seeing the artwork as an end in itself, as in the *art pour l'art* cult, he wanted it to trigger off social change: 'the rigid, isolated object (work, novel, etc . . .) is of no use whatsoever but must be inserted into the context of living social relations.'[20] Impressed by short-lived Russian experiments like Sergei Tretjakov's 'worker-writer' workshops, Benjamin even indulged in lyrical musings over 'the artist as producer'[21] devoted to collectivist practices, a communism of writing as it were: 'authority to write is no longer founded in a specialist training but in a polytechnical one, and so becomes common property.'[22]

In response to 'dialectical' criticisms levelled at him by Adorno, in 1939 Benjamin completed a second Baudelaire essay, to replace the central part of a section of the *Passagenwerk* draft entitled 'The Paris of the Second Empire in Baudelaire'. Resuming the optimism of 'The Work of Art . . .', he embarked on a distinction between the cultic, subliminal experience (*Erfahrung*) of auratic art and story-telling and the forms of alert, pragmatic experience (*Erlebnis*) developed in reaction to the shock of modern urban environments. 'Technology', he wrote, 'has submitted the human sensorium to a complex training.'[23] Much of Baudelaire's poetics was read as a 'fencing' technique, an armour to cope with the nervous collisions of life in a big city. Moreover, once placed at the behest of liberating art, technology did away with the individualistic realm of subjectivity, the cosy world of privacy within property.

In so far as it is conceived as a strategy against aestheticism and the cultic, the later Benjamin's eulogy of technological art may be reckoned a reprise of the ethicist theology of his youth.[24] He once called his ideal of a new technological culture a 'new barbarism'[25] – a dangerous label, since the idea of the technified barbarian was not alien to Nazi and proto-Nazi thought (e.g. in Ernst Jünger). More often than not, however, Benjamin had the good sense to sever his technological utopia from the vapid adumbrations of 'cultural renewal'. He subscribed to Brecht's dictum, 'communism is not radical':[26] socialism-building ought not to be confused with any cultural sea-change, or irresponsible iconoclasm towards cultural capital. In Paris, in 1926, he had become well acquainted with the work of Alexander Bogdanov, the Left communist theorist of '*Proletkult*'.[27] Like Bogdanov, he was able to see the machine as an ally rather than a foe of the worker; and like the *Proletkult* trend (quickly stifled by Leninism), he envisaged the spirit of

avant-garde art as a technical take-over from the bourgeoisie rather than a belated romantic revolt against
modernity.

Yet to conclude by showing Benjamin in such a light
presents a serious problem, for his ideological testament, to
be found in the already mentioned eighteen *Theses on the
Philosophy of History*, swarms with propositions hard to
reconcile with the Bogdanov-Brechtian line of his other
last writings. To begin with, the *Theses* reiterate all his
early animus against progress: they urge a need for pulling
the brakes of the historical locomotive – an image explicitly
employed as a rejoinder to Marx's celebrated saying that
revolutions are the locomotives of world history. Pull the
brakes on history, cried Benjamin, incensed by the Nazi-
Soviet pact of 1939. The ruling image of the theses is 'an
angel of history' (derived from a drawing by Klee owned
by Benjamin) who pays a messianic visit to the scene of
catastrophe. The angel is turned towards the past out of
sympathy for the victims of history, but 'the storm of
progress' propels him forcibly into the future (Thesis IX).
History is therefore a whirlwind spelling disaster, granting
hope only at the heart of despair.

Against the complacent evolutionist faith of mainstream
Marxism, Benjamin first adopted Kraus's motto: 'the origin
is the goal', then welded this old motif of 'hope in the past'
to a burning concern for present imperatives. Nietzsche's
presentist onslaught on antiquarian history earns a gritty
recall (in Thesis XII): 'We need history, but not the way a
spoiled loafer in the garden of knowledge needs it.' All that
Benjamin can find in the present is an ominous danger.
Whereas Rosenzweig had blamed Hegelianism for the
tragedy of World War I, Benjamin scolds 'the brothel of
historicism' for the apparent capitulation of communism
before nazism. But the upshot of his indignation was a
wholesale refusal: 'there is no document of culture which is
not at the same time a document of barbarism' (Thesis
VII). Transmitted culture – tradition – was just the spoils

carried by the victors. True humanity lay, if it lay at all, elsewhere.

Today, when counter-culture and historicism-bashing are favourite pastimes among the humanist intelligentsia, it is hardly surprising to find that the *Theses* frequently receive lavish praise as the epitome of radical wisdom on the nature of historical time. There is, however, equal reason to see them as a rather regrettable relapse in Benjamin's thought. If, following some recent readings,[28] we grant that Benjamin synthesized such diverse beliefs as the symbolist hotchpotch and naïve anti-mythical utopianism, then his 1939 *Theses* represent a surrender to irrationalism. Their critique of successive, i.e. 'homogeneous and empty', time resembles Heidegger's own theory of historicity. In Heidegger's *Being and Time* (1927) Klages's mystique of ecstasy and 'the moment' merged with a Kierkegaardian stress on 'decision'. Benjamin's *Jetztzeit* – the 'now' time, the vital presentness of a past to be redeemed by an ecstatic break in history – reminds one irresistibly of Klages's *Augenblick* as appropriated by Heidegger. The parallel infuriated Benjamin – but the fact that it was drawn even at the time was far from gratuitous.

Some modern interpreters, notably Julian Roberts, have skilfully argued that the *Theses* should not be allowed to dominate our reading of Benjamin's world-view to the detriment of the sunnier essays of his last years. Nevertheless, it is a fact that several of the main themes of the *Theses* were incorporated by Benjamin in his 1939 précis of the *Passagenwerk*: furthermore, thanks to the reminiscences of Adorno, we know that the *Theses* themselves were to provide an epistemological introduction to the *Passagenwerk*, just as the paragraphs on ideas as constellations introduced the *Trauerspielbuch*.[29] If so, the Left irrationalism of the *Theses* can hardly be minimized as something peripheral to Benjamin's thought in its final (however unfinished) incarnation. On the other hand, neither can his Brechtian identity be neglected in order to make room for the critic disgusted by 'the retrogression of society' (Thesis XI).

How then are we to assess Benjamin? As a writer he encompassed an incredible range of expressive power, from infinite delicacy to the sharpest wit. Two or three quotes from *A Berlin Childhood around 1900*, published ten years after his death, or from *One-Way Street*, should be enough to prove it: 'Like a mother who holds the new-born infant to her breast without waking it, life proceeds for a long time with the still tender memory of childhood.' 'Books and harlots can both be taken to bed.' 'Quotations in my work are like wayside robbers who leap out armed and relieve the stroller of his conviction.' Again, few modern essayists in any language can match the winged prose and the humane touch of 'Unpacking My Library'.[30] While this is not the place to dwell on the treasure of his literary criticism, it should be said that his work stands as an invitation to deep renewal in literary history, shrewdly intimating, among other things, the best moves of the aesthetic of reception, currently the most fruitful way out of the scholastics of structuralism and deconstructionism.[31]

Overall, Benjamin's literary stature is almost peerless. Further, he occupies a key position in contemporary theory because he welded the three main traditions of the counter-culture: modernism, Marxism and Freudianism. His concept of allegory gave modern art what is arguably its best legitimation to date – the idea, or myth, that modernist obscurity is not the upshot of a wilful subjectivism, the relentless effect of a 'tyranny of the imagination' long devoted to being ritually at odds with the moral and perceptual categories of the social culture, but rather the inexorable emblem of another, more genuine yet repressed humanity. Allegory in the Benjaminian sense meant that all modern art could be read as surrealism writ large: enigmatic meaning dictated by censored desire. A further, no less powerful, originality was his merger of *Kulturpessimismus* and aesthetic optimism – of a bleak view of history with a faith in artistic advancement. In this Benjamin bequeathed to the post-modern establishment of the counter-culture one of its most typical moods – though one should add in fairness that his thought on this point was far subtler than the hackneyed prejudices against modern civilization, and the gullible, superstitious progressivism of the 'experimental' cult tediously displayed by contemporary avant-garde ideology. For while in Benjamin, at least, the *odium historiae* can be understood as a response to the violence of his lifetime, in the received wisdom of today's prevailing humanism the same rejection of modern western history and most of its social values has no such excuse.

The Spirit of Negative Dialectics

Schematically, therefore, one could say that in its final stages Benjamin's thought contained a twofold message: on the one hand, there was a Bogdanovian Left communist who, instead of exorcizing *die Technik* from the soul of modern culture, fostered the use of mechanical means and Brechtian artifices to supersede the last residues of the aura and the cultic; on the other hand, there was the melancholy theorist of allegory, disposed to a more gloomy account of history. Now the most sophisticated thinker in classical Frankfurt neo-Marxism, Theodor Adorno, chose to enhance this pessimistic streak rather than the 'futurist', technological and Brechtian side of Benjamin. Throughout their crucial correspondence of 1935–8 (when Benjamin was financially dependent on grants and commissions from the Institute, then sheltering from the Nazis in America), Adorno rejected the technological collectivism of Benjamin's Brechtian aesthetics. Such an outlook, he wrote, implied the danger of an 'identification with the aggressor', for technology was part and parcel – indeed, the main embodiment – of repression.

It is easy to discern here the leitmotif of *Dialectic of Enlightenment*: instrumental reason *per se* is evil, therefore no social, progressive appropriation of technology will do. Benjamin's enthusing over *die Technik* might after all save the historical process; but Adorno saw to it that, by an

alleged collapse into an unconscious masochism ('identification with the aggressor'), this line of thought was exor-
cized, leaving the field clear for an unalloyed *Kulturkritik*.
And *Kulturkritik* viewed technological progress as no more
than the progress of barbarism.

Yet on one point Adorno's antipathy towards the Brechtian collectivism of Benjamin seems, to an extent, justified:
Adorno wanted at any price to preserve *individuality* in art
and culture. Their philosophy teacher at the University of
Frankfurt, Hans Cornelius, had taught Horkheimer and
Adorno (they actually first met at the seminar) to value
empirical subjects very highly. A neo-Kantian with strong
Austrian, i.e., Machian leanings (and as such scolded
by Lenin in *Materialism and Empirio-Criticism*), Cornelius,
besides distrusting all kinds of 'first principles' philosophies,
insisted on the need for substituting empirical individual-
ities for the lofty transcendental subjects of the German
idealist tradition. This accent on the individual was not
lost on the Frankfurtian neo-Marxists; in fact, it prepared
the ground both for their tapping of psychoanalysis and
for their cold-shouldering of big collective Subjects, like
Lukács's totality-besotted proletariat. As is forcefully main-
tained in the preface to *Negative Dialectics*, Adorno tried all
his life to use the subject against Subject metaphysics.

In aesthetics this philosophical background casts much
light on the difference between the basic stylistic preferences
of Benjamin and Adorno: whereas the former relished, as
we saw, the impersonal poetics of symbolism and surrealism, Adorno vouched mainly for expressionism, a highly
subjectivist art of loneliness and angst.[32] He was, of course,
exceedingly aware that in the rationalized culture of
modern mass society individual agency in any strong
sense had fallen into abeyance. The economy being now
'operated by society itself', its subjects were 'psychologically
expropriated', mere cogs in a social machine where the
masses are 'directed without any intervention from indivi-
duation'.[33] He thought that each individual now led a
'damaged life' (the subtitle of *Minima Moralia*, 1951): but

the greater the damage, the more the wounded, obsolete individual would become 'the custodian of truth, as the condemned against the victor'.[34] By the same token, he regarded with misgivings every modernist or proto-modernist rhapsody on individual annihilation, from Baudelaire to Stravinsky. The entire long second chapter of his *Philosophy of Modern Music* (1949) rebukes Stravinsky's primitivism as a reactionary move, the obverse of the early Schoenberg's dissolution of tonality for the sake of expression; as for surrealism, it was roundly indicted precisely for renouncing subjectivity.

The later Benjamin tended to see individuality as a bourgeois attribute, much as Adorno himself saw inward-looking spirituality in his first book (1933) *'Kierkegaard: Construction of the Aesthetic.* But for Adorno its roots went back to before the bourgeoisie. Contrasting the overwhelming domination of exchange value in America with European shame before money, he surmised on the alliance between 'feudal' vestiges and the cultural protest of art: 'the remnants of the old were, in the European consciousness, ferments of the new'.[35] Elsewhere he praised German culture and education for being long protected from the market. A paradoxical advantage of the failure of democracy in the Reich,[36] this lag allowed German culture to resist the equation of modernity with reification and its attendant demise of individual autonomy.

In view of all this stress on the psychology of individuality, one might expect Adorno's most sustained philosophical endeavours to focus chiefly on alienation and reification. However, *Negative Dialectics* marks a retreat from such themes. Realizing that 'alienation' Marxism was becoming increasingly idealist, Adorno claimed that more stress should be placed on the objective conditions of reification processes. For a moment it seemed as if, at long last, WM would be about to turn from vapid psychological generalities to the grasp of more tangible social structures. Unfortunately, the thrust of the book proved this to be more of a bark than a bite.

Negative Dialectics regards every attempt to grasp social and historical wholes as a mystification. Nevertheless, the consequence was not, as in 'positivist' social theory, to leave social theory simply scattered through separate, largely unconnected disciplines: on the contrary, critical theory was intended to work as a negating shadow of the unavailable good whole – negating, that is, as far as the existent society goes. This robbed the dialectic of all synthesis, let alone a final, crowning stage. Negativity and identity, which lived a high voltage tension in Hegel, became mortal enemies.

As the jewel in idealism's crown, Hegel's dialectic was the march of the Idea rendered by the concept, in contradistinction to romantic intuition. By contrast Adorno's dialectic was geared to the object and had a very strange relationship with conceptual thought. The core of the problem was Adorno's obsession with 'the concrete'. As Gillian Rose has shown, he attached more than one meaning to it. Three at least are worth describing: (a) first, especially in the introduction, *Negative Dialectics* speaks of the concrete as something ineffable, by nature non-conceptual – a meaning obviously closer to Bergson than to Hegel; (b) secondly, there are passages where 'concrete' points to the 'determinate negation', to objective being as the sum of many determinations – a meaning conspicuously Hegelian and referring, as in Marx, to social processes; (c) finally, 'concrete' is also used, in the spirit of Benjamin's 'ideas' (see above page 118), to denote an epistemological utopia: concepts capable of espousing the reality of experience instead of necessarily stylizing it.

Clearly (c) and (a) have in common a fair amount of irrationalism, and not surprisingly so if one remembers that the *Dialectic of Enlightenment* had described logic as 'domination in the conceptual sphere'[37] and portrayed science, the main carrier of analytical reason, as a recreation of 'myth' in so far as it implied 'the primitive superstition before brute fact'.[38] That this constituted a gross misapprehension of the nature of science, especially as presented by modern epistemology, did not bother those who hailed Adorno and Horkheimer's book as a bible of Left humanism. In fact, underlying most of Adorno's subsequent ideal of a negative dialectic was the shadow of Nietzsche, the master of misology, i.e. of the attack on logic and reason. In his *Genealogy of Morals* (1887) Nietzsche contended that 'only that is definable which has no history'; now, as has been noticed,[39] Adorno tried to make the same point about society, the medium of history. Consequently he denied himself the stability of a conceptual grasp of social structure and cultural process. Therefore his negative dialectic lacked not only direction but even content, in Kracauer's shrewd remark.[40] Conducted in the name of the highest cognitive respect for the object, the rage against identity ended up pretty objectless – dialectics turned into abstract art, as it were.

Adorno had criticized Benjamin's attempt to put montage at the service of historical materialism because of its lack of proper mediations. But what about his own mediations? Adorno habitually alternated microscopies of musical detail with sweeping, caricatural indictments of the social whole, with virtually nothing in between. Musical form in Wagner, Mahler, Schoenberg, Webern and Berg[41] is analysed with as much insight as skill; but his correlation of results with historical trends often has an arbitrary, almost eerie quality about it. Thus in the *Philosophy of Modern Music* there are a number of perceptive remarks on the stylistic fate of the dimensions of tonal music (melody, harmony, counterpoint, instrumentation, etc), yet Adorno's attempt to correlate the evolution of musical form from the classics and Beethoven to Brahms and Schoenberg with an alleged historical 'curse' visited on individuality and its artistic voice is often too fanciful and far-fetched – especially when ready-made Marxist categories are introduced. For example, few people would be persuaded that classical harmony was a sounding symbol of reification just because Adorno portentously remarks that in Berg's *Wozzeck* the full accord of C major strikes whenever there is talk of money . . .

Nor was Adorno above bending interpretation to his own convenience. For instance, he claimed that there was a kinship between the barbarism of Stravinsky's music and Nazi bestiality; then, confronted with the fact that the Nazis banned Stravinsky's works from the German repertoire, he calmly explained that in so doing they showed that they didn't want to acknowledge their own barbarism. Or take his essay on Wagner. Here Adorno has several illuminating things to say about the relationship between Wagner's music, its form and orchestration, and the Schopenhauerian pining for nirvana. Yet, as Michael Tanner noticed (*TLS* 3 July 1981), elsewhere he compares the 'glorified blood brotherhood of *Parsifal*' with Nazi secret societies, as though the Grail knights were linked by racial bonds, were 'glorified' rather than subtly criticized by Wagner and were a secret sect instead of a monastic order. Sarastro and his fellow freemasons in Mozart's *The Magic Flute* would fare much better as candidates for such a foolish comparison.

Adorno's most glaring contradiction, however, involved the very kernel of the Frankfurt world-view: the demolition of the idea of progress. 'No universal history leads from savagery to humanitarianism, but there is one leading from the slingshot to the megaton bomb.'[42] In other words, there is no progress, save for worse. Yet, we were warned, the 'untruth' of the Enlightenment lay in that, for enlightened reason, 'the process is always decided from the start'.[43] But is this not also the case when we are told that nothing counts in historical accumulation, except growth in the means of violence? By what objective criteria are we being told to ditch all the rest as bootless?

Kulturkritik invariably speaks with the voice of assertion rather than of argument. In the Adornian brand, where, even more than in the early Lukács, WM was largely reduced to stubborn, often stupid accusations levelled at 'reified' industrial society, the arrogant use of dogmatic assertion seems indeed to conceal, as Kolakowski has it, 'a poverty of thought'.[44] Such a cast of mind, it would seem, could hardly fail to quarrel with empirical research. Although he took part in devising questionnaires (including the famous 'F scale') for *Studies in Prejudice* (1945–50) co-sponsored by the Institute, the University of California and the American Jewish Committee in order to identify the social determinants of anti-semitism, Adorno eventually reached far-fetched conclusions about the relationship between prejudice and personality structure. Ironically enough, his own picture of the authoritarian personality was to be denied rather than confirmed by the extensive investigation undertaken, by Bruno Bettelheim and Morris Janowitz, in the fifth and last volume of the *Studies in Prejudice*. Once back in Germany, Adorno and Horkheimer did little to encourage empirical inquiries in social science: indeed, for all their original commitment of 'social philosophy' to the empirical, they had been downright dismissive of the worthy honing of research techniques achieved at Princeton by another exile, the Austrian sociologist Paul Lazarsfeld.

A verdict of sterility seems almost unavoidable. In Adorno's hands, dialectics turns despite itself into a formal game yielding few analytical gains – especially as regards social theory. One of the most rebarbative of contemporary thinkers, Adorno left a philosophical jargon which, in the blank resilience of its acrobatics, reminds one of deconstructionism. However, unlike deconstructionism and all the other main post-structuralisms, from Foucault and Deleuze to Baudrillard and Lyotard, negative dialectics did not embrace a nihilist denial of truth and objectivity.

Absolute negation is a privilege of art, of true art which, in our time, Adorno believed to consist of 'messages in bottles on the flood of barbarism'.[45] Whereas, in the Schillerian *Aesthetics* of the later Lukács art reflected the wholeness of man, Adorno's own *Aesthetic Theory* (1970) broke sharply with this ideal of Weimar classicism and extolled instead the 'participation in the darkness' (*Methexis am*

Finsteren) of modern art.[46] In an essay in 1962, 'On Commitment', Adorno took sides against engagement: all truly critical art was hermetic, as in Kafka or Samuel Beckett, the hero of *Aesthetic Theory*. If 'to write poetry after Auschwitz is barbaric',[47] then one must lay the ghost of Schiller: art can no longer be, *pace* Marcuse,[48] of an 'affirmative' character: the only humanism that is left compels it to depict, in tortured form, 'our satanic age'.

Short of the thwarted style of the fragment as image of the repressed, everything artistic amounted to the 'culinary', Adorno's favourite term of abuse. Culinary were the digestive, alienating pleasures of 'the culture industry' – the market-besotted machine of mass culture, which he treated with the utmost contempt. An élitist intellectual from top to toe, he never tired of excoriating 'the banausic', the vile commercial spirit of whatever art that was capable of pleasing the public at large. Although in their moral views the Frankfurtians leaned towards hedonism (an element later enhanced by Marcuse), in Adorno's hands their aesthetics exhibited a dour asceticism: only the martyrdom of form could reflect, if not mirror, the misery of modern man.

Just over twenty years ago, Lukács sarcastically referred to the Frankfurt Kulturpessimists as 'Grand Hôtel Abyss'. [49] The jibe was anything but silly, for an apocalyptic view of history was by far the real common factor among all the stars of the classical Frankfurt school. Again, as the art of the composer Leverkuhn in Thomas Mann's *Doctor Faustus* (1945) is generally taken to be a consummate metaphor of the demonic pathos built into the apocalypse of modern aestheticism, it is of some interest to recall that Adorno was said to have abetted the novelist's description of Leverkuhn's avant-garde music, which was to take the form of a brilliant parody of Schönberg's twelve-tone system. Adorno did this, of course, unawares, and was none too pleased when he found how Mann had used his help.

At any rate, Adorno's thought illustrates to perfection

our claim: the more one plunges into *Kulturkritik*, the less able one is to retrieve a decent theory of the historical process. To this extent, the Frankfurt neo-Hegelians were anything but true to the spirit of Hegel, the first great process theorist. We owe to Susan Buck-Morss a sentence exhumed from the Husserl manuscript Adorno wrote in Oxford in the mid-1930s: 'History is in the truth; the truth is not in history'.[50] In short: like Hegel and Nietzsche, Adorno was keen on historicizing culture; yet as 'truth was not in history', he deliberately refrained from offering a reconstruction of history,[51] which means that in his generation Frankfurt had no Hegel-like figure.

Since the main output of the school was social theory, such an absence was deplorable, for sound social theory seems to require a proper view of the long-term process. Furthermore, Adorno dropped the best of Hegel – the sense of process – without relinquishing the worst: the neglect of rigour and clarity. On close inspection, 'critical theory' remained 'critical' only because it purported to sustain a 'critique', and not because it ever tried to develop as analytically controlled thought. In fact, during the so-called 'positivism dispute' in West Germany of the early 1960s – a dispute chiefly between Popper and Adorno – it became clear that for the Frankfurt master social criticism was far more important than the care of his own critical tools. Ironically, the theory which, in the Marxist camp, did most to warn against the dangers of collapsing thought into praxis, drew most of its appeal from a practical posture – the anathema cast on industrial society – presented at a rather low level of theoretical rigour.

2. FROM SARTRE TO ALTHUSSER

Reacting to the news of the death of Jean-Paul Sartre (1905–80), Louis Althusser called him 'our Jean-Jacques',[52] meaning that Sartre was to our age what Rousseau had been to his: an unbending, uncompromising challenger of power. Thus homage was paid by the most un-Sartrean of thinkers to the figure who, more than any other, impersonated the intellectual as rebel in European culture since the war. The outline of his background and career as an *engagé* writer is as readily accessible as his fiction and his dramas, not least in his masterpiece of autobiography, *Words* (1963); and so we can safely address ourselves to his Marxism, and the peculiar path he took to arrive at it.

Long before turning communist, Sartre belonged to that fierce tradition of 'bourgeoisphobia' (Flaubert's word) which permeated French literature from Baudelaire to the surrealists, in Sartre's youth. Like Gide before him and Barthes after him, Sartre seemed to have tapped his own Huguenot origins to write in open defiance of both Catholic and republican bourgeois morals. But instead of extolling Gide's *acte gratuit* or, like the surrealists, the liberating power of an instinctive, spontaneous stream of consciousness, Sartre wrote in praise of 'commitment' (*engagement*), an ethics of total choice and full responsibility. Although he was trained as a philosopher, his distinctive contribution to the theory of being and the analysis of consciousness lay in the acute moral concern with which he approached such classical problems of academic philosophy.

In his first and most engrossing novel, *Nausea* (1938), the hero, Roquentin, suffers because of a heightened, painful and exemplary awareness of the incoherence of the objective world and the utter contingency of his own existence in its midst. But elsewhere a sense of absolute freedom pervades Sartrean man as he realizes that anything in the world might be otherwise. In Sartre's existentialist summa, *Being and Nothingness* (1943), the basic insight of German interpretive (*verstehen*) theory – that in order to understand human behaviour we normally have to understand a complex play of conscious ends and intentions – becomes the very structure of existence: man is his freedom, and his freedom is always actualizing itself into 'projects'. In man, existence (i.e., choice) precedes essence.

Like the phenomenology of Husserl (which he studied in

Berlin in the first year of Hitler's Germany), Sartre stressed the relation of intentionality: there is no *cogito* without a *cogitatum*, no subject without an object. However, in the Sartrean subject – the '*pour soi*' – such a correlation was to undergo a striking dramatization. The *pour-soi* is pure negativity: its essence consists in an endless annihilation of each of its objects (the '*en-soi*'). Every sojourn in an *en-soi* betrays an ugly sin ('bad faith') on the part of the subject; for the honour of the *pour-soi* is its perpetual quest for self-transcendence. No attempt was made to explain why, if existence is fundamentally choice, choosing bad faith cannot be as authentic as avoiding it.

Not even the self, seen as a substance, is allowed to lure the subject into dwelling on the reality of the given: 'man is free because it is no self but self-presence'. Consciousness is always visiting nothingness upon being; meaning lies for ever ahead of what is given. His very use of a Hegelian terminology (*pour soi*: *für sich*; *en soi* = *an sich*) testified to the fact that Sartre wished to read the problem of alienation into the phenomenon of intentionality, thereby putting the normal business of consciousness under a heavy moral burden. As a result, Sartrean freedom is real yet patently absurd: 'man is a useless passion', since no object can ever slake his thirst for authenticity.

Reading Heidegger's *Being and Time* while in a prisoner-of-war camp (1940), Sartre discovered anguish as an attribute of human existence. But while for Heidegger the anguished existent (*Dasein*) could lead to a soothing sense of Being (*Sein*) long neglected by the metaphysics of the subject, for Sartre there was no such way out: in his view, human reality was 'by nature an unhappy consciousness with no possibility of surpassing its unhappy state'.[53] Thus Sartre's nihilist ontology cast a long shadow on his call for moral engagement: for all his criticism of moral laxity, his decisionist apotheosis of freedom ended up in ethicism as *art pour l'art*.

It is hard to imagine a conceptual luggage more unsuited to lodging in Marx's inn. Yet such was the destination of

Sartre's thought: from existentialism to communist revolutionism, following a long period as a fellow-traveller throughout the cold war. As witnessed by his celebrated lecture, *Existentialism is a Humanism* (1945), Sartre was already emphasizing his concept of 'situation': freedom is always situated in time and social place, so that commitment implies involvement. Consequently, existential choices can hardly be caprices; rather they follow motivational logics, just like the gestures of aesthetic creation: freedom is a moral work of art. From involvement in abstract to the communist option, the distance now seemed narrower. Soon Sartre declared Marxism 'the unavoidable philosophy' of our time. But he did not take on board the cornerstone of the communist faith in collective salvation: historicism. In *Search for a Method* (1957), the epistemological introduction to the huge *Critique of Dialectical Reason* (1960) – which was to remain, like *Being and Nothingness* and his vast biography of Flaubert, *The Idiot of the Family* (1971–2), unfinished – Sartre warned that the idea of progress was more Cartesian than dialectical. Hence Marxism had better do without the naïve progressivism of its origins. Moreover, his Marxist treatise shared other key positions with German WM: published in the same year that *History and Class Consciousness* was reissued, the *Critique*, too, rejected both Engels's dialectics of nature and Lenin's 'reflection' theory of knowledge.

Interpreters often find much continuity between the metaphysics of freedom in *Being and Nothingness* and the central themes of the *Critique*. The Marxified Sartre defined praxis as 'purposive human activity', a social translation of 'project', and by ditching outright nearly all the objective moorings of social history (Marx's 'objective conditions'), he made 'project' triumph over 'process'. The Sartrean praxis is the sworn enemy of the 'practico-inert', all the alienating objectifications of human action. As such, it sounds pretty like the old *pour-soi* at variance with the *en-soi* in all shapes and sizes. Again, though also officially proletarian, Sartre's praxis is not, as the Lukacsian one, totality-bound: at most, it spells 'totalizations', i.e., dynamic, open-ended and precarious horizons of totalities. The reason is there to see: individual freedom goes on providing the model. No wonder the best analysis in *Search for a Method*, the least loose and repetitive section of the *Critique*, focused on the dialectic of choice and circumstance, stressing the irreducibility of the individual. For example, granted that the French Revolution in its thermidorian stage needed a military dictatorship, why Napoleon instead of any other revolutionary general? The answer, says Sartre, can be found only through a 'progressive-regressive' method, using historical materialism as well as individual psychology.

In the Sartrean brand of existentialism there was no room for collective authenticity. Having dismissed Heidegger's rather vague concept of a *Mitsein*, the nearest thing to an existential community, Sartre came to see social interaction as a Hobbesian world of rival consciousnesses, best described by the famous line from his play, *Huis-clos* (1944): *'l'enfer, c'est les autres'* (Hell is other people). He rooted existentialist ethicism in an unflinching moral solipsism. The longest text from his years of dalliance with communist politics, *Saint Genet, Actor and Martyr* (1952), rhapsodized on an arch-lonely – indeed irredeemably asocial – rebel. The *Critique*, however, found meaning and salvation in intense forms of solidarity. It all depended on the sort of group one belonged to. All of Sartre's praise went to the 'group-in-fusion', a collective, enthusiastic *pour-soi* starkly contrasted with the vile routines of the 'series'. The epitome of the serial group is the queue; the paragon of the group in fusion is the revolutionary movement.

The abundance of queues under the Soviet regime, which Sartre so doggedly defended up to the crushing of the Hungarian uprising of 1956, might have cautioned Sartre against ignoring the possibility of a serial social structure born out of high temperature revolutionary groups. Nevertheless, his abiding pessimism was quite prepared to accept such an outcome. Like rebellion, violence was to him worth trying regardless of results – indeed, even despite the fatal betrayal of revolutionary hopes. Violence is an inevitable social concomitant as long as there is 'scarcity' – a category he did not bother to clarify. Above all, however, revolutionary violence meant an ethico-ontological catharsis: it freed history, by means of transient totalizations, of the humdrum of the practico-inert. For the ongoing business of society, the prose of institutional routine, Sartre had nothing but contempt. Whenever his consciousness was ensnared by its objects, Roquentin used to grumble at their 'filthy mess'. Likewise, the Marxisant Sartre seems to abhor social 'thingness'.

So Sartre remained to a large extent a 'Cartesian' under his dialectical cloak: his praxis craved an unsoiled self-transcendence, loath to be enmeshed in things and institutions. In his thought-provoking *Adventures of the Dialectic* (1955) Maurice Merleau-Ponty (1908–61) put his finger on the wound: Sartre forgot that there is not just a dualist world of men and things, but also an 'interworld' of history and symbolism mediating between them. Yet the real ground of Merleau-Ponty's strictures was as political as it was philosophical. When Sartre was starting his march towards communism, Merleau-Ponty was writing *Humanism and Terror* (1947). A rejoinder to Arthur Koestler's classical indictment of totalitarian violence, *Darkness at Noon* (1940), the book did not baulk at vindicating red terror. Merleau-Ponty was a thinker of Catholic provenance originally influenced by the Christian existentialism of Gabriel Marcel (1889–1973). Merleau-Ponty began by 'existentializing' Hegel under the spell of Kojève (see above page 35) then embarked upon a highly sensuous version of Husserl's theory of the 'life-world' (*Lebenswelt*) in his seminal *Phenomenology of Perception* (1945) – the fountainhead of phenomenological Marxism in places as diverse as Italy and Canada. By the mid-1950s, at the time of *Adventures of the Dialectic*, he was trying to extricate the Marxism of the young Lukács from its Leninist purport with the help of Weber. To Merleau-Ponty's tentative 'new liberalism', Sartre's paean to revolutionary totalizations sounded ominously totalit-arian – a dogmatic 'ultra-bolshevism', as he dubbed it.

Serious objections have been raised against Sartre's *Critique*. An Italian critic, Pietro Chiodi, noticed that the book was at bottom a return to Hegel, since it equated alienation with objectification. The big difference was that Sartre's Hegelianism was shorn of its optimism: for the *Critique* allowed for no eventual reabsorption of object into subject.[54] Thus a truncated Hegelianism, underpinning the enduring Sartrean pathos of failure, undermined the genuineness of his Marxist conversion. At any rate, the *Critique* was not well received. There was even talk of 'metaphysical Stalinism'.[55] With structuralism already in the offing, Lévi-Strauss chided Sartre for legislating, in his preface, on a 'structural, historical anthropology'. Largely neglecting Sartre's own misgivings about historicism, he attacked the *Critique* (in *The Savage Mind*, 1962) as a stubborn example of Eurocentrism.[56]

Admittedly, by denying the existence of historical laws and rejecting economic determinism while at the same time proclaiming Marxism the highest wisdom, Sartre had given several hostages to fortune. A fine ironical point was made by Raymond Aron. The *Critique*, he wrote, showed that, contrary to Popper's belief, sticking to methodological individualism (as Sartre had; since his ontology, albeit Marxified, went on ultimately recognizing only individual action) was no guarantee against a historicist faith.[57] In addition, Sartre's long 'Socratic' insistence on the virtues of transparent consciousness and conscience, which went unabated until his *Flaubert*, was of course at odds with the coming of Jacques Lacan and his plea for a theoretical fission of the unconscious. Nor was Sartre's erstwhile hostility to psychoanalysis entirely forgotten.

As a bridge from existentialism into Marxism, the *Critique* was scarcely a success. Nevertheless, it did exert a consider-able ideological influence. Written during the Algerian war of independence and the Cuban revolution (both of which Sartre supported), it banked the fires of revolutionism over the next decade. Yet the more serious intellectual impact of Sartre's radicalism was on heretics within psychiatry like Frantz Fanon, the anti-colonialist author of *The Wretched of the Earth* (1961), and R.D. Laing, the creator of anti-psychiatry. As for social uprisings, most notably the student revolts of the mid- and late 1960s, the participants clearly preferred listening to Marcuse. After all, they longed for a romanticization of Marxism rather than a Marxification of a modern romanticism such as the philosophy of existence. But the real weakness of Sartrean Marxism has little to do with its acceptance or rejection by the spirit of '68. The plain truth is that it had only a poor analytical value – and, once more, no theory of process. Like the 'culture communism' of Lukács and his Frankfurtian progeny, Sartre's ethicist Marxism was made up of mood rather than of insight, let alone a sustained analysis of history.

Sartre's doubtful but widely publicized self-Marxification lent the international prestige of his name to a modest tradition: French humanist Marxism. As much as *History and Class Consciousness*, the *Critique of Dialectical Reason* gave pride of place to 'consciousness'. As such, it was a steady reinforcement to the anti-positivist heretic Marxists gathered around *Arguments*, a journal founded in 1956. Its main figure, Henri Lefebvre (b. 1901), had discovered Marx through Hegel and Hegel on the advice of André Breton, the surrealists being very fond of dialectics at its most 'bacchic'. Lefebvre devoted two decades to a 'critique of everyday life' hinging on the alleged ubiquity of alienation in modern capitalism. As with Sartre and German WM, his kind of Marxist approach had little in common with a critique of political economy. In *Métaphilosophie* (1965) Lefebvre went as far as taking issue with the Marxian concept of praxis; finding it too utilitarian, he pleaded for the idea of 'poiesis' as a counter-weight.

Other *Arguments* thinkers, like Pierre Fougeyrollas (*Le Marxisme en question*, 1959) or Kostas Axelos (*Marx Penseur de la Technique*, 1961), tried to correct and complete Marx with Heidegger. Their works put the French school on a par, in intent if not in achievement, with dissident Marxism in eastern Europe, where thinkers like the Czech Karel Kosík (*Dialectic of the Concrete*, 1963) were concocting suggestive borrowings from phenomenology or existentialism. Meanwhile, academic Marxism, still rare at the time in France, also leaned towards the WM conceptual paradigm, as in the case of Lucien Goldmann (1913–70; *Recherches Dialectiques*, 1959), who proposed to combine the central Lukácsian category of totality with the genetic concepts of Piaget's cognitive psychology. Finally, even the official philosopher of the French Communist Party since Lefebvre's departure, Roger Garaudy (b. 1913), sought to ground the politics of de-Stalinization on a broad-minded rehabilitation of Marxism's idealist sources.[58]

As a rule, therefore, by 1960, French Marxism was overwhelmingly *humanist*. It was also strongly *anti-historicist*, for Marxist historicism was predicated either on economic laws, a notion that smacked too much of 'positivism', or, more generally, on the assumption of more or less automatic 'contradictions' – again, something too objective and impersonal to satisfy the radical humanists' concern for the freedom of the active consciousness.

Within such a Marxist culture, the originality of Louis Althusser (b. 1918) was two-fold. First, unlike most Marxist philosophers in France, Althusser was by no means a rebellious communist – on the contrary, he extended his loyalty to the party, through May 1968 and the crushing of the Prague Spring, well until the middle of the next decade. [59] Moreover he was no humanist. Indeed, while sharing the widespread rejection of historicist beliefs, he flaunted a blunt and highly polemical anti-humanism. Marxism, he claimed, was strictly scientific; it could have no truck with woolly humanisms.

Born in Algeria, like Albert Camus and Jacques Derrida, Althusser had a Catholic intellectual background much like Merleau-Ponty's; like Sartre and Aron, he was a '*normalien*', i.e., a graduate from the Paris École Normale˙

Supérieure, where he was later to teach Michel Foucault. With him French Marxism took a resolute scholastic and scholiastic direction: it became an academic ritual of commentary on the classics of the doctrine. With only a few qualified exceptions, e.g. the work of Nicos Poulantzas (1936–79) in political sociology, the Althusserians shunned applied Marxism, sticking to endless exegeses of the master texts – by which is meant both the works of the Master, Marx, and those of the high priest of their hermeneutics, Althusser.

Yet Althusser's starting point was a rather healthy reaction against the overrating of the young Marx by the humanist Left, with all its 'alienation' cant. It seemed refreshing to hear about modes of production after so much second-rate question-begging on the dehumanization of life in modern society. With WM turned increasingly to vapid moralizing, it was a relief to hear someone treat 'man' as a pathetic fallacy leading to little knowledge. Alas though, relief was soon followed by disappointment. Althusser got rid of the humanist rhetoric only to plug Marxism into structuralist phobias. For structuralist fetishes were promptly worshipped: the indiscriminate rage against the subject, the anti-empirical bias, the arbitrary denial of continuities – the 'caesural' creed. Science, for Althusser, became first and foremost a clean break with ideology and common sense. Cognitive value came second. According to the solemn doctrine of *For Marx* (1965) and its companion volume, the collective work *Reading Capital* (1965), scientific knowledge is not a matter of grasping realities – rather, it advances through purely conceptual break-throughs. Every science is formed by an implicit set of issues – a 'problematic'; but each problematic arises from an 'epistemological break' with the muddled, unreliable conceptual situation that preceded it. Conceptual adjustment to reality 'out there' plays no rôle whatsoever. Both notions, break and problematic, belonged to the anti-empiricist epistemology of Gaston Bachelard (1884–1962); and Althusser was also familiar with its offshoots in the 'logic of the concept' of

Jean Cavaillès and the history-of-science essays of Georges Canguilhem. However, Althusser was to convert their anti-empiricism into a fully fledged, and hardly warranted, campaign against the very idea of empirical referentials in science. Althusserian science spins concepts perfectly undisturbed by the world they are supposed to explain, and thought becomes a silkworm, drawing on itself alone.

Althusser's undefended anti-realism, as well as his appalling ignorance of most modern philosophy of science (not a word about Popper or Quine, Reichenbach, Nagel, Hempel, Lakatos or Putnam) might be dismissed as merely idiosyncratic were it not for his saddling Marx with it. His real theme, in fact, save for an undistinguished course on 'the spontaneous philosophy of scientists',[60] was never epistemology *per se* but epistemology as a theoretical vindication of a specific science: Marxism, the science of history. *Reading Capital* declared the classical problem of knowledge simply unreal: any philosophy which finds intriguing the relation between knowledge and reality was deemed by Althusser sheer ideology; since 'theoretical practice is . . . its own criterion', it validates its products unaided. Knowledge is an 'effect' of the ability of the sciences to legitimize their own results by means of 'forms of proof' answerable to no other authority but their own internal rules.[61]

Now Althusser ascribed a similar view to Marx, in the Introduction (1857) to the *Critique of Political Economy*[62] – one of the few texts, along with Lenin's wartime *Philosophical Notebooks* and Mao Zedong's short essay, *On Contradiction* (1937) he accepted as part of the Marxist methodological canon. Nevertheless, in the 1857 Introduction Marx by no means presents knowledge as though it were just a 'concrete' produced in the mind; far from it, he explicitly states that the concrete is 'the point of departure *in reality*', and even adds that 'the real subject retains its autonomous existence outside the head'.[63] Althusser's comment is therefore a wilful misinterpretation, a typical example of that 'ventriloquist Marxism' that André Glucksmann equated with Althusserian theory.[64]

Unlike the eclectic humanist Marxists, Althusser always took pride in his *fundamentalism*: he described his theory as an explication of Marx's own conceptions, much as Jacques Lacan (1901–81) did with Freud's. (Althusser was in fact for a while a patient of Lacan – which apparently did not prevent him from strangling Mme Althusser in 1981; and in 1964 he wrote an article, 'Freud and Lacan',[65] which marked a turning point in the difficult relationship between Marxism and psychoanalysis in France.) Althusser sought to spell out 'the Marx of the gaps': 'symptomatic readings', analogous to psychoanalytic construals, were to elicit the deep meaning of the founder's doctrine. Above all, he tried, in the best-known pages of *For Marx*, to show how and when Marxism became both the 'science of history' and, as dialectic materialism, the basis of 'the theory of the theoretical practice'; 'Theory' with a capital T, viz. general epistemology.

For Marx located the epistemological break in Marx's work in 1845, after the Paris Manuscripts, still very much loaded with humanism, historicism and, of course, the ghost of Althusser's *bête noire*: Hegel. But critics didn't take long to point out many a humanist theme and a Hegelian motif in Marx well beyond his youthful writings, notably in the *Grundrisse* and in *Capital* itself. Thereupon, in *Lenin and Philosophy* (1968), Althusser, recognizing that the famous 1859 Preface to the *Critique of Political Economy* was still 'profoundly Hegelian evolutionist', confined the authentic Marxist Marx to his *Critique of the Gotha Programme* (1875) and his peripheral notes on the economist Adolf Wagner (1882). As François George sarcastically commented, if the views of the young Marx persisted for so long, until the very eve of his death (1883), then Marx must have managed to remain young all his life.[66] But perhaps the best gloss on it came from Althusser's own pen: in his *Reply to John Lewis* (1973) he acknowledged that his notion of an epistemological break contained just two mistakes: it was neither epistemological nor a break.[67] The grotesque story of the protracted birth of the true Marx became a signal instance of how futile, even foolish, modern Marxist scholastics could be.

Once constituted as scientific, claimed Althusser, Marxism focused on history as a 'process without subject'.[68] 'The true "subject" is . . . the relations of production (and political and ideological social relations). But since these are "relations", they cannot be thought within the category subject.'[69] It seems we are being told that because economic agents, that is, the operators of production and distribution, are performers of rôles and bearers, to that extent, of social functions in a given mode of production, there should be no question of using the subject category. Yet there is a patent *non sequitur* here. From the fact that economic analysis sees men in these rôles it does not follow at all that the notion of human agency becomes useless. Indeed, how else could one account for the actions constituting 'process' but by an empirical research on what individual subjects in their various rôles (producer, consumer, worker, owner, etc.) are up to?

Consider for instance what Marx does in *Capital*, volume III. He describes the tendency of the profit rate to fall as an unintended consequence of the rational calculations of the capitalists, who invest more and more on machinery, thereby reducing the proportion of that part of capital which is extracted from labour as surplus value. Disregarding for a moment the empirical truth or untruth of the falling rate of profit, let us attend exclusively to the conceptual side of this famous analysis. Clearly, what Marx is doing is to explain an economic process, allegedly fatal to capitalism, *by the actions of persons in charge of one of the main rôles in his plot* – the rôle of the capitalist entrepreneur. Now, while a sensible epistemologist of social science such as Raymond Boudon greatly values such a pattern of explanation, based as it is on human agency and the dialectic of outcome and intention,[70] Althusser would have us despise it, since it obviously rests on 'the category of subject'.

We tread on firmer ground when it comes to Althusser's

remarks on *causality*. He insists that true Marxism espoused a *structural* concept of causation, distinct at once both from the idea of a transitive, linear causal relation between separate events and from the (Hegelian) idea of 'expressive' causality, i.e. of effects as revealing a hidden essence of things. Furthermore, 'structural causality' is generally 'over-determined' – a notion borrowed from psychoanalysis to denote the multiplicity of variables involved in any significant social process.

But Althusser took pains to stress that social over-determination did not just mean causal pluralism. There is always a 'structure in dominance'. In practice, he and his disciples associated it with the traditional primacy of economic factors in Marxist theory, though a great deal of equivocation was spent on this point, often revolving round Engels's famous proviso about economic determination 'in the last instance'. Thus, while Balibar said that the economic is determinant 'in that it determines which of the instances of the social structure occupies the determinant place'[71] so that, for example, under feudalism the political order was autonomous because that is what was allowed by the very nature of the feudal economy, Althusser himself was far more sibylline, going as far as to contend that 'the lonely hour of the "last instance" never comes'.[72] At any rate, for those who, like the British authors of *Marx's Capital and Capitalism Today* (1977), were stimulated by Althusser's perspectives on 'structural causality' without sharing his ambivalence towards economic determination, the net result was simply to throw economic determinism into the dustbin of intellectual history.[73]

A second influential theoretical contribution from Althusser was more doubtful from the start: his reconceptualization of the Marxist doctrine of ideology. In a nutshell, he so redefined ideology that from being an illusion and a prop of class rule it became a powerful social cement without ceasing to serve class interests. Althusser further held that every society, even the communist paradise, feeds on ideology in order to work, since 'man is an ideological animal by nature'.[74] Ideology always operates through the subject, he explains; its functional model is the Christian interpellation of the individual summoned to act in accord with religious injunctions. Finally, inspired by Gramsci, but adding more than a pinch of holistic salt to Gramsci's suggestions, he introduced (1977) the concept of 'ideological state apparatuses' (ISA): church and school were depicted as means of tacit indoctrination on behalf of class-ridden social cohesion. For a class to ensure its rule, the social system as it is has to be reproduced; and the reproduction of relations of production is secured by class 'hegemony' over the ISA.[75] Thus Althusserianism quickly became the mainstay of that 'dominant ideology thesis' so closely vetted by recent sociological analysis.[76]

Inevitably, Althusserianism incurred the reproach of making Marxist social theory into something strangely akin to the 'systemic' views of Talcott Parsons's structural-functionalism, then the quintessence of 'bourgeois' sociology.[77] Ideology as a necessary, universal social glue was as functionalist a concept as any. In fairness to Althusser, the most one can say is that there was something which, along with 'theory', he partially exempted from the grip of ideology: art. A chapter in *For Marx* praised the 'materialist theatre' of Brecht, and a text in *Lenin and Philosophy* contended that aesthetic perception, though not to be confused with knowledge, makes us see 'the ideology from which [art] is born, in which it bathes, from which it detaches itself as art'.[78] Beginning with Pierre Macherey's *Theory of Literary Production* (1966), this line of aesthetic reflection was to generate a fair amount of literary criticism under structuralist-Marxist auspices.

For a time Althusser's structural Marxism passed for a powerful sophistication of Marxism in the form of a long overdue epistemology of social science. That such an impression could ever have been entertained says much about the degree of philosophical literacy in many Marxist circles, in France and elsewhere. For in reality Althusser's science-mongering was no sophistication. Rather, it was a sophistry, a pseudo-epistemology which never faced a crude and crucial contradiction, quickly detected by his very first critics: the contradiction between his stubborn denial of general criteria of scientificity (his decision simply to ignore the so-called problem of demarcation) and his claim that Marxism was the Theory of theoretical practice, as such sitting in judgement on science as a whole.[79] It is small wonder that it was not the Althusserians but their rivals in the CP led by Lucien Sève (who even rescued Hegel from Althusser's harsh dismissal) who, since the 1970s, have sustained an interesting dialogue between French Marxism and natural science.[80] To be sure, Althusser himself later dropped his former 'theoreticism'; but unfortunately the cure was worse than the sickness: for all he did then was to return to coining paltry slogans such as his definition of Marxism (in *Lenin and Philosophy*) as just 'class struggle in the field of theory'.

Yet he had begun precisely by fighting theoretical leftism, that is, the tendency to collapse Marxist theory into political praxis. About this, at least originally, structural Marxism was as fervent as Adorno, and later Habermas, in Frankfurt. E.P. Thompson, its fierce English critic, went as far as to speak of the 'poverty of theory' divorced from the empirical duties of historiographic research – by no means an unfair generalization about the Althusserian school. Moreover, Althusser's mystique of theory had a strong motivation: it aimed, as Mark Poster has it, at asserting the autonomy of the party's intellectuals against its politicians.[81] Far from amounting to a suppler political stance, however, this new kind of high-brow Marxism turned out to be quite purist and sectarian: in the 1960s, it branded Garaudy's rapprochement with the Christians as opportunist revisionism; in the 1970s, it roundly condemned Eurocommunism and the politics of alliance with the socialists (the Mitterrand-Marchais 'Common Programme').

For Althusser, significantly, Stalin's sins had little to do with totalitarian rule and ruthless ideocracy; as he claimed in *Reply to John Lewis*, Stalinism was rather a sad case of economism compounded by humanism: Stalin erred because he was obsessed with industrial growth (economism) and chose to ignore class struggle (humanism) . . . Of the iron-fisted tyrant who swallowed up the Russian market under a rigid ideocratic anti-economy, suppressing in the process whole strata such as the kulaks, not a single word. Even the Althusserian stress on clear-cut breaks between modes of production seemed to chime with the belief in the need for violent revolution.[82]

Given Althusser's relentless anti-Hegelianism, this last point sounds rather ironical. At the time of the Second International the best-known anti-Hegelian among the old Marxists, Bernstein, had claimed that the superstitious belief in the necessity of explosive transitions was something Marx inherited from his Hegelian upbringing. Hegel's fondness for abrupt qualitative change as distinct from incremental evolution had provided Marx with a frame of mind not immune, or so Bernstein thought, to the Blanquist cult of violence. The joint heritages of Hegel and Blanqui made Marx into a revolutionist rather than an evolutionist; they gave him a plutonian rather than a Neptunian view of change, favouring explosive upheavals of social fire over gradual conquests of institutional waters. Now, the irony lies in the fact that Althusser, for all his animus towards Hegel, kept the same 'plutonian' outlook. He meant to challenge the party's gradualism with a theory of history as a succession of sharp caesuras which was as volcanic-minded as the model of change in classical idealist dialectics. Apparently, the ghost of Hegel was not so easy to lay . . .

Nevertheless, all his feats of doctrinal political purism cannot detract from Althusser's role as caterer to the delicate intellectual taste of the growing intelligentsia of well-educated Left humanists. As Raymond Aron[83] perceived, structuralist Marxism, while preserving classic keywords such as production, praxis (cleverly pluralized as 'practices') and economic determination, made their content far more flexible and thereby much more palatable to a Marxisant academic public familiar with Weber and Freud, Saussure and Lévi-Strauss, Barthes and Braudel; Althusser procured a smart Marxism, worthy of the *agrégés de philo*. Above all, his was a theory which insisted on rejecting capitalism and upholding revolution without for a moment minimizing – indeed, explicitly stressing – the rôle of superstructures and the need for them. What could be more flattering to the servants of Mind, the academic cleresy?

Understandably, such an odd mix of political sectarianism and theoretical heterodoxy was often felt to be infuriatingly puzzling. In the eyes of the fiery gauchistes of the early 1970s, the Byzantine tricks of the Althusserian school just reflected the crises of both Stalinism and revisionism.[84] The notorious Maoist sympathies of the Master and his followers confirmed the Stalinist element (most humanist Marxists, by contrast, were fond of the 'Italian way'). The departures from the vulgate, including a covert agreement with Sartre's attack on the dialectics of nature and, it goes without saying, the reflection theory of knowledge, lent Althusserianism a revisionist façade. This time, however, revisionism was employed to reinforce rather than demolish myth and dogma in Marxist politics and in its misconstruction of modern history. The only reason this was less than conspicuous is that the Althusserians' navel-gazing seldom led 'theory' to engage actual history, past or present. In the end, their theory of history as science produced neither.

3. FROM MARCUSE TO HABERMAS

While structural Marxism made quite a stir among the British new Left it got a somewhat frosty reception across the Rhine. The reason is not hard to find. With a weighty, manifold tradition of *Historismus* behind them, German Marxists were unlikely to welcome the Althusserian injunction to sever theory from history. The Frankfurt school reproached Althusser for just such a severance in a special critique, *History and Structure* (1971), by Alfred Schmidt; besides, it levelled against structural Marxism the stern charge of an 'ontological regression' due to its neglect of man's fundamental historicity.[85] After all, from the outset the Frankfurtians had striven to deeply historicize Marxist categories.

Herbert Marcuse (1898–1979) was a case in point. He had begun his philosophical career by trying to out-historicize Hegel's ontology with the help of Heidegger (*Hegel's Ontology and the Foundation of a Theory of Historicity*, 1932). At the height of Althusser's fame Professor Marcuse had become a best-selling social theorist, renowned well beyond the walls of academe. He was the main guru of the wild 1960s, the prophet of campus revolutionism, from Berkeley to Berlin and Paris. Rudi Dutschke and Daniel Cohn-Bendit, the leaders of student revolt, never bothered themselves much with Althusser, but they were often said to be Marcusians. And, it must be admitted, Marcuse, more than any other aging star of WM, knew how to sing to impatient radical ears. 'All thinking that does not testify to an awareness of the radical falsity of the established forms of life . . . is not merely immoral, it is false'[86] – this kind of root and branch antinomianism sounded like the best possible prelude to insurrection. The author, moreover, had an almost impeccable pedigree. A Berlin Jew born into wealth, like Benjamin, Marcuse had been a left socialist after World War I; then he had exchanged his infatuation with Heidegger for early membership of the then rather red Institute for Social Research (1932); and eventually became the darling of the Californian Left and Berlin's Freie Universität. Nor had he ever compromised with Stalinism.

Besides, in his Frankfurt years Marcuse displayed an outlook very different from the progressive disillusionment, the despondent *Kulturpessimismus* of Adorno and Hork-heimer. His chief essays from the 1930s, since partly collected as *Negations* (1968), were highly sympathetic to the utopian element in bourgeois art and culture. Whereas mainstream Frankfurt thought focused on the stigmas of repression, Marcuse favoured the 'affirmative' side of the cultural past. Little wonder if, by 1933, writing on Marx's just unearthed Paris Manuscripts (to which he was one of the first to draw attention) he still saw labour, even nature-dominating labour, as an attribute of human essence. How un-Adornian indeed.

That, however, was just the young Marcuse. In his mature work there is nothing remotely so Promethean. Yet it is typical of him to have emerged from the 1940s, when his fellow-exiles of the Frankfurt school were plunged into utter world-historical despair, with an unscathed optimism. Only, unlike classical Marxism, he no longer found the alternative to human misery in historical development, in the contradictions of a dying social order; rather, *he turned to the psyche*. Such at any rate is the message of *Eros and Civilization* (1955). In the preface we are told that in our time psychological categories have become *political* concepts. If history had gone awry, if the Marxian prospect of proletarian revolution had fallen into abeyance, Freud would come to rescue man from capitalist alienation. What society, during the sloth of praxis, stubbornly denied our human needs, *instinct* would grant. That is why Marcuse became so angry with another ex-Frankfurtian, Erich Fromm (1900–80): for Fromm, a spearhead of the 'cultural school' in psychoanalysis, tried to free Freudian theory from instinct, replacing explanation in terms of libidinal drives by interpretations in terms of cultural conditions, and jettisoning Freud's determinism in the process. Marcuse, by contrast, showed no interest in therapeutics; all he wanted was to underscore the struggle between libido and society. He earnestly took individual psychology at a low, elemental level: 'individual psychology is . . . in itself group psychology in so far as the individual itself still is in archaic identity with the species.'[87] This way he tried to square the old Frankfurtian concern with the empirical individual (see page 131 above) with the fanciful phylogenetic concepts of the later Freud, the Freud of *Beyond the Pleasure Principle* (1920) and *Civilization and its Discontents* (1930).

Ingeniously, if not convincingly, Marcuse 'historicized' Freud's sombre view of the warring instincts of life and death by depicting work and order in modern industrial culture as slaves to an overbearing reality principle hostile to desire and gratification. Traditional repression, he claimed, still acted through objective, external coercive mechanisms, for instance threats to one's job and status. In advanced industrial society, by contrast, repression works through the psyche: it is subjective life itself that becomes an object of control and manipulation.[88] But *Eros and Civilization* pointed to a sea-change. The age of affluence which the consumer society was about to enter would enable culture to operate under a different reality principle, more humane and less bent on demanding renunciation. In the past, so much was granted to renunciation that even the first great thinker to befriend the life instinct, Nietzsche, still accepted pain as part of his human ideal. Now, Marcuse claimed, there was no longer any reason to hold out against hedonist drives. Placed under the aegis of Orpheus and Narcissus, a new libidinal civilization could 'create its own division of labour, its own priorities, its own hierarchy' at a far remove from the constraints of present arrangements.

The unabashed utopianism of *Eros and Civilization* combined themes from Fourier (redivision of labour to fit each individual's libido), Saint-Simon (administration of things to replace government of men) and Schiller (the playful mankind in an 'aesthetic state'). Overall, Marcuse proclaimed an erotic (but far from genital) and *ludic* paradise, freed from the drab ethics of performance in which we poor souls live or linger on. Social harmony and personal bliss, in such an Eden, go hand in hand. At most, Marcuse warned a fellow-dreamer, Norman Brown, there will be some tensions in the realm of Eros – but there is nothing nasty in it, he hastened to add, since they will be 'non-antagonistic' tensions. He even noted, approvingly, a far-fetched idea of Hans Sachs: the absence of technological progress in ancient Greece was due to the 'fact' that the Greeks loved the body so much. To Narcissus, Prometheus was just beyond contempt.

Unfortunately, this cheerful outlook did not last long. Less than a decade later, in *One-Dimensional Man* (1964), the libidinous elation of his treatise on Eros and culture gave way to a dismal landscape: humanity repressed in the technological cage. This time Freud was left in peace. Instead of psychoanalysis, Marcuse resumed his peculiar interpretation of Hegel originally set out in *Reason and Revolution* (1941), which transmuted the great realist into a paladin of 'negative thought' – that is, thought asserting utopian ideals in the teeth of yielding or unyielding historical realities. The lost 'second dimension' of western man was precisely everything capable of embodying the critical supersession of modern industrial culture. As for the 'new Hegel', Marcuse, he waved the flag of a 'Great Refusal' against the 'surplus repression' and the 'repressive desublimations' (chapter 3) of our late capitalist order. For *One-Dimensional Man* saw us riveted to a 'welfare-warfare society' abysmally dehumanizing since its 'contagion' with Nazism. The centre of such social hell was, of course, North America, reckoned by Marcuse to be perfectly totalitarian 'for totalitarian is not only a terroristic political coordination of society, but also a non-terroristic economic-technical coordination which operates through the manipulation of needs by vested interests.'[89] Why? Because such manipulated society also manages to preclude 'opposition against the social whole'. Naturally, Professor Marcuse considered it beneath his intellectual dignity to go and ask real people whether or not they were actually rather happy about the 'whole' – a non-terroristic one, at least – if not about each one of its parts. But then he had no need to: he happened to 'know' that real people were just manipulated zombies, brainwashed by consumption into blind compliance.

Recurrent throughout Marcuse's work was a passionate suspicion of science and technology:

The very concept of technical reason is perhaps ideological. Not only the application of technology, but technology itself is domination (of nature and men) ... specific purposes and interests of domination are not foisted upon technology 'subsequently' and from the outside; they enter the very construction of the technical apparatus ... Such a purpose of domination is 'substantive' and to this extent belongs to the very form of technical reason.[90]

The whole of chapter 5 in *One-Dimensional Man* is a quaint piece of misology, a hopelessly superannuated defence of dialectics based on the idea that, as logic works through the subsumption of the particular into the general, 'the logic of thought' is 'a logic of domination'. Then, towards the end of the book, Marcuse toys with the vision of an essentially 'different' science in a 'pacified' society.[91] But if science has to change so much, it follows that science as it now is is inherently mischievous. That such a crass epigonic sub-romanticism could ever pose as a neo-Marxism tells much about the surrender of WM to the worst of *Kulturkritik* clichés.

There is, though, an underlying continuity between *Eros and Civilization* and *One-Dimensional Man*, the two books which most endeared Marcuse to the counter-cultural Left. In neither is history seen as a vehicle of social redemption. Praxis was not a guest at the feast of Eros; nor does it condescend to bring about the 'second dimension'. The sketchy historical sociology of *One-Dimensional Man*, which constitutes the first of its three parts, makes no bones about acknowledging the irrelevance of Marx's views on class to contemporary society. Where is the working class on which the theory of surplus value was predicated? asks Marcuse. The number of blue collars is steadily dwindling. The 'physiological dimension' of exploited labour vanishes before the progress of automation. Class struggle withers away. While Marcuse felt unable to agree with Serge Mallet, the revisionist theorist of the new working classes from the *Arguments* group, that workers were voluntarily integrating themselves into hi-tech capitalism, he did share

Mallet's realization that the trend of such economy was towards determination of productivity by machines and not by individual output, which becomes anyway impossible to measure,[92] thereby destroying the very basis of the surplus-value concept, the mainstay of Marx's 'critique of political economy'. In such a 'society without opposition', technology reifies everything and everybody unimpeded.

Beyond technology's reach, however, there is just, 'underneath the conservative popular base' of our liberal industrial societies, a sizeable number of 'outcasts and outsiders'. It is with these Marcuse casts his lot. The Great Refusal belongs to the underdog, the oppressed racial minorities and the lumpenproletariat. Afterwards Marcuse enlisted rebel students and exploited peasantries of the Third World into the armies of his cultural revolution. But at the close of his 1964 book, with no uprisings in sight, he just owned that 'the critical theory of society possesses no concepts which could bridge the gap between the present and its future; holding no promise and showing no success, it remains negative'.[93] His dreary invective against modern culture draws to a close with Benjamin's motto on 'hope for the sake of those without hope'. Maybe it is worth remembering that Marcuse borrowed the melodramatic idea of an absolute refusal from Maurice Blanchot, the subtle essayist who, after a rather lengthy flirtation with fascism, wove Mallarméan poetics and Heidegger's ontology into a dazzling but profoundly irrationalist literary apocalypse.

The ecstatic applause of the counter-culture in the wake of student riots delighted Marcuse. He obliged by promptly dropping his dark views on the march of history. An *Essay on Liberation* (1969) continued to number the tamed workers lost to capitalism; but it placed high hopes on students and blacks. Marcuse reverted to the libertarian biologism of *Eros and Civilization*: instinctual urge, once again, takes over from the pseudo-Hegelianism of 'negative thought'. But as soon as the counter-culture threatened to turn into a generalized anti-culture, the philosopher began to fear its wildest militant wings. His last book, *The Aesthetic Dimension* (1978), distances itself from their new vandalism – the strident violence of what Habermas dared to call 'the fascism of the Left'.

Alas, Marcuse had himself sponsored much of their silly, dangerous contumely *vis-à-vis* institutional liberties and humane practices. Had he not, in 'Repressive Tolerance' (1965), pleaded for a replacement of liberal tolerance by a systematic bias in favour of 'enlightened' libertarianism? Had he not derided the respect for the rule of the law, likened the American police to the SS, and developed an exceedingly specious argument to the effect that while in the past many a social break-through was brought about by revolutionary violence, the conscientious application of democratic tolerance had allowed Hitler to assume power[94]? He just forgot to add that the real issue was not to show that violence was beneficial or even inevitable in pre-democratic contexts but rather that it remains necessary, and superior in effect, to democratic means, in today's liberal-democratic systems. But then, authoritarianism as such never frightened Marcuse. 'From Plato to Rousseau', he wrote, 'the only answer is the idea of an educational dictatorship'[95] – a sentence which surely made the author of the *Social Contract* spin in his grave.[96] Maybe this was the secret reason why, in *Soviet Marxism* (1958), for all his criticisms of the Leninist order, he managed to deny that the communist power élite had class interests of its own: were not Lenin's heirs just a bunch of temporarily strayed 'educational' despots?

From the start, Marcuse was the most political of the Frankfurtians. That his was a Marxism without either history or a proletariat, and that his mood of revolution without a Daybreak lacked cogency, was of little concern to the new militant radicals. What they required was a rationale for ritual revolt, not a persuasive analysis of largely imaginary evils. The essential thing was to reconnect WM with the thrills of street protest and active establishment-hatred. This Marcuse provided twice over:

by way of a euphoric libidinal utopia (even as late as his Preface to *Negations*, he was still extolling the eschatological streak in Marx), and by way of a pessimistic Refusal. Both moods suited the revolutionism of affluent society, bound to be far more 'cultural' and symbolic than social and real. The myth of widespread psycho-cultural *repression* was highly convenient: it spared the embarrassment of having to explain the diminution of actual *oppression* within our liberal, permissive social milieu. Marcuse's 'negative thought', his glorification of Refusal, became the favourite jargon of compulsive repression-bashing. Thus, the spent flame of Lukács's fervour was rekindled, together with the false Hegelianism of the spirit of *History and Class Consciousness* and Lukács's virulent anti-positivism. If ever there was a classic of *vulgar Kulturkritik* masquerading as neo-Marxism then it was Herbert Marcuse. No chance, of course, to get a theory of historical process out of such stuff. Indeed, history was twice denied: first via the crude instinctualism of *Eros and Civilization*; then, in the flattening social theory of *One-Dimensional Man*, a portrait of modern society as static as it is monolithic. And without a minimum of process, how can one have a theory of process?

Jürgen Habermas and the Holy Grail of Dialogue

The paradigm is no longer the observation but the dialogue
Habermas

The work of Jürgen Habermas is sometimes described as an attenuation of whatever radical residue was left within the 'critical theory' of the Frankfurt school. Born in the Rhineland in 1929, Habermas spent his formative years in a social and political context very different from the youth of Benjamin, Adorno or Marcuse. While they had witnessed the time of troubles of the Weimar Republic, Habermas approached middle age in the 'leftless' West Germany of the cold war. Nietzsche used to quip that the fact that so many German thinkers were, like himself, sons of clergymen predisposed them to be rather tame and quiescent in their world-view. Habermas, son of a bureaucrat and grandson of a Lutheran minister, would seem no exception to the rule: for he is often held to be the learned thinker who took the sting of subversion out of critical theory.

Yet the spark which triggered Habermas's thought was a lecture on Freud delivered by the radical Marcuse in Frankfurt in 1956, the year of Freud's centennial and of Habermas's own admission into the Institut für Sozialforschung. Marcuse, in the eyes of young Habermas, gave the old political flame of the Frankfurt school a new lease of life.[97] The gorgeous prophecy of Eros seemed to brush Horkheimer and Adorno's sultry *Kulturpessimismus* aside – and good riddance, thought the novice critical theorist.

Not that Habermas was ever a Marcusian, though. He was not a bit concerned with the instinctual basis of human nature – the theme of *Eros and Civilization* – but with the open-ended development of man, a truly Hegelian motif (see above page 43). And he had no truck, for that matter, with the Frankfurtians' neo-romantic myth of a resurrection of nature; rather, he bluntly declared it incompatible with materialism.[98] Habermas had done his doctoral work on Schelling (1954) and hence was more than familiar with romantic thought; but his overall position amounted, almost from the beginning, to 'back to the Enlightenment'. As such, it meant a sharp break with the dismal apocalyptic vision of 'negative dialectics'. In the middle of his career he did not refrain from calling Adorno's work 'an empty exercise in self-reflection';[99] in its stead, Habermas wished to promote a return to concrete social and economic analysis. In this, at least, he remained faithful to the original Frankfurt programme of 'social philosophy' (see above page 113): he sided resolutely with those who saw Marxism as a global 'critique' rather than reducing it – like Schumpeter – to a set of separable theories, some of which were endowed with scientific value.[100] Another strong line of continuity with the classical Frankfurt school was his preoccupation with the evils of 'repression' and the redeeming power of 'self-reflection'.

Habermas's first major book, *Strukturwandel der Öffentlichkeit* (Structural Transformation of the Public Sphere, 1962), breathed a very different ethos from the sore hedonism of the Frankfurt cultural critics. Rather, it took its cue from Hannah Arendt's 'Hellenic nostalgia',[101] her exaltation of a 'public space of speech and action' as the proper medium of human freedom and dignity. Studying the spread of privacy in the mores of modernity, Habermas saw the public sphere as an early bourgeois field of emancipation, initially connected with the rise of public opinion and the first stirrings of modern democracy, but nowadays threatened by the contemporary syndrome of technocratism-cum-alienation. In the world of the corporation, big science and giant state authentic public opinion had dwindled into impotence or unimportance, because major decisions are the result of deals struck by powerful interest-groups instead of reflecting sustained processes of free rational debate; and the press, given to publicity and entertainment, also shuns its informative and argumentative functions. Thus the book combined echoes of the 'culture industry' thesis, a staple Frankfurt viewpoint, with Arendt's 'civic' problematic.

The Habermasian project of restoring Marxism as a global critique placed Marxism 'between philosophy and science'. Note here the difference from the Althusserian view of Marxism as science: of historical materialism as the science of history, and of dialectical materialism as the theory of science. But Habermas's restoration of a global critique entailed in turn a full reconstruction of WM. For Habermas, the groundwork of such an enterprise had to be epistemological. Dismissing Marcusian fantasies about 'another kind of science', Habermas explicitly vindicated Kant's concern for rigorous knowledge against Hegel's hasty and scornful rejection of epistemological scruples.[102] By the same token, he refused to endorse the Manichaean caricature of science drawn by Adorno and Marcuse.

Significantly, to Habermas 'positivism' meant less a legitimation of the given than a refusal, on the part of knowledge, to reflect on man as subject of the cognitive process.

In his epistemology of social science, Habermas proceeded by five main steps, each representing a theoretical supersession of a well-known school. Step 1 played the principle of reflective analysis against Parsonian structural-functionalism, then the dominant trend of American sociology. From the point of view of the German school of cultural sciences (*Geisteswissenschaften*), Habermas claimed, Parsons's postulate of a basic harmony between the motives of social action and the institutional values of the social system was a theoretical loss, for it allowed no real room for the complex role of inter-subjectivity in tradition and society. Hence step 2: Habermas turned to the phenomenological social theory of Alfred Schütz. But Schütz in turn had overlooked the linguistic dimension of social communication. Therefore (step 3), Habermas felt compelled to complement phenomenological sociology with the later Wittgenstein's linguistic philosophy. But Wittgenstein's language-worlds are closed within themselves. Now a full sense of inter-subjectivity *in actu* implies constant contacts between different, open linguistic universes. Ergo (step 4), Gadamer's hermeneutics, stressing that *tradition* is a living *translation* of different socio-cultural horizons, supplied what was missing in Wittgenstein. However, hermeneutics, too, needs correction, for the theory of transcultural 'translation' tends to forget that language and culture are also instruments of repression. Consequently, step 5: Gadamer had to be completed with the help of Freud and of Marx's critique of ideology. Clearly, Habermas's approach to Freud was most un-Marcusian: what inspires him in psychoanalysis is its therapeutic, not at all its substantive side; he is drawn by the emancipatory potential of the ideal of self-reflection rather than by the Freudian account of psychic forces.

Such, in its barest outline, is the argument of Habermas's still untranslated *Zur Logik der Sozialwissenschaft* (On the

Logic of Social Science, 1967). But the scope of Habermasian epistemology is not restricted to social theory. The year after his *Logik*, Habermas published a more general work, *Knowledge and Human Interests* (1968). Here, criticizing Kant for holding the principle of disinterested cognition, he sets out to develop the connection, foreseen by Fichte, between interest and knowledge. According to Habermas, there are three types of science, each of them based on one major knowledge-interest: *technical* interests give rise to empirical analytical sciences; *practical* interests to historical interpretive sciences; and *emancipatory* interests to critically oriented sciences of action like economics, sociology and political theory. These sciences of action alone have *self-reflection* as their method.

Self-reflection, of course, is held to be prompted by repression. Indeed, repression is the very *raison d'être* of reflective, critical thought. It is the depth and scale of 'unequivocally identifiable suffering' stemming from repression, Habermas explains, that generates the need for a critical social science. Moreover, the concept of repression, eminently psychological as it is (in the best tradition of Frankfurt psycho-sociology) is in keeping with Habermas's 'Socratic' conviction that the reason why power relations in our society manage to continue to hold sway over us is that 'they have not been seen through'. In short, power keeps its hold on us because of our false consciousness – a classical Marxist theme.

Let us return to the three major knowledge-interests – technical, practical and emancipatory. Habermas thinks they are respectively tied up with three means of social organization: work, language and power. Hence three cognitive domains: *information*, aiming at technical control in the sphere of work; *interpretation*, ensuring the orientation of action through language within shared traditions; and *analysis*, freeing consciousness from power disguised as ideology. *Knowledge and Human Interests* ascribes one predominant epistemological model to each domain: Popper's logic of scientific discovery goes to information; Gadamer's hermeneutics to interpretation; Freud's depth psychology to analysis.

In so far as they are constitutive of scientific object domains, the three knowledge interests enjoy a *transcendental* status in Kant's sense: they denote conditions, or *a priori* forms, of knowing. But Habermas adds that they are also *empirical* in that they derive from the natural history of mankind. At any rate, as 'invariants', i.e. as deep-seated drives related to the history of the species, the knowledge-interests are a proper subject for a philosophical anthropology rather than for a mere (relativist) sociology of knowledge.[103]

We have spoken of work, language and power as practices linked to the knowledge-interests. In fact, however, nearly all of Habermas's work is built round the polarity of *work* and *interaction*, which he has borrowed from the young Hegel. As Martin Jay has shown,[104] in the course of his participation in the so-called Positivist Dispute of the mid-1960s (essentially an epistemological war between Popperians and Adornians), Habermas came to replace the early WM concept of totality by a new accent on the concept of Spirit as a field of *dialogue* instead of a unified ego. Such a concept had been adumbrated in Hegel's Jena *Philosophy of Mind* (1805). Habermas's key text in this connection is an essay, 'Labour and Interaction', written in 1967 for a *Festschrift* in honour of Karl Löwith.[105] Habermas contends that while 'work' is governed by self-evident *technical rules*, 'interaction' follows *social norms* licensed by consensus achieved through some degree of dialogue and persuasion.

In the second chapter of *Knowledge and Human Interests* the work/interaction antithesis fuels an interesting criticism of Marx. Habermas praises Marx as a social historian for the attention he paid to the interactive dimension of human strife; but he also blames Marx as a social theorist for neglecting it, for conceiving of human emancipation in terms of a process grounded on labour and technical skills alone. In short, Marx is charged with reducing the self-generating action of the species (precisely what he, Marx, credited Hegel with grasping) to a naturalistic 'synthesis through social labour' oblivious of the complex dialectics of interaction and symbolic communication.

Nor does Habermas's departure from Marx stop here. In the title essay of the collection *Technik und Wissenschaft als Ideologie* (Technology and Science as Ideology, 1968), he argues that under late capitalism several key assumptions of classical historical materialism need replacing. Since (a) science itself has become, from the 'second industrial revolution' onwards, a force of production; (b) the economy now obeys a whole array of state regulations; and (c) class conflict has been defused by Keynesian management, the critical theory of society can no longer work, as in Marx, through a critique of political economy. As early as 1960, however, Habermas warned that 'due to the introduction of elements of the superstructure into the base itself, the classical dependency relationship of politics to the economy was disrupted'.[106]

The range and degree of Habermas's epistemological concerns are surely unprecedented in the Frankfurt school. Yet it would be highly misleading to think that he has substituted them for the old stress on 'critique' and its attendant humanist ethos of *Kulturkritik*. The concept of language and communication as a medium of self-reflection – the main achievement of both the *Logic of Social Science* and *Knowledge and Human Interests* – points towards an 'ideal speech situation' as the lodestar of every interactive context among humans. Truth becomes, to that extent, a function of dialogue between truthful speakers, persons of good will: 'the truth of statements is linked in the last analysis to the intention of the good life.'[107]

A sentence from the important introduction to the fourth German edition of *Theory and Practice* (1971) encapsulates the gist of it all: 'the paradigm is no longer the observation but the dialogue'.[108] Thus the sober mystique of the dialogue, a kind of epistemological version of Arendt's public space of speech and action, replaces in Habermas the more substantive views of the good life. Language is loaded with a soteriological virtue, a salvation power which the twisted, thwarted dialectics of the Adornian idiom could only allude to in indirect and intermittent fashion. Nevertheless, the spirit of the *Kulturkritik*, however muted, still underpins such an ethic of communion through communication. This becomes patent in Habermas's diagnosis of late capitalism, *Legitimation Crisis* (1973) – to many the most accessible of all his books .

Legitimation Crisis uses the categories of work and interaction to underpin a distinction between 'system crisis' and identity crisis. The purpose of such distinction is to emphasize that the problems of steering a social system only reach a critical point when the *Lebenswelt* ('life-world') of its *socii* undergoes such a crisis that they experience their very cultural identity as deeply problematic. The book ends with an extensive discussion of the systems theory of Niklas Luhmann, a theorist with whom Habermas has been sustaining a sophisticated polemic since 1971.[109] A German Parsons, as it were, drawing on cybernetics instead of classical sociological theory, Luhmann saw system integration from a functionalist viewpoint. To him, the cohesion of the system was largely independent of social integration feeding on life-world perspectives.[110] Obviously, this approach left little room for issues of cultural identity.

But systems theory is not the only theoretical line to overlook identity crises. Marx himself had concentrated on one kind of system crisis: the economic bottlenecks created by the nemesis of competition. Habermas does not delve into the intricacies of the 'breakdown literature', namely, the by now classical debate on (a) whether or not Marx held a collapse of capitalism theory and (b) if he did, what was the nature of the breakdown process. Tugan-Baranovsky, Hilferding and Luxemburg, the earliest big names in breakdown literature, are not mentioned in *Legitimation Crisis*. But what concerns Habermas is the obsolescence of Marxian values theory in the age of hi-tech and Keynesian demand management.

His contention is that a critique of political economy

caught the point of nineteenth-century society because under liberal capitalism *social* as well as *system* integration rested on the economy: with the separation of state and civil society, class relations were institutionalized through the market; and the same impersonal market, rather than the state, was entrusted with the burden of satisfying needs. As a result, economic crises translated directly into crises of legitimation; 'system' hiccups were also lacunae in social integration. Habermas's point is that in modern state-managed societies, by contrast, social and system integration has become 'uncoupled'. The economic ideology, he claims, the principle of equal exchange, is no longer, in our midst, the ruling norm of social integration. Besides the state regularly intervenes in the economy (and hence in system integration) and the consequent politicization of class relations blurs the old polar contours of class structure. Under such circumstances, critical theory can no longer assume the form of a critique of economic thought.

The new role of the state in economic life renders Marx's categories out of focus. Therefore, Habermas shifts the analysis to the political system. Here the main systemic troubles tend to arise, as a 'rationality crisis', from the 'fiscal crisis of the state', which ensue whenever the modern, Keynesian steering state can no longer find resources to finance economic growth and the social services structure. Habermas acknowledges the possibility of this, but, unlike James O'Connor and other fiscal crisis theorists, does not overrate it. Rather, he stresses the question of legitimacy as the crucial dimension of possible crises in the political sphere. As long as people trust their steering state, 'rationality' crises all by themselves will not do much harm. 'Legitimation deficits' on the other hand would. To Habermas the modern state tries to buy off the social foci of legitimation deficits by administering shared meanings and by securing welfare through economic growth. But while the meaning-sharing can face problems derived from the incongruities between the 'community' or 'national interest' ideology espoused by the state and the realities of class structure, the attempt to fill in legitimacy gaps through growth is threatened by a deeper danger: modern culture is capable of generating social demands of a nature impossible to satisfy in economic and technocratic terms. At this juncture, the legitimation deficit which constitutes the identity crisis of the political system of late capitalism will unfold into a profound 'motivation crisis' undermining the identity of the whole of contemporary culture. In *Legitimation Crisis* Habermas believes that changes in the values of western society, as witnessed by youth movements and the spread into social culture of the *Kulturkritik* stance held for so long by most modernist art, are veering towards a general withdrawal of motivation from the needs of the capitalist system. Critics like John Hall[111] have been quick to notice a parallel between Habermas and Daniel Bell's discourse on the 'cultural contradictions of capitalism' and his stress on modernist ideology becoming, as a counter-culture creed, a growing social force.

Thus Habermas agreed, to some measure, with the motto of May 1968: 'change life'. But his endorsement of *Kulturkritik* was far from extending to the violent politics often associated with student revolt at the time. He gave his blessing to the Juso movement, the young wing of the Left among the Social democrats; but, unlike Marcuse, he forebore to encourage campus protest. Rather, he seemed to favour an old utopia of German progressivism: *Bildung* as an alternative to revolution. As he saw it, 'in the face of various sectarian enterprises, one might point out today that in advanced capitalism changing the structure of the general system of education might possibly be more important for the organization of enlightenment than the ineffectual training of cadres or the building of impotent parties'.[112] Little wonder that Habermas's 'radical reformism'[113] became for some years a target of gauchiste activism.

Two aspects at least of *Legitimation Crisis* deserve comment. The first is a historical irony that can be despatched at once. The book reflects the impact, though neither the stridency nor the spirit, of the student rebellions of the

1960s; or, more precisely, Habermas's theory of crisis, marching as it did from economic blockage and management impasses to legitimacy gaps cum cultural withdrawal, bowed to the assumption that the days of unchallenged instrumental rationality were numbered. Yet by 1973, the tide of 'cultural revolution' was already ebbing. What is more, world recession was about to launch a decade of economic and management crises deeply undermining the Keynesian wisdom that Habermas largely took for granted. If anything, the historical pendulum swung in the other direction: away from cultural discontent and towards economic worries.

Secondly, the imprint of the work/interaction dualism in *Legitimation Crisis* is conspicuous. According to Habermas, while interaction, in the guise of cultural motivation, is both what can ruin and rescue our advanced industrial society, the feats of 'work', that is of growth, technology and technocracy, cannot preserve it, for there is no way they can slake the thirst for legitimacy experienced by the increasingly ill-adjusted culture of advanced capitalism. Thus the interaction concept underpins the idea that a constant state of identity crisis has emerged in modern society, instead of the violent but episodic economic crises of earlier capitalism. But here one has to ask: where does the sociology of modernity end, and where does the old *Kulturkritik* melody begin? What is the degree of empirical support mustered by Habermas's portrait of a demotivated capitalism? More important yet, what if the capitalist order can work without much cultural faith, feeding just on a general compliance based on (a) utilitarian expectations catered for by economic growth in democratic contexts and (b) the popular realization that the existent alternatives in terms of social system are worse at delivering the goods and far more oppressive to boot? The work of some recent sociologists, notably Frank Parkin and Michael Mann, has mused over just such a possibility.

Over the last decade and a half Habermas's work has concentrated on defending his system against many criticisms. For instance, Habermas has been much exercised by claims that his concept of knowledge-interest constitutes a reduction of knowledge to technical imperatives and social needs. By stressing interests, this kind of epistemology (it was argued) saddled Habermas with the relativism of pragmatism. In the introduction to *Theory and Practice* Habermas tries to get himself off the hook. He distinguishes 'between communication, which remains tied to the context of action, and discourses which transcend the constraints of action'. Discourse is a meta-communicative level where truth claims (theoretical discourse) or norms (practical discourse) are examined.

Another considerable problem in Habermas's work up to *Knowledge and Human Interests* was the practical side of his trust in the wonderful powers of reflection. As even his able, sympathetic interpreter, Thomas McCarthy, conceded, in the theory of emancipatory knowledge-interests there was an undemonstrated identity of reason and will.[114] More specifically, a will-to-reason was postulated, presupposing a universality of self-reflection hard to square with the real situation of most of the presumed beneficiaries of enlightened emancipation. To begin with, one must quibble, as did Richard Bernstein, over the assumption of a *motivation* for self-reflection: even granting that the telos of all speech is indeed undistorted communication, still one would like to know what it is exactly that impels men to seek such ideal forms of interaction[115] – an account too scant or too dim in Habermas's own texts. Obviously, the theory of cognitive interests is too generic to qualify; for the trouble with Habermas's knowledge interests, as Nikolaus Lobkowicz has put it, is that they are interests nobody is usually interested in, in any empirically demonstrable sense.[116] Crucially, the psychoanalytic model of self-reflection could scarcely be applied to society at large.

Habermas has tried to avoid such charges by distinguishing between 'self-reflection' and 'reconstruction'. A postscript to *Knowledge and Human Interests* (1973) states that while self-reflection brings to consciousness the particulars of an individual, personal self-formative *Bildung*, 'rational reconstruction deals with anonymous rule systems' that 'do not encompass subjectivity'.[117] Habermas's idea seems to be that reconstructions relate to a *Bildung* of the species, and as such provide enabling 'frameworks' for the necessarily individual acts of reflection within interaction.

This anthropological viewpoint dictated most of the core argument of *Zur Rekonstruktion des Historischen Materialismus* (1976; partly translated as *Communication and the Evolution of Society*). Habermas's underlying purpose was to supply his dialogical ideal with a mechanism operative in man *qua* man – a 'communicative competence'[118] which would do for linguistic interaction what Chomsky's generative grammar supposedly does for individual linguistic ability. Habermas intended to show that 'the species learns not only in the dimension of the technically useful knowledge decisive for the development of productive forces but also in the dimension of moral-practical consciousness decisive for structures of interaction'.[119] The hub of the exercise was a theory of 'universal pragmatics', distinct from a merely empirical socio-linguistics.[120] 'Universal pragmatics' was just a new name for 'communicative competence', the interactive deep grammar which grounds his conception of a free, unconstrained dialogue as the main weapon of emancipation.

Habermas fleshed out the universal ethic of discourse by drawing upon the Californian philosopher John Searle's theories of 'speech-acts', which in turn were largely based on the concept of 'performative utterances' developed by Searle's early mentor, the Oxford philosopher J.L. Austin. Austin and Searle set great store by those aspects of an utterance which denote or connote the speaker's intentions rather than those which convey information about the world at large. Their speech-act school established the notion that speaking is a way of acting; but while Austin and Searle used it to discern the several kinds of acts one can perform with different kinds of utterances, Habermas's concern is with some general presuppositions underlying our uttering expressions and responding to them. Each time we perform a speech-act oriented to understanding, as opposed to serving the speaker's selfish goals, we raise 'validity-claims' grounded on reasons, so that speakers can in principle 'rationally motivate' hearers to accept those claims – validity claims being by nature 'redeemable' by means of argumentation. Thus, Habermas seeks to draw attention not only to the intentions of speakers but also to the context of the expectations they share with their hearers – the communicative framework, implicitly or explicitly dialogic, of speech-acts aimed at an understanding of validity claims. Further, he claims that discursive speech-acts always anticipate an ideal speech situation, free of force or fraud, in which every utterance fulfils four conditions: comprehensibility, truth, veracity and correctness, in the sense of being appropriate to a normative context acknowledged by both speaker and hearer. Of course, actual utterances may be lies; but even these, in Habermas's view, presuppose, if *a contrario*, the four obligations just listed. Built into false discourse there is the homage that vice pays virtue. Searle rather than Chomsky provides the conceptual grounding of universal pragmatics because Habermas finds Chomsky's theory too monologic. He also wants to replace Chomsky's innatism by a developmental view of communicative skills loosely modelled after Piaget's genetic cognitive psychology and the work of other developmental psychologists like Lawrence Kohlberg and Jane Loewinger.

Together with his emphasis on the species, the adoption of a developmental stance lent Habermas a 'differential' conception of *progress* – a far remove from the earlier Frankfurt dogmatic revulsion against evolutionary ideas. Yet in Habermasian evolution the primacy of 'interaction' over 'work', with its anti-naturalistic overtones, does not lose ground: dialogue goes on taking precedence over production, language over technology. While the Marxian theme of infrastructural determinants is rejected, the development of normative structures is deemed 'the pacemaker of social evolution'[121] again; 'the great endogenous, evolutionary advances that led to the first civilizations or to the rise of European capitalism were not conditioned but followed by significant development of productive forces'.[122]

Habermas's recent summa, a two-volume *Theory of Communicative Action* comprising 1,167 pages, in the German original, and which was begun in 1977 and published in 1981, bravely keeps the evolutionary standpoint. The huge and ponderous, often opaque *Theorie*[123] marks the culmination of what one might call, for brevity's sake, Habermas II. Habermas I revolved, as we saw, round the concepts of knowledge-interest and self-reflection. Habermas II primarily does two things: (a) he gives pride of place to the concept of communicative action – a linguistico-anthropological translation of his original Arendtian concern for the survival of a 'public sphere' as a noble realm of free human interaction; and (b) he reinforces the 'reconstructive', i.e. evolutionary, outlook he adopted in the mid-1970s.

Let us dwell for a moment on social evolution as depicted in the *Theory of Communicative Action*. In everyday interaction, it is argued, validity claims of utterances are taken for granted, since we share with our fellow-interactors a common 'life-world', a set of values and beliefs. The life-world of a given society ensures this transmission from one generation to another – the 'symbolic reproduction' of society, which is distinct from the processes of production and reproduction of goods and services – what Habermas calls 'functional systems'.

On the strength of this distinction between system and life-world as patterns of social reproduction, and of his linking life-worlds with communicative action involving validity claims and their virtual justification, Habermas sets out to correct Weber's celebrated account of cultural evolution in terms of a widespread progressive rationalization. Characteristically Habermas says that Weber erred in equating the growth of institutional differentiation with increasing rationalization. But this is because Habermas holds (so did Weber[124] – but let that pass) a concept of rationality as something more than merely instrumental, i.e. ends-and-means rationality. He calls for a shift from a predominantly teleological concept of action to a focus on the communicative.

It is Habermas's contention that throughout the cultural evolution of mankind, from clan society to our modern world, the two reproductive mechanisms, 'system' and life-world, became increasingly at odds with each other. On the one hand, 'symbolic reproduction' witnessed a rational-ization of the life-world which increasingly undermined traditional assumptions and beliefs, making communicative action more and more dependent on rational inquiry. On the other hand, the growth and complexity of 'systems' have impinged on life-worlds, threatening with their very different logic to stifle that self-same potential of communi-cative rationality. This is what Habermas terms the undue 'colonization' of the life-world by instrumental, technical rationality. In his view, here lies the root of the problem of modern culture. The *Theorie* also resumes the diagnosis of *Legitimation Crisis*, stressing that while class struggle has receded in advanced capitalism, the deepest levels of fric-tion and tension are now located in areas where the economy and the managerial state act as carriers of the above-mentioned colonization of the *Lebenswelt* – thereby provoking such reactions as the ecological and peace movements.

A key point in the discussion of the state of western civilization in the *Theorie* is the idea of an unfulfilled 'project of modernity'. The gist of the argument was summarized by Habermas himself in a lecture delivered in September 1980, when he was awarded the Adorno prize by the city of Frankfurt.[125] Habermas's starting point recalls Weber's views on rationalization as a progressive functional differen-tiation of social spheres of action: 'the project of modernity formulated in the eighteenth century by the philosophers of the Enlightenment consisted in their efforts to develop objective science, universal morality and law, and auton-omous art, according to their inner logic.' This was under-taken in the hope that the arts and sciences would promote the control of nature, further our understanding of the world and of ourselves and bring justice and even happiness into the modern universe. The trouble is, in our own time such high hopes have been shattered. The differentiation of science, morality and art has ended up in autonomous segments split off from the life-world of everyday communication – the stuff of daily life. Hence all the attempts to negate modern culture, from the heroic avant-gardes of old modernism to the present-day 'post-modern' movements. But Habermas wisely refuses to countenance the charge of 'terroristic reason' levelled against the Enlightenment tradition by the fierce anti-modern stance of such post-structuralist thinkers as Foucault and Derrida. Instead, he earnestly asks: 'should we try to hold on to the *intentions* of the Enlightenment, feeble as they may be, or should we declare the entire project of modernity a lost cause?'[126] The very fact that he dubs ideologists like Foucault and Derrida[127] 'young conservatives', who often find themselves, objectively if not intentionally, in league with the old conservative prejudices against the emancipatory drives still stemming from the Enlightenment, indicates the direction of his answer.

Habermas's courageous resistance to the post-structuralist vogue deserves our commendation. He is at present, among influential European philosophers, the thinker who argues for universalist values against a storm of wild relativisms and cynical, scarcely reasoned nihilisms. Significantly, he showed no sign of connivance at the Nietzsche cult, whereby most post-structuralists try to give themselves a philosophical pedigree. But we should begin any assessment of his impressive work by noting at once – in obedience to our guiding problematic – how he still fails to capture or recover a true sense of historical process in a manner worthy of Hegel and (partly) of Marx. For while Habermas agrees with the Enlightenment's intentions, he seems unprepared to accept its historical results. His version of the 'tragedy of the Enlightenment', to use Paul Connerton's phrase, is far more sensible, far less chillingly apocalyptic and, on reflection, less silly and melodramatic than Adorno's or Marcuse's – but in the last analysis he too sides with *Kulturkritik* rather than with a wholehearted acceptance of cultural modernity. To a degree his stance is a paradox, for he came to acknowledge progress without really accepting the direction of the process.

His worrying about the immunization of the 'life-world' against instrumental reason is a telling instance of his halfway position. Here I have to agree with one of his ablest English critics, John Hall: Habermas's pursuit of salvation ('emancipation') through knowledge-as-dialogue reeks too much of the will to 're-enchant' the world[128] – and is, to that extent, a neo-romantic outlook. Habermas recognizes that natural science has to proceed objectively; but in his hierarchy of knowledge the apex is given to a 'consensual' truth where the weight of correspondence between discourse and outer reality is almost nil. As Mary Hesse has noted, his justification of truth claims remains unclear and unsatisfactory – and even Habermas himself has somehow conceded the point.[129]

Next there is the problem of a *unified rationality* as the goal of a reflective interaction grounded on man's communicative competence. '*Können komplexe Gesellschaften eine vernünftige Identität ausbilden?*' ('Can complex societies build themselves a rational identity?') Habermas made this question the very title of his speech when the city of Stuttgart awarded him the Hegel prize, early in 1974.[130] Habermas, the philosophical social theorist, thinks they can. Social scientists are more sceptical. Thus Steven Lukes could not find anything in his work to clinch the point of demonstrating the possibility of a unified rational basis for critical theory. But if we are not shown such a basis, then there is no dispensing with the rôle of decision in moral and political thinking and therefore we have Weber's value pluralism, the everlasting war of social gods, against consensus, even procedural and dialogic as the Habermasian one is.[131]

This criticism can be extended to the epistemological

level as well. As Gerard Radnitsky has perceived, the gist of Habermas's argument is that there never is, properly speaking, an option for reason in matters cognitive; on the contrary, we always find ourselves 'in' reason, for to enter into communicative dialogic action already means to recognize critical reason as the immanent goal of true communication.[132] Since *Theory and Practice*, Habermas has actually offered this perspective as a supersession of Popper's blunt decisionism when it comes to justifying the ultimate option for critical reason in knowledge. But not everyone finds his intended supersession truly solid.

In fact, Habermas's notion that there is an 'unavoidable' rationality-thrust in whatever discourse, practical as well as theoretical in its subject matter, often entails a *non sequitur*. Habermas keeps saying that our response to validity claims implied in communicative speech-acts commits speakers as well as hearers to the pursuit of a standard rationality no less binding than those employed in logic and science. W.G. Runciman, for one, disagrees. It is one thing, he argues, to agree with Kant that when we declare something beautiful we mean that everybody else ought to like it too; but quite another to hold (as Kant never did) that such an inbuilt appeal to universality in our aesthetic judgements is binding in the same way as the rationality of logic and logic-ridden science. Now Habermas's claim that (a) standards of rationality are built into every truthful and correct dialogue about anything may be deemed the logical equivalent to Kant's famous remarks on the universal vocation of aesthetic judgements. However, his claim that (b) these standards amount to something *as binding as* logical reason is unwarranted or, at best, undemonstrated. Habermas's step from (a) to (b) is not a step, says Runciman – it is a leap.[133]

The leap seems to be somehow connected with what Perry Anderson has called the 'angelism' of Habermas's view of language, dialogue and discourse: in contrast with the French post-structuralists, who demonized language by emptying it of meaning and truth, our linguistic *Aufklärer* made speech into a truthful, reliable prop of culture as a whole, the purveyor of morality and social harmony – and, on top of all that, the driving force of history.[134] From a different angle, Anthony Giddens has also protested against the Habermasian idealization of 'interaction', which he suggests Habermas has reduced to unconstrained communication with little or no power around.[135]

Habermas's project was to restore the offensive thrust of critical theory without falling back on the naïveties of standard revolutionism.[136] Yet his para-linguistic brand of critical theory turned out to be toothless on the organizational level: ideal speech situations were only slightly less disembodied creatures than Adorno's ethereal negative thought. His very honesty in refusing both Marcuse's facile search for ersatzs of an unobliging proletariat and Marcuse's élitism left Habermas without any social carrier of his communicative utopia. One of his German critics, Bernard Willms, has even invited us to see the institutional gap in Habermas's social theory as inbuilt, since any institution implies a great deal of instrumental and technical action, and this is on the side of vile 'work', and not of noble 'interaction'.[137] But such is the judgement of the radical Left, demanding that Habermas delivers the political goods. A less partisan verdict might just point out that with him the *Kulturkritik* element central in WM became considerably less virulent and yet, for all his ambitious recovery of evolutionary perspectives, has remained up to now incapable of providing us with a true theory of historical process instead of a counter-cultural lament.

Even so, Habermasian critical theory might very well fail both as political remedy and as an account of history and nevertheless hold true as a new epistemology, at its own 'reflective' level (at a more general level, containing the problem of truth, we have already seen it also fails). After all, the core of Habermas's taxonomy of knowledge is the tier of 'reflective' sciences, where he claims to have proffered and justified a new type of cognition: critical knowledge, inspired by both Marx and Freud. Nor is that all. He makes a point of demonstrating that in order to be truly valid our normative beliefs have to constitute genuine knowledge – a perfectly debatable assumption, in fact a mirror-image of the positivist claim that if beliefs are not scientifically based they are just arbitrary preferences.[138]

Now quite apart from the aforementioned problem of assuming a generalized social motivation for participating in free discourse as the medium of emancipation, Habermas sounds implausible when it comes to ascertaining what would be the consensus of his ideal speech situations. To one of his fairest and most careful critics, Raymond Geuss, Habermas's consensual altruism appears as a very tall order indeed; for it is much more natural to suppose that participants in a free dialogue bring with them their own often jarring conceptions of values, moral and otherwise. Be that as it may, Geuss concludes that Habermas's emancipatory knowledge does not meet acceptable public criteria for successful action – a condition which Habermas himself ascribed to science in general. The requirement of publicity or inter-subjectivity cannot possibly just mean that the participants in emancipatory communication will reach consensus – it must point to something far more independent and neutral between possible, nay probable, competing candidates for consensual agreement.[139] To put it briefly: even at the 'reflective' level, 'dialogue' cannot do without at least the equivalent of 'observation'.

Reading Habermas [wrote Quentin Skinner] is extraordinarily like reading Luther, except that the latter wrote such wonderful prose. Both insist that our wills are enslaved by our present unregenerate way of life . . . Both promise that a change of heart will release us from our present bondage and bring us to a state of perfect liberty. Above all, both put their trust in 'the redeeming power of reflection' (Habermas' phrase), and hence in our ability to save ourselves through the healing properties of the Word (or discourse, as Habermas prefers to call it). But . . . we are surely entitled to something more rigorous from our social philosophers than a continuation of Protestantism by other means.[140]

Such an appraisal would be hard to better. The Parsifal of critical theory, as pure in his heart as he was valiant in exploit, Habermas captured the Holy Grail of dialogue and interaction to heal the bitter wounds wreaked by *Kulturpessimismus* upon WM. Salvation, which for Lukács was to come from revolution as grasp of totality, was now redefined to spring from higher, more humane forms of knowledge. Epistemology became soteriology, while political theory grew quietly reformist. Alas though, in the event the former lost its rationality and the latter its effectiveness.

If Habermas's rebuilding of critical theory indeed comes to grief, both as epistemology and as social theory, the consequences for WM as a whole are ominous. Mainstream WM actually meant German WM, and within the latter, after the Lukácsian comet, the prominence of the Frankfurt school is beyond question. But the Frankfurt kind of Marxism as 'critique' long laboured under two major misconceptions. First, it tended to conflate capitalism with industrial society, thereby demonizing the spread of instrumental rationality.[141] The ambivalence of classical German sociology, from Toennies to Simmel and Weber, in the face of the rise of rationalization, was converted into an open repudiation of the drift of modern culture.

The second misconception was a correlative exorcism practised on the scientific intellect. In the words of Lucio Colletti, 'Marxism, born as a scientific analysis of capitalism, discovered that science was . . . a child of capital'.[142] When this neo-romantic, decadent cast of mind was further darkened by the collapse of hope in proletarian revolutionism, 'critical theory' withdrew into an ill-disguised irrationalism. It was very well for Adorno to be scathing about 'official' irrationalisms, like the solemn pathos and the mystifying puns of Heidegger's 'fundamental ontology', but the plain truth is that he, too, put his negative dialectics into such a blind alley that the only dim light of thought-as-redemption was confined to aesthetics:[143] artistic mimesis alone kept in touch with nature and humanity, away from the fiendish spread of instrumental reason. All the worth of Habermas consists in his determination to combat this flight into unreason. And if one concludes that his revamped WM is too precarious, then it becomes difficult to resist the impression that WM is, in its philosophical complexion, incurably inimical to the spirit of critical reason.

IV

A FEW GENERAL CONCLUSIONS

Marxism is the opium of the Marxists
Joan Robinson

Western Marxism, born of the spirit of Revolution and set against the determinism of the diamat, ended up either embracing utter pessimism or espousing the vaguest of reformisms. The only major exception to this unprofitable programme – Marcuse's prescription of a Great Refusal – signified moral revolt rather than social revolution, and the same can be said to apply to Sartre's unsuccessful Marxification of existentialism. Moreover, again excepting Marcuse's pop *Kulturkritik*, political abstention was accompanied by a general dearth of fresh analysis of social realities and historical trends, especially at the economic, societal and political levels. In its most consistent efforts, WM withdrew into theory: it dwelt on the nature of social science but applied it only sparingly.

Theoreticism at the cost of sociological analysis in fact plagued WM right from the beginning. The charge alike befits Lukács's *History and Class Consciousness*, Adorno's main work, the best of Sartre's *Critique* or Habermas's oeuvre as a whole. The only instance where it would be grossly unfair to speak of theoreticism is in the case of Gramsci; but this was significantly an instance of marginal WM, of a historico-philological rather than philosophical variety. And of course all that has been suggested throughout the foregoing chapters on the unyieldingness of *Kulturkritik* to historical analysis strongly confirms the absence of historical meat in the WM stew, to the extent that WM has pre-eminently been a Left *Kulturkritik*.

186

In the main, therefore, it is hard not to subscribe to Perry Anderson's scathing verdict on WM: 'method as impotence, art as consolation, pessimism as quiescence.'[1] Qualifications would no doubt be in order, according to each thinker or school within WM, but overall the judgement is as true as it is harsh. Interestingly enough, Anderson was not alone in associating theoreticism with sterility. In 1974, in a resounding politico-philosophical interview with the *New Left Review*, Lucio Colletti warned about the prospect of the gnoseological suicide of WM: unless more concrete analysis was done, he said, creating modern successors to Hilferding's *Finance Capital* or Luxemburg's *Accumulation of Capital*, sophisticated Marxism ran the risk of becoming just 'a foible of a few university professors'.[2]

With a decade of hindsight, Marxist or Marxisant dons seem anything but few. Colletti is no longer one of them, but their number is still considerable in western academe. But let us return to the problem of theoreticism. Anderson also offered an explanation for the methodological pestilence (to borrow Weber's phrase) of WM. He ascribed it to a want of contact with political praxis.[3] I am not so sure. In Italy, for instance, the heyday of non-Gramscian WM, from the late 1960s to the mid-'70s, witnessed a frantic importation of Frankfurtian themes: repudiation of productivism, rejection of science and technology, branded as bourgeois ideology, anarchist (Marcusian) slogans, etc. Yet all this was borne by a militant '*operaismo*', an emphatically proletarian version, as it were, of the revolutionary praxis bequeathed by the spirit of May '68.

Even those who agreed with Anderson's diagnosis did not necessarily follow his valuation. Thus Russell Jacoby recognized that the plight of WM was indeed dominated by political powerlessness, yet refused to see the implicit 'dialectic of defeat' as a theoretical disadvantage. Explicitly questioning Anderson's *Considerations on Western Marxism*, Jacoby insisted that WM, with the obvious exception of his *bête noire*, Althusser, represented a healthy Hegelian stream within Marxist thought at large: a philosophical brand of Marxism as 'critique', at once more humane and more profound than the scientistic dispensations of the diamat, from Engels to Althusser. 'Unorthodox Marxism', writes Jacoby, 'is unthinkable without Hegel. The irreplaceable starting and returning points for surpassing conformist Marxism are found in Hegel. From Gramsci to Merleau-Ponty, Marxists escaped the constraints of orthodoxy by tapping Hegelian waters.'[4]

As Jacoby is the first to admit, Hegel has been used by Marxism in more ways than one. But he discerns a basic pattern, formed by two antagonistic Hegelian traditions. On the one hand, there is a 'historical' line which has valued the Hegel of open history and dynamic subjectivity, the Hegel of the *Phenomenology of Spirit*; on the other hand, there is a 'scientific' tradition which has prized the Hegel of the *Science of Logic*, relishing historical 'laws' and formalizing the dialectic into a grammar of development.[5] In short: there is the Hegel of Engels and there is the Hegel of Lukács.

Jacoby sides conspicuously with the historico-humanist tradition, and invokes it to defend WM as its main bearer among us. But the trouble with this Hegelian defence of WM is two-fold. First, it ignores rather than refutes the charge of sterile theoreticism which went together with Anderson's political strictures. Second, it takes the Hegelianism of WM too much in earnest. Ultimately WM was not that Hegelian – in fact, it was frequently most un-Hegelian in its adoption of ethicist postures. From Lukács to Marcuse and Sartre, it often played the purity of lofty ideals against the prose of the process. What Lucien Goldmann once wrote of Marcuse's *Reason and Revolution*, that it wrapped a Fichtean position in a Hegelian language, goes straight to the heart of the matter.[6] Again, Adorno (*Negative Dialectics*, pages 189–97) thought that the Lukacsian theory of reification, consciousness-minded as it was, remained a very Fichtean thing. Besides, we have now in

English at least one valiant attempt to claim that the WM of *both* Lukács and the Frankfurt school, from Adorno to Habermas, is at bottom a neo-Kantian rehearsal, doomed – *et pour cause* – to methodologism; I refer to Gillian Rose's brilliant if often elliptic *Hegel Contra Sociology* (1981, especially pages 24–36).

Should one drop the content of Jacoby's rejoinder to Anderson and still accept its point, namely, the attempt to justify WM in historical terms, as a critique darkened by defeat, a humanist resistance to the age? I think not, for two reasons. To begin with, endorsing such a view would validate the *Kulturkritik*, when all we have suggested up to here is that a true understanding of modern history does not condone the rage and despair of the enemies of modernity. But there is also the fact that the only tentative approach to a historical explanation of the evolution of Marxism available is far from confirming the connection between dialectic as critique and 'bad' times for revolution. If anything, it suggests quite the opposite.

The historical approach I have in mind was first presented in Merleau-Ponty's *Adventures of the Dialectic* (1955). We might call it the 'tidal' theory of Marxism. According to Merleau-Ponty, Marxism has known two main modes. In its youthful, revolutionary phases, it appears as a dialectic thought, giving short shrift to the 'inertia of infrastructures'. In the wake of revolutionary defeats, by contrast, it becomes stubbornly determinist and mechanist. Thus Marx himself, up to 1848, was a humanist dialectician; after the ebbing away of the 'age of revolution', in the second half of the century, he became as determinist and science-minded as to look for the 'natural laws' of capitalist production. The rekindling of revolutionary hopes after 1917 brought with it a new tide of anti-determinist dialectics – the Lukács moment. And seen from the mid-1950s, Lukács's own conversion to the official line of diamat seemed to reflect the recession of revolution in the middle decades of our century.[7]

A dozen years after Merleau-Ponty's analysis, the out-standing German Marxologist, Iring Fetscher, sketched what might be taken for an interesting sociological alterna-tive to the tidal theory. In his view, revolutionary human-ism is contingent on a certain fluidity of the social bases of the Marxist idea. Whenever collective and conscious proletarian action was replaced by powerful working-class organizations within the bourgeois social order, Marxism tended to stress its determinist aspects. The sociological truth of it is that the diamat fitted very well into that process which Aron liked to call the political education of the German workers by Marxism. Orthodox Marxism was the lay religion of unions and workers' parties whose intellectual leaders were keen on keeping non-Marxist world-views at bay – a determination very clear in both Engels (especially in the *Anti-Dühring* of 1878) and Lenin. Moreover, the elective affinities between 'organizational' Marxism and tough creeds like the diamat were reinforced by historical context. Since 'Marxist revolutions have hith-erto taken place in extremely backward agrarian countries where there could be no question of conscious action by the proletariat', revolutionary humanism has largely remained 'an episode limited to a small clique of intellec-tuals'.[8]

Nevertheless, whether one stresses the historical context, as in the tidal theory of Merleau-Ponty, or the sociological substratum, as in Fetscher's remarks on the organizational variable, Marxist ideas must still be assessed for them-selves, quite apart from the vicissitudes of their social fate. If revolutionary defeat and political isolation led to theoreticism and methodological navel-gazing, it is in those terms that WM must be examined. And re-examinations of WM have indeed been willing to face theoretical dis-cussion. The most strenuous up to now is Martin Jay's *Marxism and Totality – the adventures of a concept from Lukács to Habermas* (1984). A noted expert on the Frankfurt school, Jay gently departs from Anderson's view in that to him the sin of WM lay less in its distance from political praxis than in its élitist tendencies. Furthermore, he tends to see the Habermasian reformation as a welcome theoretical metamorphosis, which freed WM from the quagmire of *Kulturpessimismus* without falling back on the naïve chiliastic pathos of the young Lukács.[9]

However, as we have seen, Habermas's edifice is far from solid, either as an epistemology or as a social theory. And if one grants that, as a whole, WM prior to him, in so far as it pronounced on substantive history, partook of the bleak anathema cast by the *Kulturkritik* upon modern civilization, it would be no exaggeration to say that in WM a surplus-meaning was extracted from Marxism by the luminaries of a humanist cleresy at war with modernity. The result, it should surprise no one to hear, has scarcely been enriching towards our knowledge of history.

'The day of the German', said Schiller, 'is the harvest of time as a whole.'[10] If the Hegel-Marx axis was the supreme fulfilment of such an intellectual destiny, WM can be said to be a particularly perverse form of it – the collapse of a tradition of comprehensive philosophies of history into the sweeping indictments of *Kulturkritik*. It is true that immediately before the birth of WM the greatest name in German social thought, Max Weber, had challenged the classic (Hegelian) theory of process. While for Hegel the meaning of the process was the progress of freedom, and the rise of the modern West, as the last stage of world history, was to be seen as the embodiment of a higher reason, for Weber the genius of modern culture – formal rationality – was by no means an attribute of historical man; rather, it was a creation of western man and in any case enjoyed no superiority other than technical over past or alien cultures.[11] To that extent, his theory of the process was not, like Hegel's or Marx's, a vindication of modernity. Yet neither was it a repudiation of modern history, a product of the neo-romantic animus paraded by most Western Marxists.

To a large measure, the history of WM becomes a story

of betrayal – the betrayal of the gist of Hegelianism by *soi-disant* Hegelian Marxists. Obviously this does not apply to the epistemological schools of della Volpe and Althusser. The case of Althusser is one of denial rather than betrayal of Hegel, a denial which turned out to be even more sterile than the others' betrayal. But as a rule the charge of pseudo-Hegelianism holds true for the German remainder of WM, which is, after all, mainstream WM.

This is not to suggest that, in order to practise interesting, fruitful historical analysis, one has to have, if one is a Marxist, a Hegelian cast of mind: the Austro-Marxists had none, and nevertheless did make Marxist analysis grasp new domains in an illuminating way. On the other hand, it is not enough to say that WM is entitled to neglect historical analysis since it has been, in the main, a philosophers' enterprise rather than the work of historians, economists or sociologists. Marxism without history simply does not make any sense – in Marxist terms.

Perhaps the growing distance from both politics and history that marked WM helps to explain why, since about 1970 or so, radical political theory as well as the more reflective radical historiography have often worked on the tacit or even explicit assumption of a *post-Marxist horizon*. This, however, is not the place to describe such a general shift. Suffice it to say that in the main it has taken two forms: a post-Marxist radicalism in political theory, and a critique of classical historical materialism. A post-Marxist radicalism can be seen in the writings of theorists of revolution like the earlier Régis Debray (at the stage of *Revolution in the Revolution*) or Cornelius Castoriadis: they retain the concept of revolution, yet drop the Marxist analysis of the process leading to it. As for the critique of classical historical materialism, one can discern two schools of thought. The first consists in what I am tempted to call a critique of economic history, namely, the work of Immanuel Wallerstein and his followers. Wallerstein's 'world-economy' analysis is, of course, a combination of the classical theory of imperialism with the views of Ferdinand

Braudel. But the Braudelian framework of 'world-economy' history puts it at a far remove from Marxism. Unlike Marx's, Braudel's description of capitalism does not focus on modes of production, but rather on a specific kind of exchange, i.e. trade where conditions of particularly unequal competition obtain; again, Braudel tends to treat monopolistic trends, which for late classical Marxism were the dominant note of the last stage of capitalism, as the very essence of capitalism, manifested since its Renaissance beginings.[12] In addition the role of geographic determinants, crucial in Braudel's economic history, has no parallel in the Marxist paradigm.

A second wing within the new critical approach to historical materialism remains theoretical rather than historical. A thought-provoking critical examination has recently been put forward by a non-Marxist social theorist, Anthony Giddens. An outstanding Cambridge sociologist, Giddens has built his *Contemporary Critique of Historical Materialism* (1982) round the triple flag of causal pluralism, anti-class reductionism and anti-evolutionism.[13] Within the Marxist camp, however, perhaps the most influential attack on staple concepts of classical historical materialism has been the work of the English post-Althusserians Barry Hindess and Paul Hirst. To the dismay of new Left historians, their début was fiercely anti-historical, and not surprisingly, in subsequent publications they ended up by ditching the whole concept of mode of production[14] – and with it, the backbone of the Marxist theory of process. In Wallerstein's economic history the theory of process has survived, but in a distinctly un-Marxist form: in Hindess and Hirst it was abandoned outright.

Is there also a post-Marxist horizon in European, as opposed to Anglo-Saxon, radical thought? Here it is sufficient to mention just some of the key theoretical trends. In German Marxism there emerged in the early 1970s the 'state derivation debate', launched by Wolfgang Müller and Christel Neusüss.[15] Its thrust has been clearly polemical, and the polemic is directed against WM. The starting point of state-derivation theory was an attack on Habermas and Claus Offe (whose political analysis looms large in Habermas's *Legitimation Crisis*), for their severing the theory of crisis from the study of capital accumulation (see pages 171–2). State-derivation theorists stressed that the world recession which started in 1973–4 made a mockery of the Habermasian minimization of the economic crises. Rejecting approaches which are predicated on the 'autonomy of the political', they have also opposed the Althusserian assumption of largely autonomous spheres (economy, polity, etc.). In their view, far from being a characteristic of all social formations this functional differentiation of the social whole is a peculiarity of capitalism, to be explained by the *form* of class exploitation. This became the central concern of the 'capital logic' school led by Joachim Hirsch. Inspired by the German School, the British 'capital logic' theorists John Holloway and Sol Picciotto have in turn criticized the 'neo-Ricardian' Marxists. The neo-Ricardians, following Sraffa (see above page 57) got rid of Marx's labour theory of value. Accordingly, they tend to see wages (and hence, in their Marxist view, exploitation) as something determined by the power play between classes rather than 'the organic composition of capital'. The upshot is a view of politics and economics as separate spheres – the ultimate sin for capital logic theorists.

Let us call such a sin 'politism' – the undue overrating of the political, unconnected with economic mechanisms. To the capital logic school, the culprits are not just the neo-Ricardian economists; they are also WM philosophers, from Gramsci to Habermas and the Althusserians. Yet by breaking with the 'politism' of WM state-derivation, capital logic theorists do not mean to replace the autonomy of the political by good old economic determinism. 'What is required', they claim, 'is not an economic but a materialist theory of the state.'[16] As a consequence, they regard economic crises as the effect of class struggle, often giving the impression that they just rephrase the politist theme in economic guise – for which they have been taken to task by

Alex Callinicos. Recalling that class struggle was for Marx the explanandum and not the explanans of the historical process, he deplores 'the tendency on the part of so many contemporary Marxists to make the class struggle the determining element of the historical process' as 'a form of voluntarism'[17] Now voluntarism, overt or covert, has always been an approach hardly conducive to the deepening of empirical historical analysis. Therefore, if Callinicos is right, the controversy on state and capital, begun as a challenge to WM, turns out to be a hidden continuation of its chief weakness.

In the two major Latin countries with a strong Marxist culture there evolved similar theoretical syndromes of a post-Marxist nature. Thus in France the most prestigious radical thought since 1968 can be divided into two main directions. There is a radical theory of non-Marxist origins, as Michel Foucault's 'micro-physics of power'; and there are radical thinkers with a Marxist or Marxisant background, like Claude Lefort and Cornelius Castoriadis. Lefort perhaps should be deemed only a marginal case, since the main theoretical reference of his work (*Eléments d'une Critique de la Bureaucratie*, 1971) is Merleau-Ponty rather than Marx. A prolix writer, he kept churning out vague, diffuse libertarianism with little grip on sociological realities. His definition of democracy – 'the intention to face the heterogeneity of values . . . and to make conflicts into a driving force of growth'[18] – was not very far from the liberal creed, shorn of its usual juridical and constitutional sophistication.

Characteristically, Lefort broke with Castoriadis, in the late 1950s, over the question of political organization, taking a spontaneist position, a liberal leftism, as it were. Originally, however, both he and Castoriadis were post-Trotskyists: critics of Soviet communism willing to go beyond the Trotsky of *The Revolution Betrayed* (1937). Castoriadis, a refugee from the Greek civil war working for the OECD in Paris, was the moving spirit behind the chief journal of gauchisme, *Socialisme ou Barbarie* (1949–65).

Throughout the cold war it kept a robust anti-Soviet line, incurring the wrath of Sartre and other fellow-travellers of Russophile communism. The journal's theoretical weapon was the critique of bureaucracy. But unlike other ex-Trotskyists, notably James Burnham (*The Managerial Revolution*, 1941), Castoriadis did not turn his anti-bureaucratism into a flight from revolution. On the contrary: applying his concept of 'bureaucratic capitalism' to both the Soviet bloc and the advanced economies of the West, he insisted that the suppression of hierarchy was as important as the abolition of private ownership of means of production and championed self-management in industry.

This put Castoriadis at the centre of gauchiste ideology during the era of de Gaulle; May 1968 was, as is well known, much more gauchiste than Marxist and student leaders like Cohn-Bendit hailed Castoriadis alongside Marcuse. In an important sense, Castoriadis had already returned the compliment by stressing that the real crises in bureaucratic capitalism had moved from the economic basis to the political and cultural superstructures, with alienation counting for as much as exploitation: such crises played havoc with the family, youth, the meaning of work, the rôle of women, the legitimacy of the state, and so on. As one can see, gauchisme, as a reading of advanced capitalism, was not very different from the WM of Marcuse or Habermas. But the point is, Castoriadis was no longer a neo-Marxist. Instead, he was adamant on the need for a choice: 'either to remain Marxist or to remain revolutionary.'[19] Gauchisme might have begun as an ex-Trotskyism – but it ended up as a post-Marxism.

In Italy the most striking theoretical development, that of Lucio Colletti, similarly led to a clear post-Marxist outcome – though resulting in quite another politics. Colletti moved from Left communism in the early 1960s to social democratic liberalism today. His theory of social science has replaced della Volpe with Popper, shedding in the process not only dialectics but the very mythological core of Marxism: the doctrine of alienation. In a nutshell, his position nowadays says: if social science, then no (more) Marxism. In this sense, Perry Anderson's long-standing fight for Marxist history in Britain is the antipode of Colletti's sharp de-Marxification.

Yet Anderson himself – to return to Marxism in English – has come to acknowledge monumental gaps and blunders in Marxism. The closing pages of his *Considerations on Western Marxism* specify three areas 'where Marx's work appears centrally uncertain'. Anderson points out that Marx's prophecies of a breakdown (be it by social or by strictly economic mechanisms) of capitalism, as indeed his doubtful theory of value, have never been substantiated. Marx's economic catastrophism in turn made the development of a proper political theory redundant, so that Marx never offered a coherent account of the structures of bourgeois power nor understood the decisive phenomenon of nationalism.[20]

More recently, in his *In the Tracks of Historical Materialism* (1983), Anderson has gone still further. Enjoining Marxism to make 'a shift from the axis of values to that of institutions in projections of a socialist or communist future', he praises the pro-market stance of Alec Nove's remarkable and overtly revisionist book, *The Economics of Feasible Socialism* (1983). Anderson claims that 'the legacy of institutional thought within classical Marxism was ... always very weak', and rules out utopian views such as the abolition of the division of labour (Marx's borrowing from Fourier) or the replacement of the government of men by the administration of things (Marx's borrowing from Saint-Simon) as altogether incompatible with the real institutional needs of a post-capitalist society.[21]

One should not be too hasty, however, in applying the label 'post-Marxist'. Anderson would reject it, settling, perhaps, for the more ambiguous 'neo-Marxist'. On the other hand, even a deliberate post-Marxism is no guarantee of greater sociological wisdom. Consider, for example, the work of André Gorz, a contemporary of Castoriadis and Lefort. An ex-Sartrean, Gorz moved from the defence of self-management in *Les Temps Modernes* to an onslaught on the division of labour and technology as evils in themselves; he now strafes 'productivist morals' and writes more and more as an ecological Marcuse (cf. his *Adieux au Prolétariat*, 1980).

In their modern revisionism, some Marxist thinkers go as far as jettisoning even such a cornerstone of classical historical materialism as the tenet of *class struggle*. The Althusserian concept of ideology as a systemic social attribute did much to blur the notion of conflict between different class interests. As for Frankfurt theory, it largely comes down to a Marxism without class – a strange fate for theorists whose initial inspiration lay in the young Lukács's apotheosis of class consciousness. For all his belated search for ersatz proletariats, Marcuse tolled the knell of Marx's idea of the role of class when he acknowledged that the consumer society's ability to meet material needs defuses the erstwhile explosiveness of the contradiction between the vital needs of the toiling masses and capitalist class relations. Hence his typical Frankfurtian focus on other kinds of needs, *human* rather than class-bound, such as the aspiration towards instinctual gratification, creativity and the well-rounded personality – 'alienation' Marxism, in sum.

The same trend dominates the work of the now exiled neo-Lukácsian Budapest school, led by Agnes Heller. Her exegesis of Marx's moral vision (*The Theory of Need in Marx*, 1976) takes its theme from the collapse of a utilitarian theory of class based on a proletarian penury now archaic in advanced industrialism. As Jean Cohen stressed (*Telos* 33), Heller rejects the idea of class interest, tries 'to sever the theory of radical needs from class theory,' and has no use for the original Marxian link between alienation and the objectification of human powers through history – exactly the Hegelian theme in Marx's anthropological views. Obviously, such a theory of radical needs, perhaps the most beautiful flower of neo-Marxist humanism, has no use for a theory of process. Heller is far too sober to indulge in the more strident anathemas of *Kulturkritik* (the Budapest school learned from the *old* Lukács as well) – but neither is she on the side of history against the disembodied ideal.

None of our leading names in or near the post-Marxist horizon since the mid-1960s – Debray, Castoriadis, Gorz, Heller, Hirsch, Holloway, Hindess and Hirst, Wallerstein, Anderson or Colletti – is usually described as a Western Marxist. Moreover, neo-Marxists like Anderson and professed neo-classical Marxists such as Hirsch or Holloway have been as critical of WM as the ex-Marxist Colletti. This proves only that WM is not simply Marxism in the West. Rather, it was a set of heretical derivations from Marxism moulded, in its first phase (Lukács to Adorno), by the pathos of *Kulturkritik* and in the second by an 'epistemologist' bent (Althusser, Habermas); in both cases, and except for the scientist backlash of Althusserianism, the central cast of mind of WM was unmistakably 'humanist'. What made it tick was a principled opposition to the idea of Marxism as science.

Because the cluster *Kulturkritik*/humanism/theoreticism occupies the heartland of the WM theory, nothing has been said about some trends quite unrelated to it, such as the della Volpean circle in Italy around 1960, the *ouvrieriste* revolutionism theorized by Mario Tronti (*Workers and Capital*, 1966) and the naturalist attack on Marx's value concept led by Marco Lippi (*Value and Naturalism in Marx*, 1976). At any rate, Marxian economics, including the seminal Japanese branch (Morishima, etc.), is too technical and 'regional' a theoretical enterprise to compare to WM social theory, though it often harbours crucial implications for the post-Marxism problematic, as witnessed by our passing glance at the neo-Ricardian critique. Thus one of the most consistent branches within Japanese Marxist economics, stemming from Kozo Uno's *Principles of Political Economy* (1964) raises issues of direct relevance to a theory of process with causal concerns.

Nor has anything been said about Marxist thought in

national context. For instance, the major contribution of American Marxism, often ignored by European intellectuals, since the 1960s has been in economics (Paul Baran and Paul Sweezy, Robert Heilbroner), social history (Harry Braverman) and literary criticism (Frederick Jameson). But although there is by now a whole array of perceptive American interpretations of WM masters, no significant WM philosophical current has yet arisen in the USA. Finally – last but not least – the same distance from the WM cluster precluded our discussing recent developments in 'analytical Marxism' – the work of G.A. Cohen, Jon Elster and John Roemer – perhaps the most exciting theoretical work now in progress in the name of Marxism.[22]

Alas, neither a high degree of analytical rigour nor an adequate range of historical learning prevail among the kind of self-styled intelligentsia where the flowers of WM generally blossom. Modern humanists from top to toe, the enthusiasts of WM and its by-products set little store by the concerns of the historian with lessons from the past or the worries of the lucid leftist about the viability of large-scale institutional changes. WM itself taught them to pay scant attention to such trifles. Are not 'facts', as young Lukács warned, always a reactionary bogey? The WM readership seldom demands of its radical authors any credentials other than a Marxist posture with a smattering of dissidence towards the Gulag – a sort of orthodoxy in heresy, as it were. Bad or no history is really no problem. Let bourgeois critics fret about the need for restoring our grasp of process.[23] *Kulturkritik* is above all a mood, not a knowledge; and WM is by and large a *Kulturkritik* sublimated into empty theoreticism.

One thing is sure: the global output of WM never attained the wealth of fruitful perspectives on crucial issues for social science which distinguished classical Marxism between *Capital*, or the *Eighteenth Brumaire of Louis Bonaparte*, and the chief contributions of the Austrians. Remove Gramsci from the WM canon and you will find nothing to compare, even remotely, with, for instance, the pithiness of

Trotsky's writings on revolution in conditions of backwardness and unequal development, or of Bukharin's pathbreaking thematics of 'world economy' and 'state capitalism' – yet the former date from 1905–1908, and the latter were concepts built between 1915 and 1920! Social science, Marxist or not, owes infinitely more to the classics than to the vastly publicized 'sophistication' of their detractors, the 'humanist' Western Marxists.

No attempt was made throughout these pages to sketch a 'sociology of knowledge' approach to WM, locating its experiential sources within several specified social contexts – a fascinationg task, to be sure, but distinct from our purpose here. Like any other body of ideas, WM is entitled to be analysed *in itself*, without prejudicing the analysis with the results of inquiries into its class origins and social bearing. Yet there seems to be little doubt that, in order to *explain* its reception after interpreting and assessing its doctrinal content, one would do well to look for the *new intellectual demography* enjoyed by radical ideology in our midst. It is a demography whose large numbers have little in common with the tiny highbrow coteries where WM was born in inter-war Vienna or Frankfurt. And it is also a situation where radicalism has taken hold of many a strategic place in the 'symbolic reproduction' of western academe. Now that its creative period seems spent, WM is about to become a mild form of institutionalized counter-culture – the drab, jargon-ridden and highly ritualistic romanticism of the don in the land of humanities dutifully embattled against the drift of modern society. To the historian of ideas, there is not much of a riddle: all in all, the age of WM (1920–70) was just an episode in the long history of an old pathology of western thought: irrationalism.

NOTES

I. A CONCEPT AND ITS BACKGROUND

1. Cf., 'Class Consciousness' (1920) in Lukács, 1971a.
2. Mandelbaum, 1971, p.6.
3. On this point see Niel, 1945, passim.
4. Kolakowski, 1978, Vol. I, ch. 1.
5. Cf., Topitsch, 'Marxismus und Gnosis' in Topitsch, 1961.
6. Cf., Avineri, 1972, p.123n.
7. Cf., Toews, 1985, p.132.
8. See the comments by Ritter, 1957, section III.
9. Taylor, 1975, ch. 3.
10. In his entry on Hegel for the Macmillan *Encyclopedia of Philosophy* (1967), ed. Paul Edwards.
11. See his entry on Hegel in Justin Wintle (ed.), *Makers of Nineteenth-Century Culture*. (London: Routledge and Kegan Paul, 1982.)
12. Cf. Riedel, 1984, ch. 7.
13. Bobbio, 1981, p.27.
14. Taylor, *op. cit.*, p.541.
15. Gellner, 1979. p.39.
16. Cf. Roger Scruton, *The Meaning of Conservatism* (Harmondsworth: Penguin, 1980).
17. Cf. Collini, Winch and Burrow, 1983, ch. 10.
18. Kojève, 'Hegel, Marx et le christianisme', *Critique*, 1 (1946), p.360.
19. O'Brien, 1975, p.174.
20. Pelczynski, 1971, pp.230–41.
21. Fetscher, 1971, p.49.
22. On this point, see Merquior, 1979, ch. 3.
23. For a good example, see Shaw, 1978, ch. 5.
24. Cf. Henderson (1976), quoted in Hutchison, 1981, p.13.
25. From the *Critique of the Gotha Programme*; cf. Marx, 1974, p.352.
26. See his short essay on culture and socialism (1928), reprinted in *Die Forderung des Tages* (Berlin: Fischer, 1930).

27. In the *Grundrisse*; cf. Marx, 1973c, p.611.
28. *Grundrisse* (German ed.), p.161.
29. As remarked by Loewenstein, 1980, p.69.
30. Aron, 'Le marxisme de Marx' (résumé de cours, 1976–77), *Le Débat*, 28 (Jan. 1984), p.28.
31. Marx, 1976–81, vol.II, p.212; for an apt comment, see Loewenstein 1980, pp.83–84.
32. See their discussion in Thomas, 1980, chs 3–5.
33. Avineri, 1968, p.208.
34. For a concise, masterly discussion of this point, see Andrzej Walicki, 'Marx and Freedom', *New York Review of Books* (24 Nov. 1983), pp. 50–56.
35. Ibid., p. 55.
36. Joan Robinson, *New Left Review*, 31 (1965).
37. Roemer, 'Exploitation, Class and Property Relations' in Ball and Farr, 1984, pp. 209–10.
38. For the revolutionary weight of peasantries, see Skocpol, 1979.

II. THE FOUNDATIONS OF WESTERN MARXISM

1. Jaspers, *Heidelberger Jahrbücher*, 5 (1961), quoted in Konder, 1980, p.25. Jaspers attributed the authorship of the joke to E. Lask.
2. For this social and ideological background, see Congdon, 1983, intro.
3. Written between 1906 and 1909, published in Budapest in 1911; partly translated as 'The Sociology of Modern Drama' in Lukács 1965a.
4. On the Simmel/Lukács link, see the judicious comparison by David Frisby in the introduction to his translation of *The Philosophy of Money*. Simmel, 1978, pp. 15–21.
5. Cf. Congdon, *op. cit.*, pp. 52–62.
6. For his Heidelberg philosophy of art (1912–14) and aesthetics (1916–18), see the writings of their co-editor, György Markus, in Heller (ed.), 1977, pp. 192–240, as well as his article 'The Soul and Life: the Young Lukács and the Problem of Culture' in *Telos*, 32 (1977), pp.95–115, now in Heller (ed.) 1983, ch. 1.
7. But the German text had appeared since 1916 in Max Dessoir's *Zeitschrift für Aesthetik und allgemeine Kunstwissenschaft*.
8. In his foreword to a 1962 reprint of *The Theory of the Novel*.
9. For this connection, see Eva Karady's paper on Weber and

Lukács in Wolfgang Mommsen et al., *Max Weber and his Contemporaries* (Oxford: Blackwell, forthcoming).

10. Modern Sorel scholarship has done much to correct prior interpretations overstating his irrationalism. For comments on this evolution, see my article on Sorel in John Hall (ed.), *Rediscoveries* (Oxford: OUP, forthcoming).
11. Cf. Andrew Arato, 'Lukács' Path to Marxism', *Telos*, 7 (1971), p. 136.
12. Bloch, interview in *Neues Forum* (Dec. 1967); quoted in Konder, *op. cit.*, p.30.
13. Cf. Löwy, 1976, ch. 4.
14. Foreword to the 1967 reprint of *Geschichte und Klassenbewusstsein*.
15. Lukács, 1971b, pp.2–3.
16. Cf. Weber, 'Objective Possibility and Adequate Causation in Historical Explanation' part II of 'Critical Studies in the Logic of the Cultural Sciences' (1906) in Weber, 1949, pp.164–88.
17. Lukács, 1971b, p.315.
18. Cf. the judicious comments by Rudolf Schlesinger in his essay on the historical setting of *History and Class Consciousness* in Mészáros, 1971.
19. Kettler, 'Culture and Revolution: Lukács in the Hungarian Revolution', *Telos*, 7 (Spring 1971).
20. English translation in Lukács, 1973.
21. For the gist of Bloch's review, entitled 'Aktualität und Utopie' (1923) reprinted in Vol. X of his collected works (Frankfurt, 1969), see Howard, 1977, pp. 69–72.
22. Lukács, 1972, p.15 (from 'Tactics and Ethics').
23. Habermas, 1971, ch.6.
24. For quotations from Kautsky's review (1924) see Rusconi, 1968, pp.121.
25. For example, Morris Watnick in 'George Lukács: An Intellectual Biography', *Survey* 23–7 (1958–9); and Löwy, *op.cit.*, p.221–3.
26. Lukács, 1974a, p.87.
27. Cf. Bloch's 1974 interview to Michael Löwy in appendix to Löwy, *op.cit.*
28. Lukács, 1971b, p.293.
29. Ibid., p.1.
30. Cf. Adorno, 1973c, pp. 189–97.
31. Arato and Breines, 1979, p.128; Jay, 1984a, pp.106–11.
32. For a reflection of the Frankfurtian viewpoint on the scholarly discussion of Lukács, see Perlini, 1968.
33. Marck, 'Neukritizistische und neuhegelsche Auffassung der

marxistischen Dialektik', *Die Gesellschaft*, (1924), reprinted in Marck et al., 1971.

34. Kolakowski, 1978, vol. III, ch.7.
35. Cf. Schumpeter, 1954; and Löwith, 1949.
36. For the critique of historical economism, see Gramsci, 1971, pp.158–68. The sentence on the impossibility of prediction is on p.438.
37. Ibid., p.462.
38. Ibid., p.465.
39. See the comment by Cesare Luporini, 'Appunti su alcuni nessi interni del pensiero di Gramsci' (1958), reprinted in Luporini, 1974, pp.43–51.
40. This point in Gramsci's philological upbringing has been highlighted by lo Piparo, 1979.
41. Cf. Gramsci, 1971, pp.118–20; and Gramsci, 1965, pp.619–20 (letter of May 1932).
42. Ibid., pp.104–106.
43. Adamson, 1980, p.216.
44. For this point, see Boggs, 1976, p.116.
45. On this semantic shift, see Perry Anderson's learned article, 'The antinomies of Antonio Gramsci', *New Left Review*, 100 (Nov. 1976–Jan. 1977).
46. Anderson, *op.cit.*, p.26 (parenthesis added).
47. Ibid., pp.61–4.
48. Cf. Gramsci, 1971, p.227.
49. Ibid., p.108.
50. Ibid., p.108.
51. Ibid., p.365.
52. See, for instance, the discussion of intellectuals as organizers of hegemony in Sassoon, 1980.
53. Anderson, *op.cit.*, p.44.
54. By G. Galli in 'Gramsci e le teorie delle elites' in Rossi (ed.), 1975.
55. Kolakowski, *op cit.*, pp.250–51.
56. Coutinho, 1981, pp.126 and 66.
57. Cf. Tamburrano, 1963. Giuseppe Tamburrano was a moderate socialist intellectual. Not every Italian social democrat agreed with his benign view of Gramsci: for instance, the old Rodolfo Mondolfo, often considered the central figure in Italian Marxism between the death of Labriola (1904) and the publication of Gramsci's *Quaderni*, bluntly wrote that putting the party-prince 'on the throne of popular veneration' could lead only 'to totalitarianism' (Mondolfo, 'Le antinomie di Gramsci', *Critica Sociale*, 23, [15 Dec. 1963]).
58. Carl Levy, 'Max Weber and Antonio Gramsci' in *Max Weber and his Contemporaries* (see note 9).

59. Colletti, 1979, p.181.
60. Here Gramsci's views seem not very far from those of the now forgotten Russian Left communist Alexander Bogdanov (1873–1928), whose Machian epistemology Lenin flogged (without in the least refuting) in *Materialism and Empirio-Criticism* (1908). Bogdanov's *Tectology* (1922), a general theory of 'organization', claimed that automatic machinery allowed the worker, who previously just carried out alienating tasks, a decisive degree of 'control and conscious intervention'. On Bogdanov see the essay by S.V. Utechin in Labedz, 1962, pp.117–25.
61. Femia, 1981, p.232.
62. Ibid., pp.243–4.
63. On della Volpe and his school, see Fraser, 1977.
64. Cf. his essay 'Il rapporto Hegel-Marx' in Cassano (ed.), 1973, pp. 164–70.

III. THE POST-WAR SCENE

1. Cf. Tom Bottomore, introduction to Bottomore and Goode, 1978, pp. 9–10.
2. Adorno, 1967, p.31.
3. Borkenau, 1938.
4. L. Lowenthal, as quoted in Roberts, 1982, p.173.
5. Horkheimer, 1972, pp.237–8 (from 'Traditional and Critical Theory', 1937). Even those who strive to stress the radicalism of earlier critical theory are in the end compelled to acknowledge that, ultimately, from the 1930s it had only an ambivalent, 'tenuous relationship' with Marxism (cf. Douglas Kellner, 'The Frankfurt School Revisited' (a critique of Jay, 1973), *New German Critique*, 4 (Winter 1975), pp.148–52).
6. Horkheimer, 'The Authoritarian State', in Arato and Gebhardt, 1978, p.107.
7. The clash between the views of Pollock and Neumann is well told in Jay, 1973, ch.5. See also Held, 1980, pp.52–65.
8. Horkheimer, 'Zum Problem der Wahrheit' in Horkheimer, 1968, vol. I, p.256 (see Horkheimer, 1972).
9. By Buck-Morss, 1977, pp.90–99 and 102–103.
10. Benjamin, 1977, pp.29 and 32.
11. For a perceptive discussion of Klages's influence on Benjamin, see Roberts, 1982, pp. 104–109.
12. Roberts, *op. cit.*, pp.126–32.
13. On Cohen, see Willey, 1978 pp. 105–116.
14. To borrow from Wolin, 1982, p.44.

15. Benjamin, 1973a, p.256.
16. Also from the *Theses*. For a fine comment, see Peter Szondi, 'Hope in the Past: on Walter Benjamin', translated by Harvey Mendelsohn, in *Critical Inquiry*, 4 (Spring 1978), pp.491–506, an essay of 1961 reprinted in Szondi, 1964.
17. Benjamin, 1979b, p.104.
18. Benjamin, 1973a, p.224.
19. The whole German text was published by Rolf Tiedemann three years ago. Texts from it have been translated in Benjamin 1973b. For a fine analysis of the *Passagenwerk* as a whole, see Sergio Paulo Rouanet, 'As passagens de Paris', *Tempo Brasileiro* (Rio), no. 68 (Jan.-March 1982) pp.43–79 and no. 69 (April–June 1982) pp.13–39.
20. Benjamin, 1973c, p.87.
21. See the essay of that title (1934) – Benjamin's utmost Brechtianism – collected in Benjamin, 1973c. In the mid-1930s there was a sustained correspondence between Tretjakov and Brecht.
22. Benjamin, 1973c, p.90.
23. Benjamin, 1973b, p.132.
24. For this line of interpretation, see Roberts *op cit.*, p.156.
25. For instance, in 'Experience and Poverty' in Benjamin, 1977a, II.
26. Benjamin, 1973c, pp.93 and 33.
27. See note 60 to Chapter Two.
28. Roberts's being to my mind the most cogent of them.
29. Cf. Adorno, 'Charakteristik Walter Benjamins' in Adorno et al., 1970, p.26. For a fine discussion of the overlap between the *Theses* and the *Passagenwerk*, see Sergio Paulo Rouanet, 'As Passagens de Paris, I', *Tempo Brasileiro*, 68 (Jan.–March 1982), pp.47–56.
30. Cf. Benjamin, 1973a.
31. Cf Benjamin's essay 'Eduard Fuchs, Collector and Historian' (1937–8), in Benjamin, 1979, pp.349–86.
32. The point is cogently argued by Eugene Lunn (1982, pp.201–207).
33. Horkheimer and Adorno, 1972, pp.203–204.
34. Adorno, 1974, p.129.
35. Ibid., p.195.
36. Horkheimer and Adorno, *op cit.*, pp.132–3.
37. Ibid., p.14.
38. Ibid., p.93.
39. By Rose, 1978, pp.22 and 24.
40. Kracauer, 1969, p.201. On Kracauer on Adorno, see Martin Jay's 'The Extraterritorial Life of Siegfried Kracauer', *Salmagundi*, 31–2 (Fall 1975–Winter 1976), and 'Adorno and

Kracauer: Notes on a Troubled Friendship', *Salmagundi*, 40 (Winter 1978).

41. For the last three composers, see Adorno, 1973a; for Wagner, Adorno, 1981 and for Mahler, Adorno, 1960. Adorno actually went to Vienna in 1925 to study under Alban Berg.
42. Adorno, 1973c, p.320.
43. Horkheimer and Adorno, *op.cit.*, p.24.
44. Kolakowski, 1978, vol.III p.368.
45. Adorno, 1974, p.134.
46. Adorno, 1970, pp.179–205.
47. Adorno, 1967, p.34.
48. Marcuse, 'The Affirmative Character in Culture' (1936) in Marcuse, 1968.
49. In his preface to the 1962 reprint of *The Theory of the Novel*.
50. Buck-Morss, *op.cit.*, p.46.
51. On this point, see the (approving) comment by Held (1980, p.149).
52. Althusser, 1976, p.59.
53. Sartre, 1957, p.110.
54. Chiodi, 1976, passim and especially p.100.
55. See Lionel Abel's review in *Dissent* (Spring 1961), pp.137–52.
56. For a comment on his clash with Sartre on the concept of history, see my *From Prague to Paris* (forthcoming), ch.3, XI.
57. Aron, 1975, ch.6.
58. On French Marxism since the war, see Poster, 1975; Hirsh, 1981; Michael Kelly, 1982, chs. 3–5; and Jay, 1984a, chs. 9–12.
59. In 1976 he dissented, but from the party's decision to drop the principle of a dictatorship of the proletariat! It was only two years later, after the collapse of the Union de la Gauche, that he condemned the Soviet regime for the Gulag (cf. *New Left Review*, 109, [May–June 1978]).
60. Althusser, 1974.
61. Althusser, 1970, pp.52–9.
62. Cf. the third section of the essay on materialist dialectics (1963) in Althusser, 1969.
63. For this criticism, see Michael Kelly, *op.cit.*, p.133; for Marx's text, see Marx, 1973c, pp.81–111.
64. Glucksmann, 'A Ventriloquist Marxism' in *New Left Review* (ed.), 1977. Originally in *Les Temps Modernes*, 250 (March 1967).
65. Now in Althusser, 1971.
66. F. George, 'Lire Althusser', *Les Temps Modernes*, 24:275 (May 1969).
67. Althusser, 1976, p.71.

68. Althusser, 1971, p.201.
69. Althusser, 1970, p.180.
70. Boudon, 1982, ch.7.
71. Althusser, 1970, p.224.
72. Althusser, 1969, p.113.
73. Cf. Cutler, 1977.
74. Althusser, 1977, p.171.
75. Ibid., p.139.
76. For a classical critique, see Abercrombie et al., 1980.
77. This criticism is repeatedly levelled against him, for instance, by several of the co-authors of *Contre Althusser* (cf. Vincent et al., 1974).
78. Althusser, 1977, p.222.
79. Cf. among others Callinicos, 1976, especially pp.59–60, 72 and 88.
80. For a good short survey, see Michael Kelly, *op.cit.*, pp.200–206. On Sève cf. ibid., especially pp.169–72 and 191–98.
81. Poster, *op.cit.*, p.342.
82. As noticed by an ex-Althusserian, Jacques Rancière (1974, p.95).
83. Aron, 1969.
84. Cf. Jean-Marie Brohm in Vincent, *op.cit.*, p.16.
85. Schmidt, 1983, p.66 and passim.
86. From his preface to the 1960 edition of *Reason and Revolution*.
87. Marcuse, 1955, p.51.
88. Cf. 'Aggressiveness in Advanced Industrial Society', in Marcuse, 1968, pp.248–68.
89. Marcuse, 1964, p.3.
90. Marcuse, 1968, pp.223–4.
91. Marcuse, 1964, pp.166–7.
92. Ibid., pp.24–32.
93. Ibid., pp.256–7.
94. Marcuse, 'Repressive Tolerance' in Marcuse, Wolff and Moore 1969, pp.81–117.
95. Marcuse, 1955, p.206.
96. For a critical discussion of this kind of traditional nonsense about Rousseau, see Merquior, 1980, pp.35–76.
97. See his own testimony in 'Psychic Thermidor and the Rebirth of Rebellious Subjectivity', *Berkeley Journal of Sociology* 25 (1980).
98. Habermas, 1972, p.33.
99. Cf. Habermas, 'Why More Philosophy', *Social Research*, 38:4 (Winter 1971).

100. See his noted essay 'Between Philosophy and Science: Marxism as Critique' (1960), later reprinted as ch. 6 of Habermas, 1974.

101. If I may borrow this apt label from Noel Sullivan's essay on Arendt in Crespigny and Minogue, 1975.

102. For criticism on Marcuse's ideas on alternative science, see Habermas, 1968; for the vindication of Kant against Hegel epistemology, see the beginning of Habermas, 1972.

103. Cf. Habermas, 1974, pp.21 and 8.

104. Jay, 1984a, pp.473–4.

105. Reprinted in Habermas, 1968 and, in English, in Habermas, 1974, ch.4.

106. Habermas, 1974, p.237 (from the essay mentioned in note 100). He follows on this point Claus Offe's thesis about the emergence of 'political instrumentalities' largely independent from economic interests in advanced capitalist society; see Offe, 1972, passim.

107. Habermas, 1972, p.314.

108. Habermas, 1974, p.11.

109. See Habermas and Luhmann, 1971.

110. Habermas, 1976, p.131.

111. Hall, 1981, p.81.

112. Habermas, 1974, pp.31–2.

113. He uses the phrase in his introduction to Habermas, 1971b (an abridged translation of the *Einleitung* to the original German book of 1969).

114. McCarthy, 1978, pp.95 ff.

115. Bernstein, 1976, pp.223–4.

116. Lobkowicz, 'Interests and Objectivity', *Philosophy of the Social Sciences* 2 (1972), p.201.

117. Published in *Philosophy of the Social Sciences* 3 (1973). Similar ideas occur in the introduction to *Theory and Practice* quoted in note 108.

118. Cf. Habermas, 'Toward a Theory of Communicative Competence', *Recent Sociology*, 2 (edited by Hans Peter Dreitzel), London, 1970.

119. Habermas, 1979, pp.148.

120. Habermas, 'What is Universal Pragmatics' (1976), ch.1 in Habermas, 1979.

121. This is explicit in ch.3 of Habermas, 1979 ('The Development of Normative Structures'), an essay which in the German original appeared as the introduction piece of *Zur Rekonstruktion des Historischen Materialismus*.

122. Habermas, 1979, p.146.

123. For a fine summary, see John B. Thompson's review of the *Theorie*, *TLS*, 8 April 1983, p.357.

124. Much of the best recent Weber literature is in effect a valiant attempt to recall that Weber was *not* besotted by instrumental rationality; for a cogent example, see Stephen Kalberg's 'Max Weber's Types of Rationality – Cornerstones for the Analysis of Rationalization Processes in History', *American Journal of Sociology*, 85 no 5 (1980), pp.1145–79.

125. Cf. the English translation as Habermas, 'Modernity versus Postmodernity', *New German Critique*, 22 (Winter 1981).

126. Ibid., p.9.

127. For a critique of the ideology of Foucault, see Merquior 1985; and of Derrida, see my *From Prague to Paris* (forthcoming), ch.5, V and VI.

128. Hall, *op.cit.*, pp.54 and 65–6.

129. Cf. her criticisms in Thompson and Held, 1982, ch.5, especially p.114. In his reply at the end of the same volume, p.274, Habermas acknowledges that he neglected 'the evidential dimension of truth'.

130. Cf. McCarthy, *op.cit.*, p.459. For a shortened English translation see Habermas, 'On Social Identity', *Telos*, 19 (Spring 1974).

131. Lukes, ch.7 in Thompson and Held, *op.cit.*, especially p.145.

132. Radnitzky, 1970, Vol.II, pp.179–80.

133. Cf. W.G. Runciman, review of *Theory of Communicative Action*, *vol.I*, in *London Review of Books* (4 October 1984), p.19.

134. Anderson, 1983, p.64.

135. Cf. ch. 8 in Thompson and Held, *op.cit.*, especially pp.159–60.

136. For this point, see Axel Honneth's article, 'Communication and Reconciliation – Habermas' critique of Adorno', *Telos*, 39 (Spring 1979), p.46.

137. Cf. Willms, 1973, passim.

138. This point was brilliantly made by Quentin Skinner in 'Habermas' Reformation', *New York Review of Books* (7 October 1982), p.38.

139. Geuss, 1981, pp.88–91.

140. Skinner, see note 138.

141. As noted among others by Connerton, 1980, p.134.

142. Colletti, 1981, p.61.

143. This tendency in Adorno to burden art with the task of solving the impasses of philosophy and social theory begins to be openly questioned. See, for instance, Rüdiger Bubner, 'Über einige Bedingungen gegenwärtiger Aesthetik', in *Neue Hefte für Philosophie*, 5 (Göttingen, 1973) pp.38–73.

IV. A FEW GENERAL CONCLUSIONS

The epigraph comes from Robinson, 1953.

1. Anderson, 1976, p.93.
2. Colletti, *New Left Review*, 86 (July–Aug. 1974).
3. Anderson, *op.cit.*, pp.52ff. and 76ff.
4. Cf. Jacoby, 1981, p.37.
5. Ibid., pp.37–8.
6. Goldmann, 'Understanding Marcuse', *Partisan Review*, 38: 3(1971); quoted in Jay, 1984a, p.326.
7. Merleau-Ponty, 1973a, pp.63–4.
8. Fetscher, 1971, pp.178–9.
9. Jay, 1984a, pp.10–13, and ch.15 (on Habermas).
10. The quote comes from the notes for the unfinished poem 'German Greatness', of 1797, as recalled by George Armstrong Kelly 1978, p.57.
11. This is the standard and accurate interpretation of the main contrast between Hegel and Weber in relation to their substantive views. For a cogent, elegant restatement, see Pietro Rossi, 1982, especially pp.11–12 and 116.
12. Both points have been stressed in the growing Braudel literature. For a recent critical assessment, see Keith Thomas, review article in the *New York Review of Books*, (22 November 1984).
13. Giddens, 1982, passim. There is an important critical discussion in Erik Olin Wright's 'Giddens's Critique of Marxism', *New Left Review*, 138 (March–April 1983), pp.11–35.
14. Cf. Hindess and Hirst, 1975, p.312; and 1977.
15. The kick-off of the state-derivation debate was given by Müller and Neussüs in their essay 'The Welfare-state Illusion and the Contradiction between Wage-labour and Capital' now abridged as ch.2 of Holloway and Picciotto, 1978. There is a full translation in *Telos*, 25 (1975).
16. Holloway and Picciotto, *op.cit.*, p.14.
17. Callinicos, 1982, pp.156–9.
18. Lefort, 1971, p.348 (my translation).
19. From 'Marxisme et Théorie Révolutionnaire', *Socialisme ou Barbarie* 36 (June 1965). Quoted in Hirsh, 1981, ch.5, a fine concise discussion of Castoriadis's thought and its evolution. A briefer comment is in Poster, 1975, pp.201–205. For a longer analysis, covering the divergences between Lefort and Castoriadis, see Howard, 1977, chs. 9 and 10.
20. Anderson, 1976, pp.114–20.
21. Anderson, 1983, pp.104, 100 and 98.
22. Cf. G. A. Cohen, 1978; Roemer, 1982; and Elster, 1985. See also Ball and Farr, 1984, especially chs. 2 and 9.

23. I can think of two (quite unrelated) philosophers in particular: Nathan Rotenstreich (1976) and George Armstrong Kelly (1969, 1978). The first has cogently protested against the neglect of substantive issues in modern philosophy of history, showing how the latter's conscientious concentration on epistemological problems is strewn with hidden assumptions about the process – about history *qua* events, and not just history as knowledge. As for G.A. Kelly, he has forcefully emphasized the need for revitalizing our thought on the connection, so dear to Hegel, between philosophy, history and politics.

BIBLIOGRAPHY

This bibliography lists two kinds of books (articles have been given full reference in the Notes): (a) those referred to in the Notes and (b) those which, though not specifically referred to, were also important in the writing of this book. Classic works of philosophy, both ancient and modern, have been as a rule excluded (except in the case of Hegel) since they are usually readily available in English translation.

Abercrombie, Nicholas, Hill, Stephen and Turner, Bryan S. 1980. *The Dominant Ideology Thesis*. London: Allen and Unwin.

Adamson, Walter L. 1980. *Hegemony and Revolution*. Berkeley: University of California Press.

Adorno, Theodor W. *Gesammelte Werke*. Edited by Rolf Tiedemann. Frankfurt: Suhrkamp, 1970–, 23 vols.

1933. *Kierkegaard: Konstruktion des ästhetischen*. Tübingen: Mohr.

1960. *Mahler: eine musikalische Physiognomik*. Frankfurt: Suhrkamp.

1967. *Prisms*. London: Spearman. (Translation by Samuel and Shierry Weber of *Prismen: Kulturkritik und Gesellschaft*. Frankfurt: Suhrkamp, 1955.)

1970. *Aesthetische Theorie*. Edited by Gretel Adorno and Rolf Tiedemann. Frankfurt: Suhrkamp.

1973a. *Philosophy of Modern Music*. New York and London: Seabury. (Translation by Anne G. Mitchell and Wesley V. Blomster of *Philosophie der neuen Musik*. Tübingen: Mohr, 1949.)

1973b. *The Jargon of Authenticity*. London: Routledge; and Evanston, Ill.: Northwestern University Press. (Translation by Knut Tarnowski and Frederick Will of *Jargon der Eigentlichkeit: zur deutschen Ideologie*. Frankfurt: Suhrkamp, 1965.)

1973c. *Negative Dialectics*. New York: Seabury; and London: Routledge (Translation by E.B. Ashton of *Negative Dialektik*. Frankfurt: Suhrkamp, 1966.)

1974. *Minima Moralia: Reflections from Damaged Life*. London: New Left Books. (Translation by Edmund E.N. Jephcott of *Minima Moralia: Reflexionen aus den beschädigten Leben*. Frankfurt: Suhrkamp, 1951.)

1980. *Against Epistemology*. Oxford: Blackwell. (Translation by Willis Domingo of *Zur Metakritik der Erkenntnistheorie: Studien über Husserl und die phäenomenologischen Antinomien*. Stuttgart: Kohlhammer, 1956.)

1981. *In search of Wagner*. London: New Left Books; and New York: Schocken. (Translation by Edmund F.N. Jephcott of *Versuch über Wagner*. Frankfurt: Suhrkamp, 1952.)

Albertelli, Gianfranco (ed.) 1976. *Interpretazioni di Gramsci (1957–75): la problematica del marxismo*. Trento: Gruppo di lavoro 'Fenomeni Politici'.

Althusser, Louis. 1969. *For Marx*. London: Allen Lane; and New York: Pantheon. Translation by Ben Brewster of *Pour Marx*. Paris: Maspero, 1965.)

1970. *Reading Capital*. London: New Left Books. (Translation by Ben Brewster of *Lire le Capital*, with E. Balibar and others. Paris: Maspero, 1965. 2 vols.)

1971. *Lenin and Philosophy and other Essays*. London: New Left Books. (Translation by Ben Brewster of *Lénine et la philosophie*. Paris: Maspero, 1969; expanded edition, 1972.)

1972. *Politics and History: Montesquieu, Rousseau, Hegel and Marx*. London: New Left Books. (Essays translated from the French by Ben Brewster.)

1974. *Philosophie et philosophie spontanée des savants*. Paris: Maspero.

1976. *Essays in Self-Criticism*. London: New Left Books; and Atlantic Highlands, N.J.: Humanities Press. (Essays translated by Graham Lock), Contains full bibliography and includes 'Reply to John Lewis. Paris: 1973.

Anderson, Perry. 1976. *Considerations on Western Marxism*. London: New Left Books.

1983. *In the Tracks of Historical Materialism*. London: Verso Editions.

Arato, Andrew and Breines, Paul. 1979. *The Young Lukács and the Origins of Western Marxism*. London: Pluto Press.

Arato, Andrew and Gebhardt, Eike. 1978. *The Essential Frankfurt School Reader*. Oxford: Blackwell.

Aron, Raymond. 1969. *Marxism and the Existentialists*. (Translation by Helen Weaver, Robert Addis and John Weightman of part of *D'une Sainte Famille à l'Autre: essai sur les marxismes imaginaires*. Paris: Gallimard, 1969.) New York: Harper.

1975. *History and Dialectic of Violence: an Analysis of Sartre's Critique de la Raison Dialectique*. Translated by Barry Cooper of the French ed. (1973) New York: Praeger and Oxford: Blackwell.

Aronson, Ronald. 1980. *Jean-Paul Sartre: Philosophy in the World*. London: New Left Books.

Avineri, Shlomo. 1968. *The Social and Political Thought of Karl Marx*. Cambridge: Cambridge University Press.

1972. *Hegel's Theory of the Modern State*. Cambridge: Cambridge University Press.

Avineri, Shlomo (ed.) 1977. *Varieties of Marxism*. The Hague: Martinus Nijhoff.

Axelos, Kostas. 1961. *Marx, Penseur de la Technique*. Paris: Minuit.

Badaloni, Nicola. 1975. *Il Marxismo di Gramsci*. Turin: Einaudi.

Bahro, Rudolf. 1978 *The Alternative in Eastern Europe*. London: New Left Books. (Translation of *Die Alternative*. Frankfurt: Europäische Verlagsantalt, 1977.)

Ball, T. and Farr, J. (eds) 1984. *After Marx*. Cambridge: Cambridge University Press.

Bekerman, Gérard. 1981. *Vocabulaire du Marxisme*. Paris: Presses Universitaires de France.

Benjamin, Walter. *Gesammelte Schriften*. Edited by Hermann Schweppenhäuser and Rolf Tiedemann. Frankfurt: Suhrkamp, 1972– .

　1920. *Der Begriff der Kunstkritik in der deutschen Romantik*. Berne: Francke.

　1973a. *Illuminations*. Edited and with an introduction by Hannah Arendt; translated by Harry Zohn. London: Fontana.

　1973b. *Charles Baudelaire: a Poet in the Era of High Capitalism*. London: New Left Books. (Translation by Harry Zohn of *Charles Baudelaire: ein Lyriker im Zeitalter des Hochkapitalismus*. Edited by Rolf Tiedemann. Frankfurt: Suhrkamp, 1969.)

　1973c. *Understanding Brecht*. Introduction by Stanley Mitchell; translated by Anne Bostock. London: New Left Books.

　1977. *The Origin of German Tragic Drama*. London: New Left Books. (Translation by John Osborne of *Ursprung des deutschen Trauerspiels*. Berlin: Rowohlt, 1928.)

　1979a. *Reflections: Essays, Aphorisms, Autobiographical Writings*. Edited and with an introduction by Peter Demetz; translated by Edmund Jephcott and Kingsley Shorter. New York: Harcourt Brace.

　1979b. *One-way Street and other Writings*. Introduction by Susan Sontag. London: New Left Books. (Translation by Edmund Jephcott and Kingsley Short of *Einbahstrasse* [aphorisms]. Berlin: Rowohlt, 1928.)

　1982. *Das Passagenwerk* (*Gesammelte Schriften*, V, in 2 vols). Edited by Rolf Tiedemann. Frankfurt: Suhrkamp.

Bernstein, Richard. 1976. *The Restructuring of Social and Political Thought*. Oxford: Blackwell.

Bloch, Ernst. 1918. *Geist der Utopie*. Munich: Duncker und Humblot.

Bibliography

1951. *Subjekt-Objekt: Erläuterungen zu Hegel*. Berlin: Aufbau.

1954–59. *Das Prinzip Hoffnung*. Berlin: Aufbau. 3 vols. (Selections as *On Karl Marx*. New York: Herder, 1970.)

1970a. *A Philosophy of the Future*. New York: Herder. (Translation by John Cumming of *Tübinger Einleitung in die Philosophie*, I. Frankfurt: Suhrkamp, 1963–4.)

1970b. *Man on His Own: Essays in the Philosophy of Religion*. New York: Herder. Translation by E. B. Ashton of *Religion im Erbe*, Frankfurt: Suhrkamp, 1961.

1974. *Experimentum Mundi*. Frankfurt: Suhrkamp.

Bobbio, Norberto. 1981. *Studi Hegeliani*. Turin: Einaudi.

Boggs, Carl. 1976. *Gramsci's Marxism*. London: Pluto Press.

Böhm-Bawerk, Eugen von. 1975a. *Karl Marx and the Close of his System*. Edited by Paul M. Sweezy. London: Merlin (1st ed., New York, 1949; German original, 1896).

1975b. *The Exploitation Theory of Socialism-Communism*. South Holland, Ill.: Libertarian Press. (First ed. 1960. This is ch. XII of Vol. 1 of *Capital and Interest*, 1884: English translation, 1890.)

Borkenau, Franz. 1938. *The Communist International*. London: Faber and Faber. (Reprinted as *World Communism – A History of the Communist International*. Ann Arbor: University of Michigan Press, 1962.)

Bottomore, T.B. et al. (eds) 1983. *A Dictionary of Marxist Thought*. Oxford: Blackwell.

Bottomore, T. and Goode, P. (eds). 1978. *Austro-Marxism*. Oxford: Clarendon Press.

Boudon, Raymond. 1982. *Unintended Consequences of Social Action*. (Translation from the French; original edition Paris: Presses Universitaires de France, 1977.) London: Macmillan.

Braverman, Harry. 1974. *Labor and Monopoly Capital – the Degradation of Work in the Twentieth Century*. New York: Monthly Review Press.

Brazill, William J. 1970. *The Young Hegelians*. New Haven: Yale University Press.

Breines, Paul (ed.), 1972. *Critical Interruptions: New Left Perspectives on Herbert Marcuse*. New York: Herder and Herder.

Buci-Glucksmann, Christina. 1975. *Gramsci et l'Etat: pour une théorie matérialiste de la philosophie*. Paris: Fayard.

Buck-Morss, Susan. 1977. *The Origin of Negative Dialectics: Theodor W Adorno, Walter Benjamin and the Frankfurt School*. Hassocks, Sussex: Harvester.

Bukharin, Nikolai. 1969. *Historical Materialism: a System of Sociology*. Ann Arbor: University of Michigan Press; 1st ed. London: Allen and Unwin, 1926; Russian ed., 1921.

Callinicos, Alex. 1976. *Althusser's Marxism*. London: Pluto Press.

    1982. *Is there a Future for Marxism?* London: Macmillan.

Carver, Terrell. 1982. *Marx's Social Theory*. Oxford: Oxford University Press.

Cassano, Franco (ed.) 1973. *Marxismo e Filosofia in Italia*. Bari: De Donato.

Castoriadis, Cornelius (under the pseudomyn P. Cardan). n/d. *Modern Capitalism and Revolution*. London: Solidarity.

    1975. *L'Institution Imaginaire de la Société*. Paris: Seuil.

Chiodi, Pietro. 1976. *Sartre and Marxism*. Translated by Kate Soper. Hassocks, Sussex: Harvester. (Italian ed., Milan: Fettrinelli, 1965.)

Cohen, G.A. 1978. *Karl Marx's Theory of History – a Defence*. Oxford: Clarendon Press.

Cohen, Jean L. 1983. *Class and Civil Society*. Oxford: Martin Robertson.

Colletti, Lucio. 1972. *From Rousseau to Lenin – Studies in Ideology and Society*. London: New Left Books. (Translation by John Merrington and Judith White of *Ideologia e Societa*. Bari: Laterza, 1969.)

    1973. *Marxism and Hegel*. London : New Left Books (Translation by Lawrence Garner of *Il Marxismo e Hegel*. Bari: Laterza, 1969.)

1979. *Tra Marxismo e no*. Bari: Laterza.

1981. *Tramonto dell'ideologia*. Bari: Laterza.

Collini, Stefan, Winch, Donald and Burrow, John. 1983. *That Noble Science of Politics. A Study in Nineteenth-Century Intellectual History*. Cambridge: Cambridge University Press.

Congdon, Lee. 1983. *The Young Lukács*. Chapel Hill: University of North Carolina Press.

Connerton, Paul. 1980. *The Tragedy of Enlightenment*. Cambridge: Cambridge University Press.

Connerton, Paul (ed). 1976. *Critical Sociology*. Harmondsworth: Penguin.

Cooper, Barry, 1984. *The End of History: an essay on Modern Hegelianism*. Toronto: University of Toronto Press

Coutinho, Carlos Nelson. 1981. *Gramsci*. Porto Alegre: L. & P.M. Editores.

Crespigny, Antoine de and Minogue, Kenneth (eds). 1975. *Contemporary Political Philosophies*. London: Methuen.

Cutler, A. et al. 1977. *Marx's 'Capital' and Capitalism Today*. London: Routledge and Kegan Paul.

Dallmayr, Fred R. (ed.) 1971. *Materialen zu Habermas 'Erkenntuis und Interesse'*. Frankfurt: Suhrkamp.

Danto, Arthur C. 1975. *Sartre*. London: Fontana.

Debray, Régis. 1967. *Revolution in the Revolution*. Translated by Ortiz (French ed., Paris, 1967). New York: Monthly Review Press.

Desai, Meghnad. 1979. *Marxian Economics*. Oxford: Blackwell.

D'Hondt, Jacques. 1982. *De Hegel à Marx*. Paris: Presses Universitaires de France.

D'Hondt, Jacques (ed.) 1974. *La Logique de Marx*. Paris: Presses Universitaires de France.

Elster, Jon. 1985. *Making Sense of Marx*. Cambridge: Cambridge University Press.

Engels, Friedrich. 1935. *Anti-Dühring (Herr Eugen Dühring's Revolution in Science)*. London: Lawrence and Wishart.

(Translation by E. Burns from the German ed., Leipzig, 1878.)

Fakenheim, Emil. 1967. *The Religious Dimension in Hegel's Thought*. Chicago: Chicago University Press.

Femia, Joseph V. 1981. *Gramsci's Political Thought*. Oxford: Oxford University Press.

Fetscher, Iring. 1971. *Marx and Marxism*. New York: Herder. (Translation John Hargreaves of *Karl Marx und der Marxismus*. Munich: Piper, 1967.)

Fleischer, Helmut. 1973. *Marxism and History* New York: Harper. (German ed., Translated by Eric Mosbacher. Frankfurt: Suhrkamp, 1969).

Fleischmann, Eugène. 1969. *La Philosophie Politique de Hegel*. Paris: Plon.

Flynn, Thomas R. 1984. *Sartre and Marxist Existentialism*. Chicago: University of Chicago Press.

Foucault, Michel. 1980. *Power (Knowledge: Selected Interviews and other Writings, 1972–77*. Edited by Colin Gordon et al. Brighton: Harvester.

Fraser, John. 1977. *An Introduction to the Thought of Galvano della Volpe*. London: Lawrence and Wishart.

Friedman, George. 1981. *The Political Philosophy of the Frankfurt School*. London: Cornell University Press.

Gadamer, Hans-Georg. 1976. *Hegel's Dialectic*. Translated by P. Christopher Smith. New Haven: Yale University Press.

Gellner, Ernest. 1979. *Spectacles and Predicaments: Essays in Social Theory*. Cambridge: Cambridge University Press.

Geuss, Raymond. 1981. *The Idea of a Critical Theory – Habermas and the Frankfurt School*. Cambridge: Cambridge University Press.

Giddens, Anthony. 1977. *Studies in Social and Political Theory*. London: Hutchinson.

1982. *A Contemporary Critique of Historical Materialism*. Cambridge: Cambridge University Press.

Gillespie, Michael Allen. 1984. *Hegel, Heidegger and the Ground of History*. Chicago: University of Chicago Press.

Goldmann, Lucien. 1959. *Recherches Dialectiques*. Paris: Gallimard.

Goode, Patrick. 1979. *Karl Korsch: A Study in Western Marxism*. London: Macmillan.

Gorz, Andre. 1980. *Adieux au Prolétariat – au-delà du socialisme*. Paris: Galilée.

Gottheil, Fred M. 1966. *Marx's Economic Predictions*. Evanston, NJ: Northwestern University Press.

Gouldner, Alvin. 1985. *Against Fragmentation: The Origins of Marxism and The Sociology of Intellectuals*. Oxford: Oxford University Press.

Gramsci, Antonio. 1971. *Selections from the Prison Notebooks of Antonio Gramsci*. (Translated from *Quaderni del Carcere*.) Edited by Q. Hoare and G.N. Smith. New York: International Publishers.

1975. *Quaderni del Carcere*. Turin: Einaudi, 1948–51. Critical edition as *Quaderni del Carcere: Edizione Critica dell' Instituto Gramsci*. Edited by Valentino Gerratana. Turin: Einaudi. 4 vols.

1977–8. *Selections from Political Writings: vol. 1, 1910–1920; vol. 2, 1921–26*. Edited by Q. Hoare. New York: International Publishers.

Grünbaum, Adolf. 1984. *The Foundations of Psychoanalysis. A Philosophical Critique*. Berkeley: University of California Press.

Habermas, Jürgen. 1962. *Strukturwandel der Öffentlichkeit*. Neuwied: Luchterhand.

1967. *Zur Logik der Sozialwissenschaften*. Tübingen: Siebeck und Mohr.

1968. *Technik und Wissenschaft als 'Ideologie'* (essays). Frankfurt: Suhrkamp.

1971a. *Philosophisch-politische Profile* (essays). Frankfurt: Suhrkamp.

1971b. *Toward a Rational Society: Student Protest, Science and Politics*. (Translation by Jeremy Shapiro of essays written in the 1960s.) London: Heinemann.

1972. *Knowledge and Human Interests*. London: Heinemann.

(Translation by Jeremy Shapiro of *Erkenntnis und Interesse*. Frankfurt: Suhrkamp, 1968.)

1974. *Theory and Practice*. London: Heinemann. Abridged edition. (Translation by John Viertel of *Theorie und Praxis* (essays). Neuwied: Luchterhand, 1962.)

1976. *Legitimation Crisis*. London: Heinemann. (Translation by Thomas McCarthy of *Legitimationsprobleme in Spätkapitalismus*. Frankfurt: Suhrkamp, 1973.)

1979. *Communication and the Evolution of Society* (essays). London: Heinemann; and Boston: Beacon Press. (Translation by Thomas McCarthy of *Zur Rekonstruktion des Historischen Materialismus*. Frankfurt: Suhrkamp, 1976.)

1982. *Theorie des kommunikatives Handelns I–II*. Frankfurt: Suhrkamp.

1983. *Moralbewusstsein und kommunikatives Handeln*. Frankfurt: Suhrkamp.

1984. *Theory of Communicative Action, I: Reason and the Rationalisation of Society*. Translated by Thomas McCarthy. (London: Heinemann.)

Habermas, Jürgen (ed.) 1968. *Antworten auf Herbert Marcuse*. Frankfurt: Suhrkamp.

Habermas, Jürgen and Luhmann, Niklas. 1971. *Theorie der Gesellschaft oder Sozialtechnologie: Was leistest die Systemforschung?* Frankfurt: Suhrkamp.

Hall, John 1968. *Diagnoses of Our Time – Six Views on Our Social Condition*. London: Heinemann.
(forthcoming) (ed.) *Rediscoveries* (OUP).

Harris, H.S. 1972. *Hegel's Development – Toward the Sunlight*. Oxford: Clarendon.

1983. *Hegel's Development – Night Thoughts*. Oxford: Clarendon.

Hegel, Georg Wilhelm Friedrich. 1952. *Philosophy of Right*. Translated by T.M. Knox. Oxford: Clarendon.

1956. *The Philosophy of History*. Introduction by C.J. Friedrich. New York: Dover.

1964. *Political Writings* Translated by T.M. Knox. Oxford: Clarendon.

1969. *Science of Logic*. Translated by A.V. Miller. London: Allen and Unwin.

1971. *Philosophy of Mind*. Translated by A.V. Miller and William Wallace; Foreword by J.N. Findlay. Oxford: Clarendon.

1975a *Logic*. Translated by William Wallace. Oxford: Clarendon.

1975b. *Lectures on the Philosophy of World History*. Translated by H.B. Nisbet. Cambridge: Cambridge University Press.

1977. *Phenomenology of Spirit*. Translated by A.V. Miller. Oxford: Oxford University Press.

Held, David. 1980. *Introduction to Critical Theory – Horkheimer to Habermas*. Berkeley: University of California Press.

Heller, Agnes. 1974. *The Theory of Need in Marx*. London: Allison and Busby.

Heller, Agnes (ed.) 1977. *Die Seele und das Leben: Studien zum frühen Lukács*. Frankfurt: Suhrkamp.

Heller, Agnes (ed.) 1983. *Lukács Revalued*. Oxford: Blackwell.

Hindess, Barry and Hirst, Paul. 1975. *Pre-Capitalist Modes of Production*. London: Routledge and Kegan Paul.

1977. *Mode of Production and Social Formation*. London: Macmillan.

Hirsch, Arthur. 1981. *The French New Left – An Intellectual History from Sartre to Gorz*. Boston: South End Press.

Holloway, John and Picciotto, Sol (eds). 1978. *State and Capital – A Marxist Debate*. London: Edward Arnold.

Hook, Sidney. 1962. *From Hegel to Marx*. Ann Arbor: University of Michigan Press (1st ed., 1950).

Horkheimer, Max. 1947. *Eclipse of Reason*. New York: Oxford University Press.

1972. *Critical Theory: Selected Essays*. New York: Herder. (Partial translation by Matthew O'Connell et al. of *Kritische Theorie: eine Dokumentation*. Edited by Alfred Schmidt. Frankfurt: Fischer, 1968. 2 vols.)

1974. *Critique of Instrumental Reason*. New York: Seabury.

Translation by Matthew O'Connell et al. of *Zur Kritik der Instrumentellen Vernunft*. Frankfurt: Fischer, 1967.)

1978. *Dawn and Decline: Notes 1926–1931 and 1950–1969*. New York: Seabury. (Translation of *Dämmerung: Notizen in Deutschland* (as Heinrich Regius). Zurich: Oprecht und Helbling, 1934; revised and expanded edition as *Notizen 1950–1969 und Dämmerung*. Frankfurt: Fischer, 1974.)

Horkheimer, Max and Adorno, Theodor. 1972. *Dialectic of Enlightenment*. New York: Herder. (Translation by John Cumming of *Philosophische Fragmente*. New York: Institute for Social Research, 1944; revised edition as *Dialektik der Aufklärung: Philosophische Fragmente*. Amsterdam: Querido, 1947.)

Horowitz, David (ed.) 1968. *Marx and Modern Economics*. London: MacGibbon and Kee.

Howard, Dick. 1977. *The Marxian Legacy*. London: Macmillan.

Howard, Dick and Klare, Karl (eds). 1972. *The Unknown Dimension: European Marxism since Lenin*. New York: Basic Books.

Hudson, Wayne. 1982. *The Marxist Philosophy of Ernst Bloch*. London: Macmillan.

Hutchison, T.W. 1981. *The Politics and Philosophy of Economics – Marxians, Keynesians and Austrians*. Oxford: Blackwell.

Hunt, Richard. 1975. *The Political Ideas of Marx and Engels*, vol. I. Pittsburgh: University of Pittsburgh Press.

Jacoby, Russell. 1981. *Dialectic of Defeat*. Cambridge: Cambridge University Press.

Jameson, Frederick. 1971. *Marxism and Form*. Princeton, N.J.: Princeton University Press.

Jay, Martin. 1973. *The Dialectical Imagination: A History of the Frankfurt School and the Institute of Social Research, 1923–1950*. Boston: Little Brown.

1984a. *Marxism and Totality*. Cambridge: Polity Press.

1984b. *Adorno*. London: Fontana/Collins.

Joll, James. 1977. *Gramsci*. Glasgow: Fontana/Collins.

Kätz, Barry. 1982. *Herbert Marcuse and the Art of Liberation: an intellectual biography*. London: New Left Books.

Keat, Russell. 1981. *The Politics of Social Theory: Habermas, Freud and the Critique of Positivism*. Oxford: Blackwell.

Kelly, George Armstrong. 1969. *Idealism, Politics and History – Sources of Hegelian Thought*. Cambridge: Cambridge University Press.

Kelly, George Armstrong. 1978. *Hegel's Retreat from Eleusis – Studies in Political Thoughts*. Princeton: Princeton University Press.

Kelly, Michael. 1982. *Modern French Marxism*. Oxford: Blackwell.

Kellner, Douglas. 1985. *Herbert Marcute and the Crisis of Marxism*. Berkeley: University of California Press.

Kilminster, Richard. 1979. *Praxis and Method*. London: Routledge and Kegan Paul.

Knei-Paz, Baruch. 1977. *The Social and Political Thought of Leon Trotsky*. Oxford: Oxford University Press.

Kojève, Alexandre. 1969. *Introduction to the Reading of Hegel*. Translated by James Nichols. New York: Basic Books. (French ed., Paris: Gallimard, 1947).

Kolakowski, Leszek. 1978. *Main Currents of Marxism*. (3 vols) Translated by P.S. Falla. Oxford: Clarendon.

Konder, Leandro. 1980. *Lukács*. Porto Alegre: L. & P.M. Editores.

Korsch, Karl. 1938. *Karl Marx* (Translated from German manuscript). London: Chapman and Hall; and New York: Wiley.

　1970a. *Marxism and Philosophy*. London: New Left Books. (Translation by Fred Halliday of *Marxismus und Philosophie: Zugleich eine Antrikritik*. Edited by E. Gerlach. Frankfurt: Europäische Verlagsanstalt, 1966.)

　1970b. *Three Essays on Marxism*. London: Pluto.

　1977. *Karl Korsch: Revolutionary Theory*. Edited, with an introduction, by Douglas Kellner. Austin: University of Texas Press.

Kosík, Karel. 1976. *Dialectics of the Concrete: a Study on Problems of Man and the World*. Translated from the

Czech (Prague, 1963) by Karel Kowanda and James Schmidt. Dordrecht: Reidel.

Kracauer, Siegfried. 1969. *History: The Last Things before the Last*. New York: Oxford University Press.

Labedz, Leopold (ed.) 1962. *Revisionism – Essays on the History of Marxist Ideas*. London: Allen and Unwin.

Lefort, Claude. 1971. *Elements d'une Critique de la Bureaucratie*. Geneva: Droz (2nd ed., Paris: Gallimard, 1979.)

Lichtheim, George. 1961. *Marxism*. London: Routledge and Kegan Paul.

1970. *Lukács*. London: Fontana/Collins.

1974. *From Marx to Hegel*. New York: Seabury Press.

Lippi, Marco. 1979. *Value and Naturalism in Marx*. London: New Left Books. (Translation by Hilary Steedman of *Marx: il valore como costo sociale reale* Milan: Etas, 1976.)

Loewenstein, Julius I. 1980. *Marx against Marxism*. London: Routledge and Kegan Paul. (Translation by Harry Drost of *Vision und Wirklichkeit*. 1970.)

lo Piparo, Franco 1979 *Lingua Intellettuali Egemonia in Gramsci*. Bari: De Donato.

Lovell, David W. 1984. *From Marx to Lenin – An Evaluation of Marx's Responsibility for Soviet Authoritarianism*. Cambridge: Cambridge University Press.

Löwith, Karl. 1946. *From Hegel to Nietzsche*. Translated by D.E. Green. New York: Europa. (German ed. Zürich, 1941.)

1949. *Meaning in History*. Chicago: University of Chicago Press.

Löwy, Michael. 1976. *Pour une Sociologie des Intellectuels Révolutionnaires*. Paris: Presses Universitaires de France.

Lukács, Georg. *Werke*. Neuwied, West Germany: Luchterhand, 1967– .

1950. *Studies in European Realism: A Sociological Survey of the Writings of Balzac, Stendhal, Zola, Tolstoy, Gorki and others*. London: Hillway. (Translation of *Essays über Realismus*. Berlin: Aufbau, 1948.)

1954. *Die Zerstörung der Vernunft*. Berlin: Aufbau.

1963a. *The Meaning of Contemporary Realism*. London: Merlin Press. (Translation by J. and N. Mander of *Wider den missverstandenen Realismus*. Hamburg: Claasen, 1958.)

1963b. *Die Eigenart des Asthetischen*. Neuwied: Luchterhand. (2 vols).

1965a. *The Sociology of Modern Drama*. Oshkosh, Wisconsin: Green Mountain Editions. (Translation of *A Modern dráma fejlö desének története*. Budapest: Kisfaludy Társaság, Franklin, 1911. 2 vols.)

1965b. *The Historical Novel*. New York: Humanities Press. (Translation by Hannah and Stanley Mitchell of *A történelmi regény*. Budapest: Hungaria, 1947.)

1965c. *Essays on Thomas Mann*. London: Merlin Press; and New York: Grosset and Dunlap. (Translation by Stanley Mitchell of *Thomas Mann*. Budapest: Hungaria, 1948.)

1971a. *The Theory of the Novel: A Historico-Philosophical Essay on the Form of Great Epic Literature*. Cambridge, Mass.: M I T Press. (Translation by Rodney Livingstone of *Die Theorie des Romans: ein geschichtsphilosophischer Versuch über die Formen der grossen Epik*. Berlin: Cassirer, 1920.)

1971b. *History and Class Consciousness: Studies in Marxist Dialectics*. Cambridge, Mass.: M I T Press. (Translation by Rodney Livingstone of *Geschichte und Klassenbewusstsein: Studien über Marxistische Dialektik*. Berlin: Malik, 1924.)

1972a. *Asthetik*. Neuwied: Luchterhand. (4 vols)

1972b. *The Question of Parliamentarianism and Other Essays*. Translated London: New Left Books. (Selections of *Taktika és ethika*. Budapest.)

1973. *Marxism and Human Liberation: Essays on History, Culture and Revolution*, ed. by E. San Juan, Jr. New York: Dell.

1974a. *Soul and Form*. Cambridge, Mass.: M I T Press. (Translation by Anna Bostock of *A lélék és a formák*

(Kisérletek). Budapest: Franklin Társulat Nyomda, 1910.)

1974b. *Heidelberger Asthetik, 1916–1918*. Edited by György Mārkus and Frank Benseler. Neuwied: Hermann Luchterhand Verlag.

1974c. *Heidelberger Philosophie der Kunst, 1912–1914*. Edited by György Márkus and Frank Benseler. Neuwied: Hermann Luchterhand Verlag.

1975a. *Tactics and Ethics: Political Essays, 1919–1929*. New York: Harper. (Translation by Michael McColgan of *Taktika és ethika*. Budapest: Közoktatasügyi Népbiztosság Kiadasa, 1919.)

1975b. *The Young Hegel: Studies in the Relations between Dialectics and Economics*. London: Merlin Press. (Translation by Rodney Livingstone of *Der junge Hegel: über die Beziehungen von Dialektik und Ökonomie*. Zürich: Europa, 1948.)

1978. *Marx's Basic Ontological Principles*. London: Merlin Press. (Translation by David Fernbach of *Zur Ontologie des gesellschaftlichen Seins. Vol. 1. Die ontologischen Grundprinzipien von Marx*. Neuwied: Luchterhand, 1971.)

1979. *Hegel's False and Genuine Ontology*. London: Merlin Press. (Translation by David Fernbach of *Zur Ontologie des gesellschaftlichen Sens. Vol. 2. Hegels falsche und echte Ontologie*. Neuwied: Luchterhand, 1972.)

1983. *Reviews and Articles from Die rote Fahne*. Translated by Peter Palmer. London: Merlin.

Lunn, Eugene. 1982. *Marxism and Modernism: an historical study of Lukács, Brecht, Benjamin and Adorno*. Berkeley: University of Cálifornia Press.

Luporini, Cesare. 1974. *Dialettica e Materialismo*. Roma: Editori Riuniti.

Luxemburg, Rosa. 1972. *Selected Political Writings*. Edited Robert Locker. London: Jonathan Cape.

McBride, William Leon. 1977. *The Philosophy of Marx*. London: Hutchinson.

McCarthy, Thomas. 1978. *The Critical Theory of Jürgen Habermas*. London: Hutchinson.

McInnes, Neil. 1972. *The Western Marxists*. London: Alcove Press.

McIntyre, Alasdair (ed.) 1972. *Hegel – A Collection of Critical Essays*. University of Notre Dame Press.

McLellan, David. 1971. *The Thought of Karl Marx*. London: Macmillan.

1979. *Marxism after Marx*. London: Macmillan.

McLellan, David (ed.) 1983. *Marx – The First 100 Years*. London: Fontana.

Mandelbaum, Maurice. 1971. *History, Man and Reason*. Baltimore: Johns Hopkins University Press.

Marck, Siegfried et al. 1971. *Geschichte und Klassenbewusstsein heute*. Amsterdam: de Munter.

Marcuse, Herbert. 1932. *Hegels und die Grundlegung einer Theorie der Geschichtlichkeit*. Frankfurt: Klostermann.

1941. *Reason and Revolution: Hegel and the Rise of Social Theory*. London: Oxford University Press.

1955. *Eros and Civilization: A Philosophical Inquiry into Freud*. Boston: Beacon Press.

1958. *Soviet Marxism: A Critical Analysis*. London: Routledge.

1964. *One-Dimensional Man: Studies in the Ideology of Advanced Industrial Society*. Boston: Beacon Press; and London: Routledge.

1968. *Negations: Essays in Critical Theory*. Boston: Beacon Press; and London: Allen Lane. (Partial translation by Jeremy Shapiro of *Kurtur und Gesellschaft*. Frankfurt: Suhrkamp, 1965. 2 vols)

1969. *An Essay on Liberation*. Boston: Beacon Press; and London: Allen Lane.

1970. *Five Lectures: Psychoanalysis, Politics and Utopia*. Boston: Beacon Press; and London: Allen Lane. (Translation by Jeremy Shapiro and Shierry Weber of *Psychoanalyse und Politik*. Frankfurt: EuropäischeVerlagsanstalt, 1968.)

1972a. *Studies in Critical Philosophy*. Boston: Beacon Press; and London: New Left.

1972b. *Counterrevolution and Revolt*. Boston: Beacon Press; and London: Allen Lane.

1979. *The Aesthetic Dimension: Toward a Critique of Marxist Aesthetics*. London: Macmillan. (Translation by the author of *Die Permanenz der Kunst: Wider eine bestimmte Marxistische Aesthetik*. Munich: Hanser, 1977.)

Marcuse, Herbert, Wolff, Robert Paul and Moore, Barrington. 1969. *A Critique of Pure Tolerance*. London: Jonathan Cape.

Marx, Karl. 1956. *Selected Writings in Sociology and Social Philosophy*. Edited by Tom Bottomore and Maximilien Rubel; translated by T. Bottomore. London: Watts.

1967. *Writings of the Young Marx on Philosophy and Society*. Edited and translated by Lloyd D. Easton and Kurt H. Guddat. New York: Anchor Books.

1970. *Critique of Hegel's 'Philosophy of Right'*. Edited by Joseph O'Halley. Cambridge: Cambridge University Press.

1973a. *Political Writings II: The Revolutions of 1848*. Edited by David Fernbach. London: Penguin.

1973b. *Political Writings III: Surveys from Exile*. Edited by David Fernbach. London: Penguin.

1973c. *Grundrisse*. Translated by Martin Nicolaus. London: Penguin.

1974. *Political Writings I: The First International and After*. Edited by David Fernbach. London: Penguin.

1975. *Texts on Method*. Edited and translated by Terrell Carver. Oxford: Blackwell.

1976–81. *Capital: A Critique of Political Economy*. Introduced by Ernest Mandel; translated by David Fernbach and Ben Fowkes. London: Penguin.

Masaryk, Thomas. 1972. *Masaryk on Marx*. Edited by Erazim Kohák. Lewisburg, Pennsylvania. (Abridged translation of *Die philosophischen und sociologischen Grundlagen des Marxismus*, Vienna, 1899.)

Merleau-Ponty, Maurice. 1962. *Phenomenology of Perception*. New York: Humanities Press; and London: Routledge.

(Translation by C. Smith of *Phénoménologie de la perception*. Paris: Gallimard, 1945.)

1969. *Humanism and Terror: An Essay on the Communist Problem*. Boston: Beacon Press. (Translation by John O'Neill of *Humanisme et terreur: essai sur le problème communiste*. Paris: Gallimard, 1947.)

1973a. *Adventures of the Dialectic*. Evanston, Ill.: Northwestern University Press. (Translation by J. Bien of *Les Aventures de la Dialectique*. Paris: Gallimard, 1955.)

1973b. *The Prose of the World*. Evanston, Ill.: Northwestern University Press. (Translation by John O'Neill of *La prose du monde*. Edited by Claude Lefort. Paris: Gallimard, 1969.)

Merquior, J.G. 1969. *Arte Sociedade em Marcuse, Adorno e Benjamin*. Rio: Tempo Brasileiro.

1979. *The Veil and the Mask: essays on culture and ideology*. London: Routledge and Kegan Paul.

1980. *Rousseau and Weber: two studies in the theory of legitimacy*. London: Routledge and Kegan Paul.

1985. *Foucault*. London: Fontana.

(forthcoming) *From Prague to Paris: structuralist and poststructalist itineraries* (London: Verso).

Mészáros, István. 1979. *The Work of Sartre, I: Search for Freedom*. Atlantic Highlands, NJ:

Mészáros, István (ed.) 1971. *Aspects of History and Class Consciousness*. London: Routledge and Kegan Paul.

Miller, James. 1979. *History and Human Existence: From Marx to Merleau-Ponty*. Berkeley: University of California Press.

Mommsen, Wolfgang, J. Osterhammel and S. Wimster (eds.) (forthcoming) *Max Weber and his Contemporaries*. London: Allen & Unwin.

Mouffe, Chantal (ed.) 1979. *Gramsci & Marxist Theory*. London: Routledge and Kegan Paul.

Nemeth, Thomas. 1980. *Gramsci's Philosophy: A Critical Study*. Brighton: Harvester.

Niel, Henri. 1945. *De la médiation dans la philosophie de Hegel*. Paris: Aubier.

Bibliography

New Left Review (ed.) 1977. *Western Marxism – A Critical Reader*. London: New Left Books.

Nove, Alec. 1983. *The Economics of Feasible Socialism*. London: Allen and Unwin.

O'Brien, George Dennis. 1975. *Hegel on Reason and History – a Contemporary Interpretation*. Chicago: Chicago University Press.

Oakley, Allen. 1983. *The Making of Marx's Critical Theory: A Bibliographical Analysis*. London: Routledge and Kegan Paul.

Offe, Claus. 1972. *Strukturprobleme des kapitalistischen Staates*. Frankfurt: Suhrkamp.

Papaioannou, Kostas. 1983. *De Marx et du Marxisme*. Paris: Gallimard.

Parkinson, G.H.R. 1977. *Georg Lukács*. London: Routledge and Kegan Paul.

Pelcynzki, Z.A. (ed.) 1971. *Hegel's Political Philosophy: Problems and Perspectives*. Cambridge: Cambridge University Press.

Pelczynski, Z.A. (ed.) 1984. *The State and Civil Society – Studies in Hegel's Political Philosophy*. Cambridge: Cambridge University Press.

Perlini, Tito. 1968. *Utopia e Prospettiva in György Lukács*. Bari: Dedalo.

Plant, Raymond. 1973. *Hegel*. London: Allen and Unwin.

Poster, Mark. 1975. *Existential Marxism in Postwar France: from Sartre to Althusser*. Princeton N.J.: Princeton University Press.

Rader, Melvin. 1979. *Marx's Interpretation of History*. New York: Oxford University Press.

Radnitzky, Gerard. 1970. *Contemporary Schools of Metascience*. Gotebong: Akademiförlaget.

Rancière, Jacques. 1974. *La Leçon d'Althusser*. Paris: Gallimard.

Reichelt, Helmut. 1973. *La Struttura Logica del Concetto di Capitale in Marx*. Bari: De Donato. (Translated by

Francesco Cappelloti from *Zur logischen Struktur des Kapitalbregriffs bei Karl Marx*. Frankfurt: Europäische Verlagsanstalt, 1970.

Riedel, Manfred. 1984. *Between Tradition and Revolution – the Hegelian transformation of political philosophy*. Cambridge: Cambridge University Press. (Translated from *Studien zū Hegels Rechtsphilosophie*. Frankfurt: Suhrkamp, 1969.)

Ritter, Joachim. 1982. *Hegel and the French Revolution – essays on the Philosophy of Right*. Translation from the German edition (Cologne: Westdeutscher, 1957) by Richard Winfield. Boston: M I T.

Roberts, Julian. 1982. *Walter Benjamin*. London: Macmillan.

Robinson, Joan. 1953. *On Re-Reading Marx*. Cambridge: Cambridge University Press.

Roemer, John. 1982. *A General Theory of Exploitation and Class*. Cambridge, Mass.: Harvard University Press.

Rose, Gillian. 1978. *The Melancholy Science – an introduction to the thought of T.W. Adorno*. London: Macmillan.

1981. *Hegel Contra Sociology*. London: Athlone Press.

Rosen, Michael. 1982. *Hegel's Dialectic and its Criticism*. Cambridge: Cambridge University Press.

Rosen, Stanley. 1974. *G.W.F. Hegel – an introduction to the science of wisdom*. New Haven: Yale University Press.

Rosenzweig, Franz. 1976 *Hegel e lo stato*. Bologna: Il Mulino. (Translation by Anna Lucia Künkler Cianotto and Rosa Curino Cerrato. of *Hegel und der Staat*. Aalen: Scientia Verlag, 1962.) 1st ed., 1920.

Rossi, Pietro. 1982. *Max Weber: Razionalità e razionalizzazione*. Milan: Il Saggiatore.

Rossi, Pietro (ed.) 1975. *Gramsci e la cultura contemporanea*. (2 vols) Rome: Riuniti (1st vol. pub. in 1969).

Rotenstreich, Nathan. 1976. *Philosophy, History and Politics: Studies in Contemporary English Philosophy of History*. The Hague: Martinus Nijhoff.

Rouanet, Sergio Paulo. 1983. *Teoria Crítica e Psicanálise*. Rio: Tempo Brasileiro.

Rubel, Maximilien. 1974. *Marx critique du Marxisme*. Paris: Payot.

Bibliography

Sartre, Jean-Paul. 1948. *Existentialism and Humanism*. London: Methuen. (Translation by Philip Maiet of *L'Existentialisme est un humanisme*. Paris: Nagel, 1946.)

1950. *What is Literature?* London: Methuen. (Selection translated by B. Frechtman of *Situations II*. Paris: Gallimard, 1948.)

1957. *Being and Nothingness*. London: Methuen. Translation by H. Barnes of *L'Etre et le néant: essai d'ontologie phénoménologique*. Paris: Gallimard, 1943.)

1958. *The Transcendence of the Ego: an Existentialist Theory of Consciousness*. London: Vision Press. (Translation by Forrest Williams and Robert Kirkpatrick of *La Transcendance de l'ego: esquisse d'une description phénoménologique in Recherches philosophiques* 6, Paris: 1936–7.)

1964. *Saint Genet, Actor and Martyr*. London: W.H. Allen. (Translation by B. Frechtman of *Saint Genet, comédien et martyr*. Paris: Gallimard, 1952.)

1964b. *The Words*. New York: Braziller. (Translation by B. Frechtman of *Les Mots* (autobiography). Paris: Gallimard, 1963.)

1974. *Between Existentialism and Marxism*. London: New Left Books. (Translated by J. Matthews of selections from *Situations VIII (Autour de 68)* and *IX (Mélanges)*. Paris: Gallimard, 1971.)

1976. *Critique of Dialectical Reason: Theory of Practical Ensembles*. London: New Left Books and Highlands, N.J.: Humanities Press. (Translation by Allan Sheridan-Smith of *Critique de la raison dialectique: vol. 1. Théorie des ensembles pratiques*. Paris: Gallimard, 1960.)

Sassoon, Anne S. 1980. *Gramsci's Politics*. London: Croom Helm.

Schmidt, Alfred. 1983. *History and Structure*. Boston: Institute of Technology, Massachusetts. (Translation by Jeffrey Herf of *Geschichte und Struktur: Fragen einer marxistischen Historik*. Munich: Carl Hanser, 1971.)

Schmidt, Alfred and Rusconi, Gian Enrico. 1972. *La Scuola di Francoforte – origine e significato attuale*. Bari: De Donato.

Schroyer, Trent. 1973. *The Critique of Domination*. New York: Braziller.

Schumpeter, Joseph A. 1954. *History of Economic Analysis*. London: Allen and Unwin.

Searle, John. 1969. *Speech Acts: An Essay in the Philosophy of Language*. Cambridge: Cambridge University Press.

Shaw, William H. 1978. *Marx's Theory of History*. London: Hutchinson.

Shklar, Judith. 1976. *Freedom and Independence – A Study of Hegel's Phenomenology of Mind*. Cambridge: Cambridge University Press.

Simmel, Georg. 1978. *The Philosophy of Money*. London: Routledge and Kegan Paul. (Translation by Tom Bottomore and David Frisby of the 2nd German ed. of 1907; 1st ed., 1900.)

Singer, Peter. Oxford: 1980. *Marx*. Oxford: Oxford University Press.

Skocpol, Theda. 1979. *States and Social Revolutions – A Comparative Analysis of France, Russia and China*. Cambridge: Cambridge University Press.

Slater, Phil. 1977. *Origin and Significance of the Frankfurt School*. London: Routledge and Kegan Paul.

Sorel, Georges. 1976. *From Georges Sorel*. Edited by John Stanley. New York: Oxford University Press.

Sraffa, Piero. 1960. *Production of Commodities by Means of Commodities – Prelude to a Critique of Economic Theory*. Cambridge: Cambridge University Press.

Stepelevich, Lawrence S. (ed.) 1983. *The Young Hegelians – an anthology*. Cambridge: Cambridge University Press.

Szondi, Peter. 1964. *Satz und Gegensatz*. Frankfurt: Insel.

Tamburrano, Giuseppe. 1963. *Antonio Gramsci: La vita, il pensiero, l'azione*. Bari: Laterza.

Taminiaux, Jacques. 1984. *Naissance de la Philosophie Hégélienne de l'État*. Paris: Payot.

Tar, Zoltán. 1977. *The Frankfurt School – the critical theories of Max Horkheimer and Th. W. Adorno*. New York: Wiley.

Taylor, Charles. 1975. *Hegel*. Cambridge: Cambridge University Press.

Thomas, Paul. 1980. *Karl Marx and the Anarchists*. London: Routledge and Kegan Paul.

Thompson, E.P. 1978. *The Poverty of Theory and other essays*. London: Merlin Press.

Thompson, John B. and Held, David (eds). 1982. *Habermas – Critical Debates*. London: Macmillan.

Tiedemann, Rolf. 1965. *Studien zur Philosophie Walter Benjamins*. Frankfurt: Europäische Verlagsanstalt.

Toews, John Edward. 1985. *Hegelianism – the path toward dialectical humanism*, 1805–1841. Cambridge: CUP (1st ed., 1980).

Topitsch, Ernst. 1961. *Sozialphilosophie zwischen Mythos und Wissenschaft*. Partly translated as *Per una critica del marxismo*. Roma: Bulzoni Editore. Neuwied: Luchterhand.

Tronti, Mario. 1966. *Ouvriers et Capital*. Paris: Christian Bourgeois Editeur. (Translated by Y. Moulier, 1977.)

Tucker, Robert. 1961. *Philosophy and Myth in Karl Marx*. New York: Cambridge University Press.

Ulam, Adam B. 1960. *The Unfinished Revolution – Marxism and Communism in the Modern World*. London: Longman.

Uno, Kozo. 1980. *Principles of Political Economy: Theory of a Purely Capitalist Society*. Translated by Thomas Sekine. Brighton: Harvester. (Japanese ed., 1964)

Vincent, Jean-Marie. 1976. *La Théorie Critique de l'Ecole de Francfort*. Paris. Galilée.

Vincent, Jean-Marie et al. 1974. *Contre Althusser*. Paris: 10/18.

Wallerstein, Immanuel. 1974. *The Modern World-System – Capitalist Agriculture and the Origins of the European World-Economy in the Sixteenth Century*. New York: Academic Press.

Wartofsky, Marx W. 1977. *Feuerbach*. Cambridge: Cambridge University Press.

Weber, Max. 1949. *The Methodology of the Social Sciences*. (Translation by Edward Shils and Henry Finch of Part of *Gesammelte Aufsätze zur Wissemschftslebre*. Tübingen: Mohr, 1922.) New York: Free Press.

Weil, Eric. 1970. *Hegel et l'État*. Paris: Vrin.

Wellmer, Albrecht. 1971. *Critical Theory of Society*. New York: Seabury Press. (Translation by John Cumming of *Kritische Gesellschaftstheorie und Positivismus*. Frankfurt: Suhrkamp, 1969.)

Willey, Thomas E. 1978. *Back to Kant – the Revival of Kantianism in German Social and Historical Thought, 1860–1914*. Detroit: Wayne State University Press.

Willms, Bernard. 1973. *Kritik und Politik*. Frankfurt: Suhrkamp.

Wolfe, Bertram. 1965. *Marxism: 100 years in the life of a doctrine*. New York: Dial.

Wolff, Kurt H. and Moore, Barrington, Jr. (eds). 1967. *The Critical Spirit: Essays in Honor of Herbert Marcuse*. Boston: Beacon Press.

Wolin, Richard. 1982. *Walter Benjamin – an Aesthetic of Redemption*. New York: Columbia University Press.

Wood, Allen W. 1981. *Karl Marx*. London: Routledge and Kegan Paul.

Worsley, Peter. 1982. *Marx and Marxism*. London: Tavistock.

Zelený, Jindrich. 1980. *The Logic of Marx*. Oxford: Blackwell. (Translation by Terrell Carver from *Die Wissenschaftslogik bei Marx und das Kapital*. East Berlin: Akademie, 1968.)

LANDMARKS IN WESTERN MARXISM

1923	Lukács: *History and Class Consciousness*
	Korsch: *Marxism and Philosophy*
1928	Benjamin: *One-Way Street*
1947	Horkheimer and Adorno: *Dialectic of Enlightenment*
1948–51	Gramsci: *Prison Notebooks* (posth.)
1949	Adorno: *Philosophy of Modern Music*
1954	Bloch: *Das Prinzip Hoffnung*, I
1955	Merleau-Ponty: *Adventures of the Dialectic*
	Marcuse: *Eros and Civilization*
1959	Goldmann: *Recherches dialectiques*
1960	Sartre: *Critique of Dialectical Reason*
1963	Kosík: *Dialectic of the Concrete*
1964	Marcuse: *One-Dimensional Man*
1965	Lefebvre: *Métaphilosophie*
	Althusser: *For Marx*
	Althusser et al.: *Reading Capital*
1966	Adorno: *Negative Dialectics*
1968	Habermas: *Knowledge and Human Interests*
1969	Colletti: *Marxism and Hegel*
1970	Adorno: *Aesthetische Theorie*
1973	Habermas: *Legitimation Crisis*
1982	Benjamin: *Das Passagenwerk* (posth.)
	Habermas: *Theory of Communicative Action*

INDEX